Put Work In Its Place

Bruce O'Hara is the director and founder of Work Well, Canada's first Work Option Resource Centre. Over the past ten years he has helped hundreds of Canadians negotiate more flexible working arrangements — including many people who said, "My employer will *never* give me what I want."

O'Hara has also received national attention as the author of *Working Harder Isn't Working: How we can save the environment, the economy and our sanity by working less and enjoying life more.*

Bruce O'Hara works three days a week — and loves it!

Put Work In Its Place

How to redesign your job
to fit your life

Bruce O'Hara

New Star Books
Vancouver
1994

An earlier version of *Put Work In Its Place* was published in 1988 by Work Well Publications, Victoria, B.C.

Edited by Judith Aldritt McDowell and Audrey McClellan
Cartoons by Graham Harrop
"Spotlights" in Step Two by Kathy English
Index: Jeannie Ma
Cover: Kris Klaasen / Working Design
Cover illustrations: Barbara Klunder

Printed and bound in Canada by Best Gagné Book Manufacturers
1 2 3 4 5   98 97 96 95 94
First printing, November 1994

Publication of this book is made possible by grants from the Canada Council, the Department of Communications Book Publishing Industry Development Program, and the Cultural Services Branch, Province of British Columbia.

Canadian Cataloguing in Publication Data

O'Hara, Bruce, 1952-
  Put work in its place

  Includes bibliographical references.
  ISBN 0-921586-40-X

  1. Part-time employment.   2. Hours of labor, Flexible.
3. Job sharing.   4. Telecommuting.   I. Title.
HD5109.O53 1994   331.25'72   C94-910864-2

Contents

How to Use This Book   IX

Step One: Thinking Clearly About Work
Sorting Out the Baggage of the Past   3

Step Two: Surveying Your Options
Nine Ways to Have the Best of Both Worlds   13
Job Sharing   17
Permanent Part-Time   27
Leaves of Absence   35
V-Time   44
Banked Overtime   49
Phased Retirement   56
Flextime   63
Compressed and Modified Workweeks   69
Telecommuting   75

Step Three: Choosing Your Time
Taking Stock of Your Life   87
Making More Time in Your Life   101
Getting More of What You Want   106
Shaping Your Free Time to Fit Your Plan   112

Step Four: Deciding About Money

What Can You Afford?   117

What Will Happen to Your Benefits?   123

Step Five: Designing A Program

First Steps   131

Job Sharing   141

Permanent Part-Time   149

Leaves of Absence   154

V-Time   161

Banked Overtime   169

Phased Retirement   175

Flextime   179

Compressed and Modified Workweeks   188

Telecommuting   193

Step Six: Getting What You Want

Planning Your Next Move   201

Writing an Individual Proposal   208

Writing a Collective Proposal   224

Step Seven: Putting Work In Its Place

Expediting the Approval Process   243

Implementing Your Program   247

Evaluation and Follow Up   251

Special Cases And Further Resources

Work Options as an Alternative to Layoffs   257

Options for Job Seekers   260

Compensatory Benefit Leaves   264

The Flexible Workplace   271

Dead Heroes: Men and Work   275

Further Resources   283

Index   292

Put Work In Its Place

How to Use This Book

A healthy balance between work and personal life is so satisfying and so rewarding that those who have achieved it often find it hard to believe they were ever willing to settle for less. They are also aware that the benefits of putting work in its place are not merely self-centred; the whole and happy person is an asset to family, friends, co-workers, and the community.

In the 1950s, a large majority of North American households consisted of a husband who worked full time outside the home, a wife who was a full-time homemaker, and one or more dependent children. The standard Monday-to-Friday, nine-to-five workweek was designed for this traditional family pattern. It was not designed to suit the dual-earner families, single parents, and older workers who make up most of today's workforce.

As a result, many North Americans are feeling burned out from a work pattern that doesn't fit their needs. They want more time for family, volunteer work, friendship, travel, and hobbies. They want time for a life outside of work. If you are one of those individuals, or think you might be, this book is for you.

During the past twenty years, a whole range of practical new working arrangements have gradually come into use. *Work options* are voluntary, employee-initiated arrangements designed to reduce or restructure worktime. Unlike the more traditional types of part-time work, work options usually carry hourly pay rates equal to full time, full employment rights, and a share of benefits prorated to the proportion of worktime. The scope of options now in use includes job sharing, permanent part-time, V-Time (voluntary reduced work-time), banked overtime, phased retirement, leaves of absence, flex-time, compressed workweeks, and telecommuting.

If designed properly and used under the appropriate circumstances, all of these options can benefit both employees and employers. Between them, the new options can accommodate almost any work schedule imaginable. As well, when overworked individuals work less it opens up new jobs for the unemployed.

Futurists estimate that the flexible working arrangements described in this book will be the norm for almost everyone within fifteen to twenty years. You don't have to wait that long; you have in front of you a complete tool kit for achieving freedom, flexibility and balance — now.

As the director of Work Well, Canada's first Work Options Resource Centre, over the past ten years, I have helped many Canadians arrange new working hours that better meet their needs. Three generalizations have emerged from this experience:

❶ **You are more likely to get what you want in a work schedule if you take the time to find out exactly what you want and need.**

❷ **If you begin by investigating the full range of options available, you will be in a better position to select the option best suited to your needs.**

❸ **A well-thought-out, written proposal will greatly enhance your chances of getting exactly what you want.**

Put Work In Its Place will take you through the seven-step process that Work Well clients have found to be most effective:

Step One: Thinking Clearly About Work examines the cultural baggage many of us carry about work. It is designed to help you free yourself from outdated attitudes so that you can choose the schedule you *really* want.

Step Two: Surveying Your Options describes nine types of new work schedules and includes criteria for helping you decide if a particular option is appropriate for you. It also provides a mini-profile of each option in practice. If you read all the mini-profiles, you will get a good picture of the basic options and how they can be combined or modified to meet a diversity of personal situations.

Step Three: Choosing Your Time helps you create a balance in your life — a balance that better reflects your own priorities.

Step Four: Deciding About Money helps you deal creatively with the financial implications of changing your work schedule.

Step Five: Designing A Program takes you through the process of restructuring your job so that you can get the work schedule you want and still meet your employer's needs. Each chapter in this section contains specific advice on one of the nine options.

Step Six: Getting What You Want describes the crucial factors of producing and presenting a successful proposal.

Step Seven: Putting Work In Its Place shows how to get through the approval process quickly and how to implement your new schedule.

Special Cases and Further Resources expands on a number of special issues related to work options and provides a list of additional information sources.

Getting the balance you want in life is not an easy process or a quick one. It requires effort and careful thought. In many cases, success also requires courage and persistence. Time and time again, however, those who have been through the process report that the results are well worth the effort.

Note on the New Edition

An earlier version of *Put Work In Its Place* was an instant hit when it was published in 1988. This new edition has been fully updated with current information and resources. [**AMERICAN READERS:** *Put Work In Its Place* **also proved popular in the U.S., so the new edition includes notes in this format which provide U.S. equivalents for Canadian information.**] Two items that have not been changed in the new edition are Graham Harrop's cartoons and the "Spotlight" mini-profiles in Step Two. Both received such an enthusiastic response it seemed best not to mess with success.

STEP ONE

THINKING CLEARLY ABOUT WORK

Sorting Out the Baggage of the Past

Work is a lot like sex — it's hard to think clearly about it when your emotions are involved. Although work is primarily a source of income, it also has a big influence on our feelings. It affects our sense of self-worth and our sense of who we are. We structure our time around work, and work determines many of our social contacts.

It's hard to think clearly about work because the subject is surrounded with emotionally charged and frequently contradictory ideas, images, values, and judgments. Before we can know what we really think about work, we have to sort through all the things we have been told we *should* think and feel.

Many of our ideas about work reflect deep-seated values from the past, some of which have outlived their usefulness. The values we attach to work are more than a response to present-day realities; in large part, they are a response to voices from the various stages of human history. A quick look at the past will help put these "voices" into perspective.

Work in the Hunter-Gatherer Economy

For upwards of one million years, or more than 99 percent of our history on this planet, human beings lived in small nomadic tribes that hunted and foraged for food. They had few possessions because

every possession was an extra burden to carry as they moved around
from place to place in search of food.

As a way of gathering food, the nomadic life was inefficient because land used this way could support only a few people per acre.
However, it was very efficient in terms of work, because people ate
only what nature provided. Anthropologist Marshall Sahlins has
estimated that nomadic people spent an average of 20 to 25 hours
per week on activities we would call "work."

For most of human history, people worked only half the time that
we work today. If you are one of those people who feel you've
worked enough by Wednesday afternoon, perhaps you are hearing
an ancient voice from deep within your psyche. You may be re-
sponding to a genetic prompting based on a million years of history.

Work in the Agricultural Economy

Roughly 10,000 years ago, many tribes in various parts of the world
ceased living as nomads. They began to plant crops and tend ani-
mals. Because they were not moving around so much, it was easier
to accumulate possessions. Although growing food required more
work, the supply was more dependable. It also meant that more
people could survive on a smaller area of land.

Many of our values originated in the agricultural era. In the agricultural economy, work was not the only — or even the most important—element in people's lives. Other spheres of activity were given
equal or greater value.

Religion, for example, was extremely important. In those days,
religion was the focus of a web of communal activities requiring
active participation. During the Middle Ages, up to 180 religious
holidays were celebrated every year; most of the population of
Europe did not work on those days.

Extended family structure meant that nurturing the young, caring
for the old, and tending the sick all took place within the family.
Celebration and self-expression were also public, participatory activities. Work was only one of a range of activities through which
individuals developed a sense of identity, worth, and purpose.

The strong societal values we attach to family and church may seem out of proportion to the time we actually devote to them today. However, they are not so disproportionate if we see these values as a hungering for the communal structures we once had but have largely lost.

Before the industrial revolution, people satisfied most of their economic needs through a complex set of social contracts rather than through exchanges of money. People thought of wage labour as an intrusion of economic values into an area that is more properly personal. The lingering notion that paid work creates "wage slaves" and that paid activities are not as "pure" as those we provide for free, both reflect the values of pre-industrialized society.

Work in the Industrial Economy

By the early 1800s the introduction of steam power and the spread of factories had transformed the economic base of Western society. New technology threw millions of people out of work. High unemployment drove down wages, so workers had to work long hours to earn enough to live. By 1825 the average workweek had increased to more than 75 hours. Even young children worked twelve hours a day, six and a half days a week. This unprecedented obsession with work trivialized and pushed aside activities which had previously enjoyed equal social and cultural value.

Social historians have a rule of thumb that a culture's deepest values originate 100 to 150 years in its past. Today's virtues are the central life lessons and moral prescriptions adopted by our great-great-grandparents. Their lives were dominated by labour; work was, of necessity, the paramount virtue.

North America was more strongly affected by the nineteenth century obsession with work than was Europe. America was a frontier continent. What traditions we have came from the homesteading pioneers. The endless task of settling a new land prepared us to accept industrial-strength overwork as normal. This perhaps explains why Europe has longer vacation times, more worktime flexibility, and fewer dual-earner households — Europe never fully lost

... CERTAINLY IT'S A DEPARTURE FROM THE MOTHER-WORKS-FATHER-STAYS-HOME   FATHER-WORKS-MOTHER-STAYS-HOME SYNDROME...

the traditions of a balanced lifestyle. North America's deepest moral values were formed during the most overworked century in all of humanity's million-year tenure on Earth.

By early in the twentieth century, the harshness of the industrial economy began to soften. Successive campaigns for shorter work-times reduced unemployment, which in turn drove wages up. Wages rose to the point where a single wage earner could support himself, his spouse, and children. A well-defined division of sex roles occurred; the man worked outside the home and the woman worked inside the home.

Over time, a rigid ideology of gender became established around this new pattern: men were ordained to be the breadwinners, women the caregivers. Perhaps one way to keep perspective on the idea that "a woman's place is in the home" is to remember that the gender roles we think of as "traditional" are less than 100 years old.

Work in the Service Economy

In the twentieth century, rising labour costs have led to the increasing use of machines to replace human labour in the production process. Because fewer and fewer workers are needed to make things, more and more of the workforce has become involved in selling things and providing services — education, banking, entertainment, health care, and so on.

Paid work has supplanted activities that were formerly part of a social matrix. Childcare became the province of professional teachers, and caring for the infirm, the domain of the medical community. Self-expression devolved into a paid entertainment industry. Human concern and support became the bailiwicks of counsellors and therapists. Sport was largely given over to professional athletes. Even charity became a professional activity. Unpaid activities had little status; people became "just housewives" or "just volunteers."

As the economy shifts away from production and towards services, most of the new jobs are being created in areas that have traditionally employed women. Women began entering the labour force in large numbers in the 1950s. By the late 1980s, women were filling three out of four new jobs. Today, we are still in transition from an industrial economy to a service economy, and thus find ourselves caught between two worlds.

Our present systems of work scheduling were designed for an industrial era in which the paid workforce was largely made up of men with stay-at-home wives. In the 1950s the average male wage earner worked 40 to 50 hours a week, while his spouse spent a similar amount of time keeping house and caring for their children. The rest of the time was available for family activities and entertainment.

A different social pattern had emerged by the 1980s because of rising expectations and inflation in the cost of living. Today's pattern is for husbands and wives both to work 35 to 50 hours per week outside the home, with their "free time" spent on housework and child care. Although the new pattern has raised family income, it has also brought increasing levels of divorce, alcoholism, child abuse, suicide, stress-related illnesses, and psychiatric disorders.

As we move from an industry-based economy to a service-based economy, the mismatch between the structures of the workplace and the needs of the workforce can be expected to cause increasing levels of social breakdown. In the 1990s, many of us feel like square pegs in round holes. Maybe because that's what we are.

Work in the Economy of the Future

The workplace continues to change with increasing rapidity. Current estimates are that automation and computers will eliminate roughly one-half of current jobs in the next twenty years. Women are expected to continue entering or re-entering the workforce in large numbers.

Several futurists have estimated that by the early 2000s, the average workweek will fall to 20 hours. The expected new family pattern is that husbands and wives will each work about 20 to 25 hours a week for pay and spend a similar amount of time on domestic tasks, leaving the rest of the time available for family activities, hobbies, and entertainment.

There are two scenarios as to how this new pattern will come about. If we continue on our current course, the rapid pace at which technology is eliminating jobs, combined with women's continued re-entry into the workforce, will make for rising levels of unemployment. High unemployment, in turn, will push down wages. Eventually the economy will slide into a 1930s-style depression. Shorter workweeks will then be essential within any workable program to restore health to the economy.

A happier prospect is that Canadians will organize a national movement to implement shorter working times before that happens. Sharing the work will reduce unemployment. Lower unemployment will, in turn, make for higher wages. Increased consumer spending power will make for a more prosperous economy. (For more on this issue, see my book *Working Harder Isn't Working*.)

The push for shorter workweeks will be driven by social changes as much as by economic ones. In his book *New Rules*, pollster Daniel Yankelovich documents a profound shift in social values. North Americans used to operate primarily out of what he terms "an ethic of success." For most people, being successful — having a big car, a "good" job, a fancy house, and the envy of one's neighbours — was the goal of life.

Increasingly, however, North Americans are shifting to what Yankelovich calls "an ethic of self-fulfilment." Instead of asking, "How can I be successful?" people are asking, "What gives meaning, satisfaction, and value to my life?" Instead of assuming that some prepackaged picture of success will make them happy, people are starting to make their own decisions about what is most important in life. Today, many of these individuals are asking for new work schedules; more can be expected to do so in the years ahead.

Progressive corporations, as well, are finding they need to look at more flexible work hours. John Naisbitt, co-author of *Re-Inventing the Corporation*, notes that in a fast-changing service economy, a corporation's most important asset is no longer its machinery or its financial base, but its employees. Companies that attract and retain the best people are at an advantage; flexible work schedules are becoming an important tool for attracting and keeping good workers.

So the good news is that more sensible work schedules are on their way. The bad news is that it may take fifteen years before they are widely available. If you are not prepared to wait that long, this book is for you.

Reshaping Our Values

What lessons can we derive from history that will guide us in developing a healthy attitude toward work?

It is okay to want to work less. For the greater part of human history, people have worked less than they do now. For all we know, our desire for more leisure may be built into our genes.

It is okay to want to work. People often feel guilty for working when work is not financially necessary. However, in a society that is as obsessed with work as ours, it is important to recognize that work is one of the few legitimate paths to status, social connection, and a sense of self-worth.

It's okay to want not to work. History tells us that paid work doesn't have to be the centre of life. There are many ways to make a contribution to the community. We needn't allow our cultural bias to blind us to other possibilities for self fulfilment.

Change isn't easy. We live in a culture that assumes there is something wrong with people who are not devoted to work. Your boss may share this view. Change under such circumstances requires persistence, patience, and a willingness to challenge the status quo.

The gender revolution is not over. Women have moved into the workforce in large numbers, but they are working within structures designed for men. Intellectually, men have accepted the idea that they should be more involved with parenting and housework; in practice, many men are still locked into attitudes and workplace structures that make work the focus of their lives. Until men are also liberated, women's liberation will have little practical value.

Balance is important to health. People are more likely to remain sane and happy when they have a number of meaningful roles and activities. Our society tends to be emotionally unhealthy because so many people establish their identities exclusively through work.

You are not alone. A Conference Board of Canada survey found that about one-third of working Canadians would like to work less. If you would like to change the role of work in your life, your ideas are not aberrant; they are the way of the future.

STEP TWO

INTRODUCING WORK OPTIONS

Nine Ways to Have the Best of Both Worlds

During extended trials in American, European, and Canadian companies, the following nine work options have proved to be practical alternatives to the 40-hour week.

- **Job sharing**: two or more people share one full-time position, with prorated salary and benefits.
- **Permanent part-time**: less than full time, but with seniority rights, promotion opportunities, prorated benefits, and hourly rate of pay equal to full time.
- **Leaves of absence**: authorized periods of time away from work without loss of employment rights.
- **V-Time**: a voluntary time/income trade-off that allows employees to reduce work hours by 5, 10, 20 or 50 percent for a specified period of time.
- **Banked overtime**: programs whereby overtime pay may be converted to time off work.
- **Phased retirement**: employees approaching retirement qualify for a gradually reduced workweek without loss or reduction of pension benefits.
- **Flextime**: employees work a standard number of hours each week within flexible starting and quitting times.
- **Compressed workweek**: employees work a standard num-

ber of hours within fewer days — for example, 40 hours a
week in four, ten-hour days.
- **Telecommuting**: employees work at home part of the time,
  in some cases communicating with the office through a
  computer linked to a modem.

It is also possible to develop major or minor variations on each of
the above options, depending upon the nature of the job, the needs
of the employee, and the needs of the employer.

How available are work options? The survey data in the table
below is adapted from *The Corporate Response to Workers with Family
Responsibilities* by Helene Paris (Ottawa: Conference Board of Canada, 1989).

Employers are embracing work options for very practical reasons.
The effectiveness of work options in alleviating various human resource problems is outlined in the chart on the next page (statistics
are from the same 1989 Conference Board of Canada Survey).

Narrowing the Field

Some work options will work better for you than others. Use the
following rules of thumb to help narrow the field.

PERCENTAGES OF ORGANIZATIONS OFFERING WORK OPTIONS		
WORK OPTION OFFERED	FORMALLY	INFORMALLY
Job sharing	8.5%	10.7%
Permanent part-time	25.3%	4.2%
Banked overtime	42.5%	26.9%
Flextime	31.1%	17.6%
Compressed workweeks	23.5%	4.8%
Telecommuting	1.7%	8.8%
Shorter workweeks	13.9%	6.4%
Shorter workdays	9.9%	4.3%

EFFECTIVENESS OF WORK OPTIONS IN ALLEVIATING HUMAN RESOURCE PROBLEMS

Option / HUMAN RESOURCE PROBLEM	Job sharing	Permanent part-time	Banked over-time	Flextime	Compressed workweeks	Telecommuting	Shorter workweeks	Shorter workdays
Recruitment	83.8	82.6	42.8	75.8	79.8	90.6	81.3	80.4
Retention	79.1	79.1	60.4	76.1	79.8	78.1	79.7	78.3
Absenteeism	89.4	80.2	50.7	81.0	83.2	90.9	85.9	82.6
Tardiness	83.6	75.8	25.0	74.7	78.1	84.9	78.5	71.7
Employee stress	78.8	70.0	53.5	72.8	71.3	81.8	71.9	71.7
Employee morale	77.3	77.8	56.6	75.0	74.2	75.0	74.6	71.7
Employee loyalty	61.5	65.6	49.1	58.9	55.4	59.4	57.1	58.7
Productivity	68.2	69.2	36.2	70.5	63.8	65.6	69.8	65.2
Quality of performance	58.5	56.8	30.7	57.8	57.6	66.7	56.3	58.7

The percentages in the table combine the responses of organizations that felt the work options were "effective" or "very effective" at alleviating problems.

- If you want to cut your worktime by 40 percent or more, look at **job sharing** and **permanent part-time**;
- If you want a slightly shorter workday or workweek, consider **V-Time** or **permanent part-time**;
- If you want longer vacations or an extended period of time away from work, look at **V-Time** and **leaves of absence**;
- If you want to work fewer hours in the years before you retire, look at **phased retirement. Job sharing, permanent part-time, V-Time,** or a **leave of absence** may also meet your needs;
- If you want to take time off in place of overtime pay, consider **banked overtime**;

- If you want to change your schedule without reducing your hours of work, look at **flextime**;
- If you would prefer to work longer days but fewer of them, the **compressed workweek** may be suitable;
- If you want to do all or part of your work from home then see **telecommuting**.

When you have decided which option you like best, read the description of that option in Step Two. If you are not sure how much time you need or how large a cut in hours you can afford, complete Steps Three and Four first. Then go to Step Two.

The information in Step Two will help you decide if the option is right for you and how well it would work in your job. If two or more options seem equally workable, look at them again with the following questions in mind:

? *How well does the option suit your needs?*

? *How easy would it be to get your employer to agree to it?*

Job Sharing

Job sharing is a work arrangement in which two or more (but usually two) people agree to share the duties, wages, and benefits of one full-time job. The work may be divided on a time or task basis; benefits are usually prorated. Although the job sharers work part time, the job remains a full-time position in the eyes of the employer.

Job sharing first became popular in Europe after the Second World War. Since then it has been used extensively in Europe and the United States. In Britain, for example, a 1986 Equal Opportunities Commission determined that over one-third of local authorities at the city, borough, and country levels provided job-sharing opportunities for professional, administrative, technical, and clerical staff.

In the United States, various studies have shown that the number of employers offering job sharing has grown by healthy percentages every year. The practice now extends into health care, education, the legal profession, construction, manufacturing, wholesale and retail trade, insurance, real estate, and government. Similarly, a 1986 New Ways to Work survey indicated that 35 states allowed job sharing, and federal agencies have programs and procedures designed to support it.

Research on the prevalence of job sharing in Canada has been limited, but a 1989 Conference Board of Canada survey of Canadian employers showed that, of those who responded, 8.5 percent had formal policies allowing job sharing and another 10.7 percent allowed it informally.

People decide to job share for a variety of reasons, but the most common one is a desire to have more time for caring for children at home. Parents of young children often find full-time work incompatible with the demands of home and family.

Many women leave the workforce while their children are young, and they often have a hard time re-entering at a later date. Job sharing helps to avert this problem by allowing mothers of young children to keep their position at work while having more time at home. Today, a growing number of fathers also want to spend more time with their children.

Job sharing also appeals to people who need large blocks of time to devote to some activity outside the workplace. This includes artists, writers, and people who are starting their own businesses. Others wanting to upgrade their skills or develop a new career may need time during the day to attend courses at college or university.

People in high-stress jobs may decide to job share for health reasons. Job sharing may also be the answer for people whose work is highly repetitive and boring, or for an older person seeking comfortable re-entry into the workforce. If appropriate pension arrangements are available, job sharing can be an ideal way to phase into retirement.

There are many different ways to share a job. In some arrangements, the partners divide the duties of the job along well-defined lines and work almost independently of one another. In other arrangements, the partners share all duties and work closely together as a team. Sometimes, but not always, one partner routinely fills in if the other partner is ill. Many job sharers trade blocks of time with each other in order to get longer vacations, or in order to attend special events. In other situations, time trade-off is discouraged or expressly forbidden. Schedules vary greatly, as well. Some job sharers work half-days; others work half-weeks or alternate weeks, alternate months, or even alternate years. Sometimes job sharers divide hours unequally; for example, one partner might work three days a week and the other partner works the remaining two. Occasionally, three people will share two full-time jobs. In Victoria, British Columbia, three teachers successfully shared two full-time teaching positions: two worked 60 percent of the time and the other worked 80 percent of the time.

Parent/student job sharing is another interesting variation. In this model, a parent of school-age children shares a job with a university or college student. The parent works full time except during Christmas, Easter, and summer holidays, at which times the student takes over. This arrangement gives the parent time with the children when they are home from school and helps the student to earn money for education. In Job Sharing for Youth programs, organizations make job sharing available as an option to all entry-level employees, as long as the job-sharing partner is an unemployed young person. Job Sharing for Youth programs give young people a chance to enter the workforce gradually. The programs are also an ideal form of job training because the young person gets instruction and back-up from the experienced partner.

Job sharing and work sharing are not the same, although the two terms are often used interchangeably. Job sharing is a voluntary arrangement which individual employees may request in order to meet their personal needs for additional free time. Work sharing is an involuntary arrangement in which the employer attempts to avoid layoffs by cutting hours of work, usually with the agreement of a union or other employee organization. Work sharing does not necessarily mean that two workers share the duties of a specific job. In fact, most work sharing programs involve an across-the-board cut in the hours of all employees.

When discussing job sharing with your co-workers, your union, or your supervisor, it is important to make sure that they understand these differences between job sharing and work sharing.

What Do Employers Think of Job Sharing?

More and more employers are becoming sympathetic to the idea of job sharing. Those who are innovative or who have had some experience with it are usually more receptive. Employers with experience in job sharing are aware of the advantages that come from having the benefit of two people's energy, ideas, and enthusiasm.

Nevertheless, most potential job sharers will need a pioneering spirit and should expect to work hard at designing a proposal that will mutually benefit themselves and their employers. Employers who are conservative and resistant to change will be reluctant to accept the idea of job sharing because they have never tried it and have not experienced its advantages. In most cases, their reluctance is based on legitimate concerns. Will job sharing disrupt the smooth flow of the work involved? Will job sharing mean more work for management personnel? Will job sharing cost the company more money for employee benefits and training programs?

If you hope to convince your employer to let you share your job, even on a trial basis, you would be wise to design a program which clearly addresses these concerns, and others like them, and to present your request in the form of a written proposal.

What Do Unions Think of Job Sharing?

Many unions, particularly those with a high proportion of female members, are becoming sensitive to the need for alternate work arrangements. Some unions will actively campaign for the right to job share. Other unions still oppose job sharing because they equate it with part-time work which, traditionally, has not been advantageous to the employee in terms of rights, benefits, and job security.

Union contracts that rule out part-time work make job sharing difficult or impossible. However, as job sharing becomes more popular and accepted, unions are recognizing the need to support members who request job-sharing arrangements. This support can and should take the form of negotiating contract terms that create job-sharing opportunities with full employment rights, equal hourly rates of pay, and prorated benefit packages.

Would Job Sharing Suit You?

The process of setting up a job-sharing arrangement may involve a considerable amount of time, research, and persuasion. It also involves a significant loss of income. Before you begin, it is important to consider your motives and your ability to deal with all the circumstances involved in sharing a job.

If you are thinking of sharing your job, you should look closely at

Spotlight on Job Sharing

Maureen Dewhurst and Jill Evans share the position of Program Placement Officer at Western Community Outreach, an employment centre near Victoria. As counsellors, they match the skills and interests of special needs clients with wage-subsidized employment opportunities. Once a contract has been negotiated, Maureen and Jill continue to monitor the placement and provide ongoing support to their clients.

Maureen and Jill split the week between them. One partner works Monday and Tuesday, the other works Thursday and Friday. They work together on Wednesday morning and spend part of this cross-over time updating each other on new contracts and other client-related information. Their schedules are designed so that they each get an equal number of statutory holidays, and they also get complete benefit packages, prorated for half time.

Maureen used to administer the program by herself on a full-time basis. However, at one point she came close to resigning because of the stress associated with the job and her desire to spend more time with her young son. Her supervisor suggested that she follow the example of another staff member and try job sharing.

Maureen's supervisor knew that compatibility is a key factor in successful job sharing, so she advised Maureen to participate in the selection of her job-sharing partner. Maureen reviewed resumés and conducted her own interview with short-listed candidates.

After more than a year of job sharing, Maureen and Jill agree that their partnership works because they are "on the same wavelength." They also share a good sense of humour, and they trust each other to do the job well. Since they began job sharing, other staff have commented on their energy and productivity. According to one staff member, the position they share is so demanding that job sharing is the only way that anyone could handle it.

The arrangement has only one minor drawback. Since Maureen and Jill work different days of the week each month, other staff members sometimes find it hard to remember which partner will be in the office on a particular day without first consulting the appointment book.

Maureen is glad she chose job sharing instead of resigning. "I've never been happier in any job!" she says. "It's the best office I have ever worked in."

your personal needs in the areas of time, money, career development, authority and responsibility, and work habits.

■ TIME

Job sharing generally works best when both partners keep to a regular work schedule. Your schedule may involve working half-days, half-weeks, or even half-years, but it should be consistent and predictable in order to avoid confusing co-workers, clients, or supervisors.

The option of trading time with a partner makes job sharing more flexible than most traditional forms of part-time work, but if you prefer a highly flexible schedule you may feel dissatisfied in a job-sharing arrangement. If you are looking for a great deal of freedom to determine when and how much you work, you would be better off working on call, or as a self-employed contractor or consultant.

For help in assessing your needs for time, see Step Three.

■ MONEY

Because most job-sharing arrangements involve working half time and earning half pay, you will find it easier if you have a relatively well-paid job or a working spouse who is earning a good income. If not, you will have to look carefully at ways to limit your expenses enough to get by on a reduced income. For more information about money, see Step Four.

■ CAREER DEVELOPMENT

For people who do not want to give up work in order to have a family or pursue outside interests, job sharing can be an ideal compromise, but there is a cost involved. Few job sharers get promoted unless they are willing to return to full-time work. This is not to say that job sharers never get promoted. Sometimes two heads are so much better than one that job sharers create an unbeatable combination. However, experience to date indicates that employers are more likely to promote individual, full-time workers than job-sharing teams. It is important to question yourself carefully on this point. If getting ahead is important to you, you may find that job sharing is not in your best interest.

■ AUTHORITY AND RESPONSIBILITY

Some people find satisfaction in having the authority that goes with full responsibility for important tasks or projects. These people often have difficulty working in cooperative situations where they are required to share responsibility and authority. They enjoy the status and rewards that go with being the boss. Their motivation depends to a large extent on getting full credit for their own achievements. They like clearly demarcated areas of responsibility and will object to taking the blame for someone else's errors.

Other people prefer working shoulder-to-shoulder in a team setting where there is a constant exchange of ideas and no one person is in charge. These people can handle the process of sharing responsibility for decisions and the lack of individual authority that is a feature of a cooperative working arrangement. They are more concerned about getting good results than about who gets either the credit or the blame. They seem relatively indifferent to the kudos that go with a star performance. They are also willing to shoulder part of the blame for problems, even though they might not be directly responsible.

Before setting up a job-sharing arrangement, it is important to establish which of these two types you most closely resemble. Do you like to do things your own way? Do you need the reinforcement that comes from getting individual approval for your work? Do you dislike sharing blame as well as authority? If so, you should approach job sharing cautiously, making sure that you can set up an arrangement which suits your personal needs and working style.

Some job-sharing agreements are defined in such a way that each partner is responsible for a distinct and separate set of tasks or projects. This allows the partners to work more or less independently, to make unilateral decisions in their own areas of responsibility, and to reap the rewards they have earned on their own merits. Even so, the partners must always recognize the need for regular communication and for techniques or strategies which will ensure that relevant information is shared effectively.

In many cases, however, job sharing means working coopera-
tively on tasks or projects for which the partners are jointly responsible. One person may pursue the project to a certain point, at which
time the other person takes over and continues working along mutually agreed-upon lines.

Some jobs will lend themselves to either arrangement, but most
will be best suited to one or the other. If you have a choice, you can
decide on an arrangement that suits your personal style and look for
a partner whose needs and style of working are compatible with
your own. However, if you prefer working independently, and your
job does not lend itself to clear divisions of responsibility and authority, you should probably reconsider the whole issue of job sharing.

■ WORK HABITS

Although some jobs are easier to share than others, the more important consideration is often not the job itself, but whether the partners
are temperamentally suited to the challenge of making the arrangement work. Here are some of the factors that influence the success
of job-sharing partners.

Flexibility. Flexibility is at the top of the list of qualities essential
for job sharers. Job sharers must be willing to accommodate their
work habits and points of view to those of their partner. If you like
to run the show and are not prepared to negotiate over differences
with your partner, job sharing could prove difficult.

Organization. Job sharing cannot work without good organization. The ability to plan ahead and work within an orderly system of
procedures is essential. Do you have the necessary organizational
skills to make job sharing successful? Do you put files away when
you are finished with them? If you dislike planning ahead, and work
best in the midst of a pile of papers and coffee cups, you may find
job sharing incompatible with your style of organization.

Collaboration. Job sharing requires an ability to collaborate on
making decisions, assigning tasks, and evaluating outcomes. You
may have to complete projects or tasks you did not initiate, or let
your partner take over responsibility for tasks you would prefer to
do yourself. Try to assess whether or not you feel comfortable con-

sulting with others and taking advice rather than doing the job your own way.

Communication. The success of job sharing depends upon open and honest communication. A job-sharing partnership must be a close working relationship between people who are prepared to deal frankly with each other's needs and opinions. You are likely to run into problems if you find it difficult to say "no" or to criticize another's work.

Would Job Sharing Work in Your Job?

Most jobs can be shared if the partners are committed and compatible. Supervisory positions can be more difficult to share than other jobs. However, through Work Well, I have heard of many instances of successful job sharing by supervisory personnel — for example, a head nurse, a college president, and the executive director of a social service agency.

So far, most job sharers have been women employed in white-collar, professional jobs, largely because these employees are most likely to enjoy a financial position that allows them the freedom to work less. In other kinds of positions, job sharing is often equally practical. Although the numbers are smaller, instances of successful job sharing can be found within most occupational areas.

It is usually necessary to go through the process of designing and proposing a job-sharing arrangement in order to know definitely whether it will work in any particular job. See Step Five for detailed instructions on designing a job-sharing program.

Spotlight on Job Sharing/ Permanent Part-Time

When Dr. Olga Dudek started to practise in Victoria in 1981, she was the city's only female dentist. Dr. Dudek has also set another precedent: she is the first dentist in Victoria to split a practice.

Even when she was in dental school, Dr. Dudek knew that she wanted to practise half time so that she could raise a family. She found a willing and compatible partner in Dr. Trudy Rey. In the beginning, the two dentists decided to experiment with the arrangement for three months. Once it appeared the partnership was going to work, they went on to sort out practical details of scheduling and staffing.

Both dentists have separate case loads (except for patients who need emergency treatment), and the office is open six days a week. Each partner works three of the days. They also rotate every four weeks so that both partners work two Saturdays every month and have two full weekends off. This arrangement accommodates patients who can only make appointments on certain days of the week, especially Saturdays.

Each dentist has her own staff who rotate their days according to her schedule, but there is some overlap for those who want to work four days a week. The dentists and their staff communicate mainly by leaving notes for each other at the end of each rotation. In addition, Dr Rey and Dr. Dudek meet for lunch once a month. They organize frequent potluck dinners that give all the staff members a chance to socialize and discuss their work. Because some members of the two staffs are in the office on the same days, they can work together to organize jobs relating to housekeeping, equipment maintenance, and ordering of supplies.

Dr Dudek is convinced that sharing her practice has significantly reduced the stress commonly associated with dentistry. She also believes her income wouldn't be much higher if she were working full time; higher overheads and income tax would probably offset additional earnings.

With two young children and a house under construction, Dr. Dudek thinks working full time would be impossible. Job sharing also gives both partners the flexibility to take long leaves. Dr. Rey took three months off to travel while Dr. Dudek covered for her. In Dr. Dudek's words, "Most people have to wait until retirement to realize such a dream, but a partnership makes it possible at a much earlier stage of life."

Permanent Part-Time

Permanent part-time work is less-than-full-time work that:

- Pays hourly rates equal to full time;
- Provides full seniority rights, based on a reduced number of hours;
- Includes a benefit package that represents a prorated portion of full-time benefits;
- Assumes that the employee is a committed and permanent member of the workplace team, with full access to further training and opportunities for career advancement.

Permanent part-time is one of the most flexible and widespread work options. Because it is such a familiar feature in the workplace, permanent part-time is often more acceptable to unions and employers than some of the lesser-known options.

The permanent part-time category of workers has grown rapidly over the last fifteen years, partly because an increasing number of personnel managers have realized that some of their most valuable employees do not want to work full time, or cannot, for one reason or another. For many employers, creating permanent part-time positions has solved the problem of how to reliably cover peak periods and extended hours of service.

Work schedules can vary from a few days a month or a few weeks of the year to regular half-days or a regular four-and-a-half day week, and everything in between. The most popular schedules appear to be two-day or three-day weeks at seven-and-a-half hours a day, or five-day weeks at four to six hours a day.

Permanent part-time, sometimes called *career part-time*, has been around for many years. Initially, employers made part-time employment an exception for valued employees of long standing who wanted to work less for health or personal reasons. In some cases, the employer would agree to a part-time arrangement simply because the person was too hard to replace. In some fields, particularly female-dominated occupations such as nursing or teaching, well-qualified professionals have had reasonable success in creating permanent part-time arrangements.

Other occupational areas vary widely in the degree to which permanent part-time work is available. In most large organizations, a few people will be on permanent part-time, even if the option is not generally available. Some industries use permanent part-time extensively: within the unionized supermarket industry, for instance, permanent part-time is both widely available and well paid. Some organizations approve of permanent part-time in theory but severely restrict it in practice; the Canadian government has been notorious in this regard. In a number of male-dominated fields such as logging and mining, permanent part-time is so rare that few companies have policies to cover it.

The treatment accorded to permanent part-time workers also varies greatly. In some teaching and nursing contracts, workers on permanent part-time get full benefits rather than prorated benefits. (In a number of cases, giving full-benefit packages to part-time workers has backfired; although a few part-time workers get excellent benefits, management severely restricts access to permanent part-time because of the increased costs.) In the majority of permanent part-time arrangements, however, employees get benefits proportional to their hours of work. Frequently, the shape of the benefit package is uneven; one permanent employee who works half time may receive full medical and dental coverage but no pension; another may get full pension benefits but have to pay medical and dental plan premiums.

People who work half time or more usually receive the most benefits. For people working less than half time, rights and benefits may be so minimal that the distinction between permanent part-time and casual part-time is virtually meaningless.

What Do Employers Think of Permanent Part-Time?

Thirty years ago the majority of the workforce was made up of full-time workers, predominately married men with wives at home, and young singles of both sexes. The only part-time work available was casual employment at the lower occupational levels. Generally speaking, employers viewed part-timers as a peripheral part of the workforce. Most part-time work was geared for teenagers and students. For the employer, hiring students was a cheap way to handle peak periods or to get the Joe-jobs done. For the student, part-time jobs provided work experience and some pocket money, but they were not the main source of support.

During the 1950s and 1960s, employers developed a number of basic assumptions about part-time work.

- Part-time workers were peripheral, casual, and expendable;
- Part-time workers were not self-supporting, so offering low wages and minimal job security was an acceptable practice;
- Part-time workers were under the financial umbrella of their parents or their spouse, so they didn't need any benefits;
- Work was not the main focus of a part-time worker's life; the employer could not expect a long-term commitment or a professional attitude from part-time staff;
- Part-timers were only temporary workers, so there was no point in providing them with training or opportunities for advancement.

Today, many employers consciously or unconsciously view part-time employment in terms of these traditional assumptions. Sometimes this perception is deliberate and self-serving on the part of employers. As often as not, however, employers have simply failed to notice that the nature of part-time work has changed over the years. The more casual, peripheral, and expendable part-time work-

ers of 30 years ago have been replaced by permanent part-time workers who are:

- Working to provide basic family income, not to earn pin money;
- Committed professionals, working as hard as other employ-ees;
- Self-supporting adults with as much need for job security and employee benefits as other employees;
- Highly productive on the job because they are not spread too thin or operating beyond their limits;
- Permanent members of the labour force and, consequently, a good investment for ongoing training and career develop-ment.

As an adult who wants to work less than full time, your task is to help your employer and co-workers recognize the difference be-tween yourself as a permanent part-time employee and the casual part-timer of the past. Using the term "permanent part-time" is a way to emphasize this difference. It is a way to establish a new concept in your supervisor's and co-workers' minds which differentiates be-tween the kind of employee you are and out-dated assumptions about part-time work.

By calling yourself a permanent part-time employee you may ac-complish a lot — or nothing. If your employer simply pastes *perma-nent part-time* over the mental file that used to say *part time*, nothing will change. If, on the other hand, you can persuade your supervisor to open a new mental file and begin to fill that file with information about who you are, what your needs are, and what your contribution to the workplace could be, it will make a world of difference to the way you are treated. A well-written and persuasive proposal for permanent part-time status can be the key to shifting your em-ployer's attitude.

This difference in thinking stands to benefit both you and your employer. Treating you as a casual worker may cost your employer less in wages and benefits, but it often means that you are underused in terms of your potential contribution to the organization.

Spotlight on Permanent Part-Time

Jackie DeRoo is the manager of corporate planning for the Bentall Group, a large construction and real-estate development firm based in Vancouver. She manages the system the company uses to prepare budgets and develop strategic and operational plans.

Before going on maternity leave to have her second child, Jackie asked permission to reduce her full-time position to an average of three-fifths time. She also wanted to do more of her work from home.

In her proposal, Jackie described how some of her functions could be delegated to other staff. She also described what new arrangements would be needed in the areas of support staff, salary, benefits, and the method of recording her hours. She assessed the costs of installing home telecommuting equipment and also included a detailed timetable to show how her hours would fit in with the varying demands of the planning process.

Because Jackie's supervisor considered her a highly valued member of the management staff, he accepted her proposal for a minimum two-year period. He agreed that the nature of her planning responsibilities was ideally suited to working part time according to a pre-arranged schedule that would allow regular staff meetings. Although the company pension plan had no category for permanent part-time employees, the pension committee approved Jackie's request for the company to continue its contributions on a prorated basis. The company also agreed to prorate her extensive benefits package.

Jackie's new arrangement has worked well on all fronts. Her supervisor says she is just as effective in her job as she used to be, and has no doubts about her continued commitment to her work. Jackie's new secretary also works three-fifths time, and is happy with this schedule because her husband works shifts and she can spend more time with him.

Because of some unique extra planning demands that no one foresaw, Jackie actually worked closer to four-fifths time during her first year on part time, but after that she was able to reduce her work hours to the level she prefers. Because Jackie's arrangement has been so successful, her supervisor says the company will probably be prepared to approve other part-time proposals if similar circumstances arise.

What Do Unions Think of Permanent Part-Time Work?

Many union leaders operate on similarly outdated ideas of what part-time work is, thinking of part-time workers as teenagers and housewives out to earn pocket money — and take jobs away from "real" workers. If you belong to a union that resists part-time employment, your first challenge will be to convince your co-workers, your union representative, and your union executive that there is a marked distinction between traditional part-time workers and today's permanent part-time employee.

Other unions oppose part-time work on the grounds that part-time workers have often been exploited in the past. In many cases this attitude creates a self-fulfilling prophecy; such unions ignore part-time workers or deny them union membership, and in the absence of solid union support, part-timers in those organizations are then vulnerable to exploitation.

You can respond to this circular logic by pointing out the benefits that progressive, responsive unions have achieved by using the permanent part-time concept. Critics of part-time employment often use the retail sector as an example of how badly part-time workers are exploited. Yet unionized, permanent part-time supermarket clerks in the United Food and Commercial Worker's Union (UFCW) enjoy good wages, an extensive benefit package, and seniority rights. The UFCW and other progressive unions do not fear an expansion of part-time work because they have fought to ensure fair treatment for their permanent part-time members.

Would Permanent Part-Time Suit Your Needs?

Because so many different schedules are possible, most people can find a variation of permanent part-time that suits their needs. However, people often fail to anticipate some of the hidden factors that can create problems. Consider the following questions carefully before you decide to switch from full time to part time.

? *Are you prepared for the possibility of negative reactions from co-workers and supervisors?*

Workplaces vary a great deal in their tolerance of differences. In some settings, co-workers and supervisors will see your part-time status as a positive indication of innovation, creativity, and flexibility within the organization. In other workplaces, part-time status might be resented.

You may sense that co-workers and supervisors think you are not serious about your career because you are not working full time. When an opportunity for promotion arises, you may be passed over. Although you may eventually establish your credibility as a committed worker through good job performance, in the short term you might have to accept loss of status and promotional opportunities as a necessary cost of working fewer hours.

Your wage and benefit package is a good indicator of your employer's attitude to permanent part-time. If you are getting fair treatment on the economic front, you are less likely to encounter prejudice elsewhere. However, if your employer expects you to take a cut in your hourly wage or to give up a disproportionate share of benefits, you can probably expect to be treated less fairly in other ways as well.

? *Are you prepared to let others take over some aspects of your job?*

Working fewer hours almost always means giving up some control over your job. It may mean letting go of tasks you find rewarding. If you're not around when a last-minute decision is made, you can't be consulted. You will also miss out on some of the news and office gossip. If you enjoy being at the centre of things, you may have to deal with the feeling of being an outsider.

? *Are you prepared to accept a schedule that meets the demands of the job rather than your own personal schedule?*

Some jobs offer limited opportunities for a change in working hours. You may be able to get the amount of time off that you want only if you take it at times that suit the needs of your particular job.

? *How will working part time affect your pension?*

If you have several years of full-time service invested in a pension plan, switching to part time could be a costly option in terms of lost income at retirement. This is especially true if you shift to part-time status in the years immediately before you retire.

Make sure that you have protected your pension before cutting your hours of work. Pension benefits can always be protected, and most employers are willing to make the necessary arrangements. If yours is not, working part time could ruin your plans for a secure retirement.

Would Permanent Part-Time Suit Your Job?

Many jobs are relatively self-contained. People who work as shift nurses, switchboard operators, assembly-line workers, hotel clerks, and air traffic controllers all have well-defined duties that fit into prearranged blocks of time. Because continuity is not a big factor, such jobs can be easily adapted to permanent part-time.

Also suitable are jobs in which the tasks can be organized into separate cases or projects. Social workers, lawyers, hairdressers, chiropractors, architects, and police duty officers can usually reduce their hours of work by redistributing or limiting the number of clients or projects they accept.

In jobs that demand a lot of continuity, part-time work may cause disruption within the rest of the organization. People whose jobs involve supervising or coordinating the activities of full-time workers, or who serve as resource or support people for others, will find a part-time schedule difficult to manage. In these situations, small cuts in worktime (a four-day week, for example) may be feasible if mechanisms for good communication are part of the program. Where larger reductions in worktime are desired, job sharing is a better choice for people in supervisory positions or jobs that focus on the transfer of information.

Leaves of Absence

A leave of absence is a period away from work without loss of employment rights. Reasons for taking a leave include family problems, mental health breaks, further schooling, community service, or extended vacations. Leave may be paid or unpaid, depending upon the circumstances and the employer. The employer may continue to pay for fringe benefits, but not always.

Leaves of absence are ideal for taking a number of days, weeks, or months off work on a one-time basis. For time off on a recurring basis—one month out of every six, for example—the V-Time option might be a better alternative. Job-sharing arrangements can sometimes accommodate the need to be away from work for extended periods of up to six or eight months out of every year.

Leaves of absence fall into two categories: compensatory benefits and discretionary leave. Compensatory leaves include sick leave, maternity leave, parental leave (for care of sick children), compassionate or bereavement leave, vacations, and statutory holidays. In some workplaces, forward-thinking employers are granting such additional benefits as paternity leave for fathers of newborn children, and adoption leave for parents of newly adopted children.

Compensatory leaves are rights of employment; they are available to all employees in a given workplace. Compensatory leaves are almost always the product of negotiation between an employer and a union or an employee association. Individuals have little power to bring them about. (For more information, see the chapter on Compensatory Benefit Leaves, page 264.)

Rights to compensatory leave are spelled out in written guidelines or in collective agreements. If you are not sure what your rights are, ask your personnel department or union representative. You may be surprised to discover that your employer's personnel guidelines cover some compensatory leaves that are not widely known.

Work options usually come under the category of discretionary leave. This kind of leave is not a right of employment. Management grants permission for discretionary leave on a case-by-case basis. Discretionary leaves include personal leave, extended leave, educational leave, "time-buyer plans," and sabbatical leaves.

Types of Leave

Before making a request for a leave of absence it is important to consider the types that are available, as well as the possible consequences of taking any one of them.

■ PERSONAL LEAVE

Personal leave, also known as *leave without pay*, *temporary leave*, *leave of absence*, or simply *leave*, is any time away from work that is not covered under other leave programs.

Whether you want time off to climb in the Andes, have a face-lift or a hair-transplant, enrol in a three-month acting course, or take the children to Disneyland, you are asking for personal leave. If your workplace has no specific policies for illness, bereavement, maternity, paternity, or adoption leave, you will have to negotiate time off for these purposes within the framework of existing personal leave policies.

Personal leave is almost always leave without pay; that's the bad news. The good news is that you can structure a personal leave to fit your individual needs. Because there is no paycheque attached, personal leave is not an employee benefit. This means that your request does not need to qualify under a company-wide program, nor does it set a precedent for other employees.

Although personal leave is usually unpaid, many workplaces allow employees to go on receiving benefits while on leave. Benefits frequently continue for up to 90 days, but they may go on longer if the leave is granted for health or educational reasons. Leaves which last longer than 90 days are usually handled under provisions for extended leave.

In a few cases, personal leave may be mandated as an employee benefit (meaning that management is required to approve requests for leave if the employee gives appropriate notice) though management can sometimes refuse a request on the basis of operational considerations. Inconsiderate employees can abuse the right to request personal leave and inflexible employers can abuse the right to deny it. Some programs follow a middle course by giving supervisors authority over requests for personal leave, at the same time either appointing an arbitrator to negotiate disagreements or by submitting them to a grievance process.

■ EXTENDED LEAVE

Most large organizations have extended leave policies that pay neither wages nor benefits but guarantee employees a job when they return to work after an arranged absence of several months to a year. Extended leaves have a variety of names including *indefinite leave, inactive status, leave without pay,* or *care and nurturing leave.*

Seniority rights are usually suspended during extended leave, and pension arrangements are put on hold; the employee stays on the pension plan but does not accrue any additional time of service while on leave. Some organizations will allow employees to self-pay employment benefits while on extended leave.

Although extended leave policies guarantee that employees will have a job when they return, it may not be the same job they had before they went on leave. Employees on leave may be required to give notice of their intent to return. (The required period of notice is frequently 90 days.)

For the employer, extended leave policies are relatively inexpensive. Costs are limited to finding and training a replacement. However, being able to take extended leave without pay can be invaluable for the person who needs a long period of time off work, whether it is to care for young children or infirm relatives, to take additional training, to travel the world, or to engage in missionary service. For

this reason, it is worthwhile to include provisions for extended leave
in collective agreements or personnel policy manuals.

■ EDUCATIONAL LEAVE

Educational leave comes in various shapes and sizes, depending
upon the policy of the employer. It can be paid or unpaid, and it may
or may not include continued benefits. Sometimes educational leave
is offered as an employee benefit with well-defined eligibility requirements. It may also be available at the discretion of management.
In some cases, employees are allowed to count the time spent attending approved courses as though it were time at work.

Educational leave is seldom treated as a separate program on its
own. More often, it falls under other programs such as training or
orientation. The personnel policy manual may, for example, define
certain short courses or classes as being part of an employee's standard duties. Among these would be emergency first aid courses, updates on safety procedures, and so on.

Permission to attend courses or educational programs that are
only marginally job-related is often covered in the guidelines for
personal leave. Leave for the purpose of attending courses that are
not job-related may be included in the extended leave guidelines.
Leave to attend school for longer periods (six to eighteen months)
while on the company payroll is usually included in the guidelines
for sabbaticals. Some organizations will help employees self-fund
their educational leave by facilitating participation in time-buyer
plans.

■ TIME-BUYER PLANS

Time-buyer plans allow employees to defer part of their income to
a later date so that they can self-fund a sabbatical. Time-buyer plans
have been available in the teaching field for many years under
five-for-four or *deferred salary* plans, which receive special treatment
from Revenue Canada. [**AMERICAN READERS: Americans can
create informal time-buyer plans — but the I.R.S. does not have a
comparable tax-shelter arrangement for deferred income.**]

In a typical five-for-four plan, a teacher would work full time at

Spotlight on Leaves of Absence

Rudy Van der Vegt is a teacher in the Greater Nanaimo School District who runs an alternate school for Native teenagers. In addition to teaching all subjects, he is responsible for the practical operation of the program — "from transportation to cooking breakfast occasionally."

Four years ago, the Nanaimo school board offered all senior teachers in the district a year's leave of absence and approximately $8,000 in lieu of their regular salary. This generous offer was part of an innovative scheme to reduce costs and prevent layoffs of new teachers during an unusually tight fiscal year.

Rudy decided to take advantage of the offer and, with the help of their savings, he and his wife and daughter travelled for a year in Asia. Because their living expenses were low, they actually spent less that year than they would have if they had remained at home.

Rudy and his family enjoyed the experience so much that when he returned to work, Rudy decided to participate in the Deferred Salary Leave Plan available to all teachers in the district. Under this plan, a teacher agrees to defer a fixed percentage of salary for a certain number of years. The school district holds the money in trust and invests it in a specified financial institution. During the period of leave, the teacher receives payments from the plan instead of a regular salary. The plan also pays for sick leave credits, superannuation deductions, and premiums for fringe benefits.

During the first year, Rudy decided to defer one-third of his salary, but that was too difficult to manage, so for the second and third year he is taking three-quarters of his salary. At the end of the third year he will be able to draw 80 percent of his present salary, which he will use to take his family on another trip to Asia. The school district won't guarantee him the same job when he returns, but he will be offered a position in the same salary range somewhere in the district. This is a chance he is prepared to take, although he is pretty sure he will be able to get his present job back as he did after the previous leave.

Rudy calls the plan a form of "enforced savings." When he returns from his Asian expedition, he plans to contract for his third leave.

80 percent of salary for four years and then take the fifth year off on the deferred earnings, plus interest. Deferred earnings held in trust by the employer or kept in a separate trust account are not taxed until received by the employee.

If you wish to exercise a time-buyer option, you should get specific details from Revenue Canada (phone numbers for the office nearest you are listed in your city's telephone directory). A useful guide to deferred salary plans in Canada is *The Time-Buyer* by Don Abrams.

■ SABBATICALS

Sabbaticals are paid leaves granted for the purpose of education, research, community service, or a mental health break. Within university and college communities, professors can usually claim a year's sabbatical at half or three-quarters salary after every six years of full-time teaching. Most academics use their sabbaticals to write or do research, though some may use the time to study for an advanced degree.

Several major Canadian and American corporations make social service sabbaticals available to selected employees. For example, an executive may remain on the company payroll for several months while directing a fundraising campaign for the United Way. In some high-stress jobs (parole officers, for instance) periodic sabbaticals may be offered as a way of avoiding burnout.

Employers rarely grant sabbaticals unless they foresee some benefit to themselves in terms of good public relations for the organization or an improvement in the health or professional status of an employee.

Would a Leave of Absence Suit Your Needs?

As you have seen, the conditions surrounding leaves vary greatly, depending on the type of leave, the policies of the employer, and the terms of any collective agreement. Different kinds of leave have significantly different effects on income, benefits, seniority, and the right to return to the same job.

In each of these areas it is important to establish both what you want and what you would accept. In your proposal you can ask for what you want; if that is granted, everything is wonderful. If your employer will only give you part of what you want, you will need to be clear on what is feasible for you — and what's not.

■ INCOME

Can you make a good case for paid leave? Educational leave for work-related schooling may be either fully or partly paid. If you take a leave of absence to head a fundraising campaign, it's good publicity for your employer, and you can use that argument to justify staying on the company payroll. Leaves associated with family responsibilities are sometimes negotiated into collective agreements; make sure you are given the correct information about this. Consider carefully whether you can afford to take unpaid leave if that is all that is available.

■ BENEFITS

Some leave arrangements come with full fringe benefits whereas others require that you cover the cost of benefits while you are off work. Many collective agreements make provision for benefits to be covered during short-term leaves, but longer leaves may not be covered. Again, consider whether you could afford the time off work if it involves covering the cost of fringe benefits out of your own pocket.

■ SENIORITY

Depending upon your particular agreement, you may or may not accrue seniority while you are off work. If you do not accrue seniority, how many people will pass you on the seniority list while you are away? Will this have any effect on your job security or the duties assigned to your job? Most people on leave continue to accrue seniority, but if that is not available would you still want to exercise this option?

■ RIGHT TO RETURN

You may not be guaranteed the right to return to the same position, particularly if you take an open-ended leave. Consider how important this factor is to you. If you feel that it is essential to keep your present position, you may want to make your leave proposal contingent upon being able to resume your current duties.

Would a Leave of Absence Work in Your Job?

The answer to this question depends upon whether or not you can make satisfactory arrangements to ensure your work gets done while you are gone. This might require finding a temporary replacement or arranging to delay your work until you return.

Think about your job in light of the considerations raised in the previous discussions about job sharing and permanent part-time. Also, consider the following questions:

? *Do you have unique skills or characteristics that are essential to the performance of your duties? (This could include a diverse contact network, long-established client relationships, or, in the case of a graphic artist, a distinctive style.)*

? *Are you involved in a project (or projects) that would make it difficult for you to turn your responsibilities over to someone else? Would the person taking over require a prolonged period of orientation and training?*

If the answer to any of these questions is "yes," your employer will probably resist a request for a leave. However, that is not necessarily a reason for giving up.

? *If you were in an accident or became seriously ill and needed to be away from work for several weeks or even months, how would your employer cope? Would a co-worker or a part-time employee take over your responsibilities? Would several people share your duties?*

Would your employer hire an outsider to fill your position temporarily? Would your work be put on hold until you returned?

Nobody is indispensable. If you were away on sick leave for an extended period, your employer would have to find a way to deal with the situation. Granting your request for a leave may be difficult, but it is unlikely to be impossible. Besides, if you are really irreplaceable, your employer should be interested in keeping you healthy and satisfied, even if that means doing without you for a while.

V-Time

In 1976, the Santa Clara County Employees Union in California conducted a survey of employee needs. Among other things, the survey revealed that a significant number of workers wanted to reduce their hours, even if it meant a corresponding loss of income. However, the pattern of responses was not uniform. Some employees wanted no change in worktime. Among those who wanted to work less, needs varied in terms of both when and how much they wanted to work.

In response to this survey, the union developed a proposal for a new work schedule called *V-Time*, which is short for *voluntary reduced worktime*. The program established rules for a time/income trade-off which would give employees a range of choices for reducing their hours (and their income) by a fixed percentage over a set period of time.

Management initially vetoed the concept. Then in 1980, the passage of Proposition 13 resulted in lower property taxes in California, and the county was faced with the need to trim its budget. As an alternative to laying off employees, management agreed to experiment with V-Time.

Individual employees, the union, and management all benefited from the program. In the years since, V-Time has been used by numerous state, county, and city governments in the United States. In Canada, the province of Québec was one of the first to promote V-Time in both the public and private sectors. The key elements of a V-Time program are:

- **A variety of time-off choices, defined as a percentage of full time.** Some programs have as many as twelve possible options. In a fairly typical program, the range of time-off choices would be 2.5, 5, 10, 20, 25 and 40 percent of full time.
- **A choice of time off in the form of a shorter workday, a shorter workweek, or extended vacation time.** The table below illustrates a sample range of work options, assuming a 40-hour week as the baseline.
- **Income prorated in direct proportion to hours worked.** Employees retain benefits although some may be prorated, particularly for large reductions in worktime.
- **Approval by the employee's immediate supervisor required for participation in the program and the form of time off.** Most programs have an appeal process or arbitrator to help employees and supervisors reach agreement.
- **Periodic opportunities for enrolment and renewal.** These usually occur every three, six, or twelve months, although some programs are continuously open for applications. Employees have the option to return to full-time hours at the end of any enrolment period.

Employers often resist V-Time proposals initially, but if they can be persuaded to offer the program on a temporary or trial basis, their resistance often turns quickly to support. They discover that V-Time is an inexpensive way to improve employee morale and reduce burnout. This in turn increases productivity and reduces absenteeism.

SAMPLE RANGE OF V-TIME OPTIONS			
PAY REDUCTION	HOURS OFF/DAY	DAYS OFF/ MONTH	WEEKS OFF/YEAR
2.5%	12 minutes	.5	1.25
5%	25 minutes	1	2.5
10%	45 minutes	2	5
20%	1.5 hours	4	10
25%	2 hours	5	12.5
40%	3.25 hours	8	20

Spotlight on V-Time

David Parsons and Jacalyn Hamilton are environmental planners with the B.C. Ministry of the Environment. Their work involves assessing the environmental impact of proposed commercial and industrial projects and designing plans to safeguard the environment.

David Parsons also owns a farm, and V-Time lets him take every Friday off so that he and his family can spend more time there. David says his V-Time schedule is "delightful because it allows me to do things that are important to me outside the job."

Jacalyn Hamilton cares passionately about both her work and her children, and V-Time lets her feel good about both. "I would have great difficulty working at all," she says, "if this option were not available."

The V-Time program at the Ministry of the Environment has been in operation since 1983. At that time the department was facing the prospect of layoffs, and one employee was about to lose his job. Some of his co-workers offered to work less so the department would have money to provide another salary. Since the program started, six employees have elected to shorten their workweek by between 10 and 40 percent. They can always return to full time if they give twenty days notice. Participants get full medical and dental coverage, and most other benefits are prorated, including sick leave and holiday pay.

V-Time is no longer necessary in order to avoid layoffs, but the program has been continued by popular demand. Now the money that the department saves from V-Time goes to hire short-term contract staff for special projects and busy times.

Everyone agrees that V-Time has resulted in a "great improvement in staff morale." In the opinion of Branch Manager John Dick, "The V-Time participants have been some of the most productive employees." He thinks the program has either "maintained or enhanced" their productivity. Problems with the program have been minor. The branch manager and the payroll clerk both have to do some extra work to accommodate the nonstandard schedules, and one participant found that a V-Time schedule requires flexible daycare arrangements.

However, Jacalyn Hamilton is satisfied with her schedule, and David Parsons says, "Without reduced hours, I was always squeezing things, always on a treadmill. I'm a much happier person now."

V-Time can be a way to keep valued employees who might leave because they are under too much pressure. For companies in a difficult financial situation, it can be a creative alternative to layoffs. Why force people out of work when some employees want to work less?

Would V-Time Suit Your Needs?

V-Time programs are popular with employees because they allow more time off without a huge loss of income. Pay cuts are in a range that many people can afford, whereas job sharing or permanent part-time usually mean a big drop in pay. Though the amount of free time gained is moderate, V-Time is flexible enough to meet a variety of needs.

Parents of preschool or school-age children often choose the option of a shorter workday. For others, an extra day off a month or a few extra weeks of vacation can make the difference between surviving and burning out. Because golf courses, riding stables, tennis courts, and other recreational facilities tend to be less crowded in the middle of the week, a mid-week afternoon can be an ideal time for a break from the workplace.

V-Time is appropriate for anyone who wants a small cut in working hours on an ongoing basis. V-Time also allows individual employees to choose different schedules for their time off. This feature accommodates a wide range of uses for free time, from parenting and further education, to volunteer work, recreation, and travel. V-Time programs usually include the option of returning to full time at the end of any twelve-month period — an important protection in case you need to return to full time for financial reasons.

V-Time is a payroll and personnel system meant to serve an entire work unit. If you're wanting only to change your own work schedule, a proposal for permanent part-time would be a simpler way to meet your needs.

Setting up a V-Time program is a lot of work. However, if several employees want to reduce their hours, a collective proposal for V-Time would be easier than each person making a separate proposal for part-time work. A group proposal would also simplify management's task. If you think you would have difficulty getting your employer's agreement to permanent part-time, making a group V-Time proposal might increase your chances of success.

V-Time can be attractive to unions because it makes work options available to all employees on equal terms while allowing room for individual needs and differences. Your union may be willing to help design a collective V-Time program. The support of a strong union can make a big difference in discussions with your employer.

In addition to giving workers greater flexibility, V-Time can also play an important role in avoiding layoffs. When layoffs are threatened, it often turns out that enough employees would prefer to be working less to accomplish the same payroll savings. A carefully designed V-Time proposal from a group of employees can be the catalyst that gets an organization thinking creatively about alternatives to layoffs. (For more information, see the chapter Work Options as an Alternative to Layoffs on page 257.)

Would V-Time Work in Your Job?

In deciding whether your job could be tailored to fit a V-Time schedule, ask yourself the following questions:

? *What effect will your temporary absences have on your job?*

? *What will happen to your work when you are away?*

? *How can you minimize disruption for others?*

Because the cuts in worktime are usually small, V-Time adapts well to most jobs. In fact, if you often get sick because you are overloaded and burned out, going on V-Time may help you get more work done.

If you are planning to cut your worktime by more than 5 percent, you will need to plan on shedding some of your responsibilities or delegating them to others. Having more time off will not do you much good if it means overloading yourself during working hours.

Banked Overtime

For many Canadians, mandatory overtime is a burden — the difference between having a manageable workload and an unmanageable one. As one exhausted employee put it, "I'm sick and tired of being sick and tired." While banked overtime does not eliminate this problem, it is usually easier to get than a ban on overtime.

Banked overtime gives workers the right to take paid time off as compensation for working extra hours. The idea of banked overtime is not new. It has been around for years, both formally in organized programs and informally as a matter of mutual consent between employees and employers.

Formal programs with adequate relief staffing are generally effective at compensating employees adequately. Informal arrangements are often less successful. In many cases, banked overtime exists only on paper: employees are entitled to compensatory time off, but in practice they never get it because there is never a convenient time for the employer.

Well-organized programs avoid this problem by hiring full-time relief staff to fill in for employees who are taking compensatory time off. Employees book their compensatory time according to the availability of relief staff. In order to even out the pressure on replacement staff, firms with known peak periods often allow anticipatory time off, which means using compensatory time off before it has been earned. Good systems also have an overtime arbitrator and a grievance committee.

HOW DO YOU FEEL ABOUT BANKED OVERTIME...?

Would Banked Overtime Suit Your Needs?

Banked overtime can be useful if you do not want to work more than 40 hours a week but, at the same time, do not care too much when you put in your time. Banked overtime is even more attractive if, for personal reasons, you would prefer to work weekends and have more free time during the week. For instance, you might prefer to work on Sunday when the golf links and ski slopes are crowded, then take Thursday or Friday off so you can golf or ski without lining up. If you like to camp or fish, you may be able to exchange weekend work for additional vacation time.

On the other hand, if it is important to keep your work from interfering with your weekends and evenings, you won't be satisfied with banked overtime. The only solution for you would be either a ban on mandatory overtime or the addition of a weekend relief shift at your workplace. At one of its Ontario plants, for example, 3M Canada added a weekend shift that works twelve hours Saturday and twelve hours Sunday and gets paid for 40 hours. This arrangement keeps the plant open seven days a week, avoids overtime, and is popular with both the weekday and the weekend shifts.

If you are accustomed to working overtime and getting paid for it, you may have grown used to the extra income. In that case, banked overtime may not have much appeal. If you are not sure how banked overtime would affect your finances, pay special attention to Step Four: Deciding About Money. Remember, too, that the tax collector takes a big chunk of your overtime earnings.

Would Banked Overtime Work in Your Job?

The crucial element in a successful banked overtime program is adequate relief staffing. If you are going to start banking your overtime, who will relieve you when you want to take your compensatory time off? How long would it take to train your replacement, and would that person also be able to relieve other employees with similar jobs?

Spotlight on Banked Overtime

David English is a research technician with the Tides and Currents Section of the Canadian Hydrographic Service located at the Institute of Ocean Sciences in Sidney, B.C. He installs and services tide gauges in the western Arctic and then collects and processes the data. During the winter months he also does undersea diving to retrieve research instruments placed along the Pacific coast.

David spends two or three months every year travelling, doing field-work, and this means he builds up considerable overtime. His contract allows him to take his banked overtime either in cash or as compensatory leave. Although the majority of David's male co-workers are married with children, they typically choose to convert their overtime into cash. David decided to take a different approach. Because he has to be away so much, he wanted to spend more time at home with his two young daughters during the months when he isn't doing fieldwork. To make this possible, he decided to use his banked overtime to take every Friday off.

One of his daughters goes to pre-school, so David takes her to school on Fridays and sometimes does a duty day with the other parents. David's wife works part time, and the fact that he is home on one of her working days helps to reduce childcare expenses. Because he enjoys carpentry, David prefers to do his own house repairs rather than pay someone else to do them. He can use his Fridays off to work on the house, and this leaves the weekend free for family outings.

David's decision to take more time off happened to coincide with a new development in overtime policy within his division. Because overtime pay-ments were exceeding the amount allotted in the budget, staff were re-quested to take a portion of their overtime in compensatory leave. David's supervisor thinks staff will eventually become used to the idea of taking more leave, and he hopes they will follow David's example. He says that other staff have been able to adjust their workloads to accommodate David's four-day week because it is predictable.

David's wife likes the choice he has made. "It gives the children a chance to be with him all day," she says. "The prospect of spending long weekends together also helps me accept fieldwork better." David agrees. "Fieldwork can be hard on families," he says. "Compensatory leave is one way that I can do my job and still spend more time with my family."

It is obviously easier and more economical for an employer to offer banked overtime if a relief person can cover for several employees. For this reason, banked overtime works best for factory jobs, clerical work, construction jobs, police work, firefighting, and the medical professions.

If your job is a one-of-a-kind position, banking overtime will be harder. Your replacement would require a great deal of training if your work involves a unique talent or skill, or if your job is built around ongoing relationships (for example, psychotherapy or social work).

If you are on salary, you probably do not get paid for overtime. In that case, you will likely have difficulty negotiating banked overtime with your employer regardless of the kind of work you do.

If you want to institute a banked overtime program at your workplace, you will need the help of your union or at least a well-written proposal — unless, of course, you are fortunate enough to have an employer who is willing to look at the high human cost of excessive overtime.

The Politics of Overtime

Overtime may or may not mean more money in the employee's weekly paycheque. Either way, the practice of using overtime on a regular basis causes serious problems for workers, for employers, and for society at large.

- Workers are under more stress and have less time to spend with their families;
- High levels of overtime result in higher rates of turnover, absenteeism, accidents, and health problems;
- High use of overtime translates into higher rates of unemployment. The Swedish experience suggests that banked overtime and relief staffing could provide jobs for up to 4 percent of the Canadian workforce;
- A 1994 Statistics Canada survey suggests that overtime use in Canada has been increasing, particularly for senior workers, pushing older workers to the edge of burnout — or

beyond — while younger workers languish in underemployment or unemployment.

If overtime has such negative consequences, why does it figure so prominently in our economy? Why do so many employers refuse to ban overtime or to hire relief staff to deal with peak periods? Overtime is desirable for a number of reasons.

- It adds greatly to a firm's flexibility in handling peak periods, equipment breakdowns, and rush orders;
- It allows companies to get more production out of the same overhead;
- Overtime pay is a significant and necessary part of many workers' income;
- Overtime often helps consumers get goods and services faster.

In addition, there are a couple of hidden economic reasons why employers rely on overtime.

Salaried employees often work extra hours without compensation. In many organizations the official workweek for salaried employees is 40 hours, but the expected workweek may be 50 hours or more. Promotions are reserved for *committed* employees, that is to say, those who put in a lot of extra hours for free. Because most salaried workers are not unionized, it is difficult to organize against this kind of exploitation. Although provincial labour codes offer some protection (at least on paper), individuals acting alone to withstand this practice are vulnerable to being blacklisted within their organizations.

Overtime represents a significant saving in the cost of benefits. A full benefit package adds roughly 40 percent to the cost of wages; these costs are covered within an employee's first 40 working hours. As there are no additional benefit costs attached to overtime, when employers pay overtime pay to a regular employee rather than hire relief staff, it results in a substantial savings on benefit costs. Even if an employer pays a 50 percent premium for overtime, the 40 percent saving on benefits makes overtime only slightly more expensive than hiring extra staff. In addition to benefits, the cost of hiring extra staff must include training and, in some cases, severance pay.

In discussions of overtime, some employers may have a hidden agenda based on these unacknowledged economic benefits, and for this reason may adamantly refuse to ban overtime or to hire relief staff to cover peak periods. Other employers may agree to a banked overtime program, but only reluctantly, and sometimes only under strong pressure from a union. Be prepared for this resistance.

Employers who resist replacing overtime with relief staff have not recognized the full costs of excessive overtime, which include lost productivity, increased absenteeism, accidents, burnout, and high rates of staff turnover. While these costs typically dwarf the apparent savings that result from overtime use, they are less visible on a company's balance sheets. Employers can't know for sure how much of their low productivity or high absenteeism is due to excessive overtime and how much is from other causes. The costs of high turnover and accidents may not even be tracked as accounting categories.

Often the central task in getting employers to adopt a banked overtime program is to help them become aware of the less visible costs of overtime. Relief staffing is a better policy — not just for the individual worker, but for the employer as well.

Phased Retirement

Phased retirement is a catch-all name for a variety of programs which enable older workers to reduce their work hours in the years preceding full retirement. Many people experience retirement as a sudden shock, a loss of identity and self-worth. Phased retirement programs give older workers time to develop new roles, relationships, avocations, and interests before they retire from the workforce.

Sometimes older employees work fewer hours only in the six months before they plan to retire. Sometimes the reduction starts five years before retirement. Sometimes the phasing period lasts ten years or more.

Most people choose to work a shorter workweek, but phased retirement can also take the form of extended vacations. Reductions in worktime vary from 10 percent to 50 percent. Sometimes the phasing is progressive — for example, from a four-day week at age 62, to a three-day week at age 63, and half time at age 64. Most phased retirement programs include pre-retirement planning courses, some kind of pension protection, and training for the retiring employee's successor.

Phased retirement is rapidly becoming standard practice in Europe. In Sweden, for instance, any worker over age 60 can collect a partial pension while working half time. In North America the idea of phased retirement is still relatively unknown, so if you want to take part in a phased retirement program, you will probably have to initiate it yourself.

Models of Phased Retirement

Phased retirement programs can be designed in several ways; the following are the five most common models.

■ COMPANY-PAID PROGRAMS

Some companies give workers who are approaching retirement age extra vacation time or a shorter workweek with no loss in pay. Because such programs are expensive to the employer, the benefits tend to be relatively short term (six months to one year). Although this is not really enough time to prepare for retirement (particularly when time off takes the form of a longer vacation), these programs involve no loss of either income or pension.

■ EMPLOYEE-PAID PROGRAMS

In this approach, older workers are allowed to reduce their work hours if they agree to take a proportionate cut in salary. Pension contributions are usually based on the full-time salary in order to avoid any effect on the employee's pension after retirement. Though this approach results in a loss of income, it has several advantages:

- The arrangement can be designed for individual cases;
- The arrangement permits substantial flexibility in the length of the phasing period and the amount of reduced worktime;
- The arrangement is usually easier to negotiate than other forms of phased retirement because it costs the employer less.

■ PARTIAL PENSION SCHEMES

A few Canadian organizations, such as the University of Alberta, use an approach that is popular in Europe and the United States. Partial pension schemes allow workers past a certain age (usually 55 or 60) to start collecting a small pension to help cover the income lost by

Thinking Clearly About Retirement

Most Canadians will spend close to one third of their adult life in retirement. Whether these are the best years or the worst depends in large part on thoughtful preparation and planning. It also depends on how realistically we view this new stage of life.

Most people have some fears about retirement: "I'll feel useless," "I won't have enough human contact," "I'll be bored," or "I'll get sick and senile." Many people run away from these fears by throwing themselves whole-heartedly into their work. These people are pretending that they will never retire. For them retirement comes as a traumatic and sometimes fatal shock.

Fears about retirement should be seen as inner messages that say "Pay attention. You have some problems to deal with." Realistic planning for retirement means facing your fears and finding solutions to your concerns. The solutions may involve initiating new relationships, developing new interests and activities, or learning how to take better care of your health.

Most people also have fantasies about retirement: "I'll be able to sleep late," "We'll travel all the time," "I'll be able to (play golf, go fishing, visit the grandchildren, etc.) whenever I want." These are all ways of saying, "Life may be lousy now, but everything will be wonderful when I retire."

People who fantasize about retirement are likely to be bitterly disappointed. After three months of non-stop travel (or golf or fishing), they feel bored and jaded. Realistic planning for retirement involves testing our fantasies in practice. It means abandoning illusions and acquiring habits and skills that will make our dreams come true.

It is a fundamental human need to feel useful. How are you going to meet that need in retirement? The wisdom, personal skills, and judgment you have acquired in more than half a century of living are important assets. Retirement provides a tremendous freedom to work for love, not money. Coming to grips with retirement involves finding new ways to make a contribution to the world.

It's difficult to develop new interests, relationships, activities, and skills while working full time. This is particularly true for men, because men in our society are encouraged to define themselves entirely in terms of their work. For people over the age of 50, phased retirement can be a chance to practise for the real thing.

working part time. Under such an arrangement, older employees could work 60 percent time, which is a three-day week, and still take home 80 to 90 percent of their regular paycheque. In terms of cost, partial pension schemes are often a satisfactory middle ground for both the employer and the employee.

■ INTEGRATED OPTION PLANS

Options like V-Time, job sharing, personal leave, or permanent part-time can be adapted to allow phasing into retirement. Only two changes are required: courses in pre-retirement planning should be offered to older workers, and the pension plan should be changed to allow contributions based on full-time salary.

■ POST-RETIREMENT WORK POOLS

Some companies offer retired employees temporary or relief jobs and/or short-term contracts for special projects. This arrangement gives retired workers extra income and a chance to stay involved for as long as they need or want to be. Employers often find this approach to relief staffing both less expansive and more effective than using temporary workers or consultants.

Would Phased Retirement Suit Your Needs?

Some people use phased retirement as a preparation for full retirement, but for most people the pay-off is more immediate. They simply enjoy the opportunity for free time now. By age 50 or 55, many people have paid off the house and their children have left home. They have less need for a full-time income. Often people at this age feel less need to prove themselves through work; they are more interested in doing what pleases them. The need to spend time with family and friends, or on volunteer commitments, relaxation, hobbies, or a second career seems much more urgent.

For many people, phased retirement offers the opportunity to enjoy the kind of balanced life they have always wanted. It is one of the few socially acceptable ways of having a life that is not dominated by work. However, phased retirement has some drawbacks worth considering.

? *Are you prepared for the possibility of being taken less seriously on the job?*

Some of your colleagues might envy you because you are working fewer hours than they are. Inside, they might be thinking, "I wish I had the guts to take some time for myself and my family the way Harry has." But, this may come out as something like "Old Harry can't cut the mustard anymore. They've already put him out to pasture." In some organizations your status may actually improve by working less, but in others you may notice subtle or not-so-subtle signs of discrimination.

? *Are you prepared to share some of your duties?*

In a phased retirement program you will probably be sharing your duties with your successor. That's fine if you get along with that person. If not, the experience could be awkward or downright painful. In that case you might be wise to make your participation in a phased retirement program contingent upon finding an acceptable partner/successor.

? *How much loss of income can you afford?*

In phased retirement, your income could shrink as much as 50 percent, depending upon how much you want to work and the kind of arrangement you negotiate. The more expensive the arrangement is for your employer, the less likely you are to get the deal approved. The trick is to find a middle ground that you and your employer can both afford.

? *How much of your pension can you afford to lose?*

Most phased retirement plans are designed so that your company pension will be the same as if you had worked full time right up to retirement. In partial pension schemes, however, there is some loss of pension income, usually on the order of 5 to 10 percent. In the unusual case that your employer cannot or will not adjust the pension plan to meet your needs, your pension could conceivably be cut by up to half. It is important to know what your bottom line

Spotlight on Phased Retirement

Ken Waldock is a computer analyst who works for Victoria General Hospital in the Management Information Services department. As he approached the age of 65, Ken wanted to reduce his hours from full time to part time. He asked for permission to decrease his worktime gradually over a two-year period to 22.5 hours per week. Since this arrangement also met the needs of the department, his manager agreed.

At that time, the Management Information Services department was changing over from IBM equipment to a new DEC system, and new staff were to be trained to work with the DEC equipment. However, because the information systems in the hospital were being transferred one department at a time, the hospital still needed a programmer with experience on the IBM system. Ken's desire to reduce his hours fitted perfectly with the hospital's plans to phase into a new computer system.

Ken says phased retirement has been a boon to him, but he admits his case and circumstances were special; he had been with the hospital for only two and a half years as a casual full-time employee, so he had no pension plan or benefits package. That made negotiations easier.

Ken and his manager had to work out a new employer-employee relationship. Instead of keeping him on staff as a part-time employee, the department gave Ken a two-year contract as a computer consultant. For the first year he worked 30 hours a week, later reducing his schedule to 22.5 hours a week, or 4.5 hours a day. He usually works from 7:30 to noon every morning, but he can rearrange his work hours if he wants to take a long weekend.

For Ken, the major advantages of phased retirement are the continued income and the opportunity for mental stimulation. He also feels more in charge of his own life than he did when he was working full time. Within his arrangement, he can organize his own work hours as long as he fulfils his commitment to his client-departments. If he works more than 22.5 hours per week, he gets paid for his time. Despite the fewer hours, Ken feels just as involved with his work as he did before. However, now that the two years are almost up, he feels more prepared to retire. When there are no longer any departments using the IBM system at the hospital, Ken says that he will take a holiday and then look around for some other part-time opportunities.

is for pension income so you can walk away from any phased retirement offer that does not meet your needs.

? *Are you an all-or-nothing person?*

Most people dislike drastic change, but some people thrive on it. If you are the kind of person who handles a crisis better than incremental adjustments, you can probably handle full retirement better than a gradual disengagement.

Would Phased Retirement Work in Your Job?

It is possible to design a phased retirement schedule that will work for almost every job, including management positions. In a few cases it will be necessary to transfer to a different job in order to be eligible for phased retirement, but this is the exception rather than the rule.

For smaller reductions in worktime (5 to 30 percent), the criteria are essentially the same as for V-Time. The criteria for job sharing apply to larger cuts in working time.

Flextime

Flextime is the term used to refer to flexible working hours. Employees on flextime work a fixed number of hours every day or week, but they can choose their own starting and quitting times. For example, one employee working an eight-hour day might start at 8 a.m. and finish at 4 p.m.; another employee in the same department and working the same number of hours might begin at 9 a.m. and finish at 5 p.m. In the most flexible programs, staff can work a different schedule each day and "bank" hours from day to day or week to week.

Flextime was developed in 1967 by a West German management consultant named Christel Kammerer. She devised the scheme to solve a problem at an aerospace research and development centre near Munich. Lateness and absenteeism had increased because more employees had started to own cars and were driving to work over roads that could not handle the increased traffic.

Kammerer's flextime innovation produced the anticipated improvement in traffic flow, but managers were surprised at the extent of overall benefits: absenteeism declined by approximately 40 percent, overtime dropped by about 50 percent, employee turnover was reduced, tardiness disappeared, and morale rose sharply.

After that, flextime spread fairly quickly throughout Europe and eventually made similar progress in the United States. About 30 percent of Canadian and American firms now have part of their workforce on flexible hours. (Some flextime programs are known by generic terms like *flexitime* or *flexible hours*.)

Spotlight on Flextime

Katherine Rempel is the office administrator for the Victoria branch of National Life of Canada, an insurance company. She is one of two office staff who provide office support services for the branch manager and eight sales representatives.

Katherine works from 8 a.m. to 4:30 p.m. and her office partner works from 8:30 a.m. to 5 p.m. They are both taking advantage of a company-wide flextime schedule introduced by the head office of National Life in Toronto. Under the National Life flextime program, all staff must be on duty between the core hours from 9:30 a.m. to 11:30 a.m. and from 1:30 p.m. to 3:10 p.m. Flexible hours are from 7:15 a.m. to 9:30 a.m. and 3:10 p.m. to 6:15 p.m. In a large city, the company's flextime program helps staff avoid the worst of the rush hour. By providing extended office hours, it also helps the company with the need to conduct business between a number of time zones. The branch office in Victoria has special needs, however, so its employees have somewhat less flexibility in the hours they work.

Because only two people are available to answer phone calls, one person must be in the office early in the morning in order to receive head office calls from Toronto. Someone also has to be in the office after 4:30 p.m. to take local phone calls. From the company's point of view, it makes good sense to stagger the hours of the two office staff in Victoria.

Katherine is satisfied with her hours because she describes herself as a natural early bird; even a 7:30 a.m. start is not too early for her. By finishing her work at 4:30, she can be home by 5 p.m. and have the whole evening to spend with her family. As a single parent for many years, she has been able to cut her childcare costs by working an early schedule. At work, Katherine enjoys at least an hour when she can concentrate without a lot of interruptions. Since there are no peak periods, she and her office partner can adjust their lunch hours to suit themselves as long as one person is always available to answer the phone.

Flexibility is limited in a small office, but fortunately Katherine doesn't have to contend with the heavy rush hour of a large city. She prefers an early schedule, and she is pleased that in her sixteen years with insurance companies, that option has always been available.

Most flextime schemes use the following terms and concepts:

- Bandwidth — the period between the earliest starting time and the latest quitting time.
- Flexible starting time — the period within which employees can begin the workday (for example, between 7 a.m. and 10 a.m.).
- Flexible quitting time — the period within which employees can end the workday (for example, between 3 p.m. and 6 p.m.).
- Core time — the period when all employees must be at work (for example, between 10 a.m. and 3 p.m.).
- Mid-day flexibility — the period during which employees may be away from work (for example, between 11 a.m. and 1 p.m.).

Flextime is based on the assumption that employees will work a standard number of hours; pay periods are also based on this assumption. Some adjustment is necessary when there is a difference between salaried hours and actual hours. These adjustments are made at the end of accounting intervals, which are called "settlement periods." Some systems require employees to adjust their work hours in order to come out even at the end of each settlement period.

SAMPLE PROGRAM

With mid-day flexibility:

7 A.M.	10 A.M.	NOON	2 P.M.	3 P.M.	6 P.M.
flexible starting time	core time	mid-day flexibility	core time		flexible quitting time

Without mid-day flexibility:

7:30 A.M.	10 A.M.		2 P.M.	5:30 P.M.
flexible starting time		core time		flexible quitting time

These are called "zero balance" systems. Other systems allow employees to carry an excess or deficit of hours from one settlement period to the next.

In systems with no carry-over provision, flexibility increases with the length of the settlement period. If the settlement period were one day, for example, you would have to arrange your starting and quitting times (or your lunch hour) so that you worked the required seven or eight hours that day. If the settlement period lasted four weeks, you could work different amounts from day to day and week to week as long as you had credit for working the required 140 to 160 hours at the end of the four-week period.

Accounting is simple in zero balance systems, but they don't have much flexibility for dealing with fluctuating workloads or changes in the responsibilities employees have outside of work. *Hours banking* provides this kind of flexibility. Hours banking means adding or subtracting, at the end of each settlement period, any surplus or deficit of hours from the employee's account in the hours bank.

Hours banking can have significant benefits, including extra days off. For example, if you are salaried for 35 hours per week and you work an average of 7.5 hours each day, you would earn one full day off every fourteen working days. With hours banking, you could take every third Friday off.

Many systems have rules that ensure adequate coverage. Certain individuals may be designated to cover lunch hour or the beginning or end of the business day. If hours banking is allowed, days off must sometimes be booked in advance on a rota system in order to guarantee essential coverage.

Would Flextime Suit Your Needs?

Flextime allows you to change your schedule without any reduction in your hours, your paycheque, or your benefits. For many people, especially commuters, this is an attractive option. If you must now commute in the thick of the rush hour, flextime may help reduce your commuting time.

Other advantages include the ability to tailor your workday to your children's school schedule. Whether you are an early bird or a

... YOU WERE ASKING ABOUT FLEXTIME, BRAWNLEY...?

night hawk, flextime can make a big difference to your comfort and your efficiency on the job. Flextime with hours banking can satisfy your need for a long weekend every so often if you do not mind working an additional half-hour every day.

If you have peaks and valleys in your workload, you may spend some of your time struggling to catch up and the rest wondering what to do with yourself. In that case, flextime can function as an informal version of banked overtime. You can work late when things are hectic, and take time off when the workload is light, without any effect on your paycheque.

If your basic problem is overwork, flextime won't lighten your load although it may drastically reduce the time and effort you spend commuting. Many people mistakenly think that flextime will make their job easier, but that is not the way it works. If you are overloaded or burned out you should consider a work option that involves working fewer hours.

Would Flextime Work in Your Job?

Flextime is not practical for all jobs. If your job requires constant interaction with other staff members, you probably need to work the same hours as your co-workers. Flextime is usually not possible for assembly line workers. However, if you work independently a lot of the time, flexible hours will not present many problems. Most office jobs can be adapted to fit into a flexible schedule.

Flextime is also appropriate if you have some discretion in the scheduling of your workload. Professionals like social workers, chiropractors, and investment counsellors can often book appointments to coincide with a flexible schedule. If you are a member of a response pool of telephone operators, sales representatives, or shipping clerks, for instance, flextime will work if it is designed to ensure adequate staff coverage.

If flextime cannot work in your job, you could look at the possibility of V-Time, banked overtime, or a compressed workweek, particularly one that involves staggered hours.

Compressed and Modified Workweeks

Riva Poor's 1970 book *Four Days, Forty Hours* sparked a flurry of experiments in rearranging the 40-hour workweek. Of the many versions tried, four have gained fairly widespread acceptance:

- The 4/40 compressed workweek comprises four ten-hour days each week. Common variations are four, 9.5-hour days and an alternating schedule of three ten-hour days and four ten-hour days.
- The 3/38 compressed workweek comprises three 12.5-hour days each week.
- The modified workweek makes each workday 45 to 50 minutes longer, depending on scheduled hours, with every other Friday off.
- Staggered hours comprises five standard eight-hour days every week, but with a choice of starting times.

Let's look at each of them in turn.

■ THE 4/40 COMPRESSED WORKWEEK (4/40 CWW)

In 1970, approximately 40 North American firms were using the 4/40 CWW. Three years later, an estimated 3,000 companies had implemented such a plan. By the late 1970s CWW was beginning to receive a mixed press. Although the CWW is still popular (between one and three million North Americans are still working a compressed work-week), there are some limits to its usefulness. One indication of the difficulties of early CWW programs is the fact that nearly 30 percent are discontinued shortly after implementation, five times the rate for flextime.

For employees, a compressed workweek has the advantage of making every weekend a long one. CWW also lessens commuting time by reducing the number of commutes and, sometimes, by allowing workers to avoid rush-hour traffic.

The disadvantages are the fatigue and increased risk of accidents associated with a longer working day. Extended work hours are especially hard on older workers and parents of young children.

The compressed workweek is usually an across-the-board arrangement in factories and institutional settings like hospitals and airports. In most cases, all employees have to participate, including those who find the schedule a hardship or an inconvenience. Office workers can sometimes negotiate an individual 4/40 workweek, particularly if they work independently most of the time.

Initially, employers thought that CWW would increase productivity and reduce absenteeism, but there is little evidence to support this. Employers do like the fact that a compressed workweek reduces set-up and clean-up time. Sometimes it also provides more efficient shift coverage.

A compressed workweek is often effective in providing extra coverage for peak workloads. For example, chronic care hospitals require around-the-clock coverage. This can be handled by three eight-hour shifts. Since the bulk of the work comes between 8 a.m. and 6 p.m., this period could be covered by a ten-hour shift. (Employees usually work three ten-hour days one week and four ten-hour days the next, for a 35-hour average workweek.)

On the negative side, employers may find that the CWW creates communication problems with customers, suppliers, and parts of the organization that remain on a five-day week.

Spotlight on Compressed Workweek/Permanent Part-time

Brenda Ruttan and Sandra Green are registered nurses in the Medical Cardiology Unit of Royal Jubilee Hospital in Victoria. Both nurses are single women in their twenties; neither has children. Both work twelve-hour shifts on a full-time compressed workweek schedule. A typical rotation involves four days or nights on followed by five days off.

Brenda likes having several days off in a row so that she can more easily visit out-of-town friends and family. Both nurses also spend less total time preparing for and commuting to work. On the job, the longer shift makes it easier to organize their daily tasks and complete their charting. Sandra believes that they can provide more continuity of care because they deal with the same patients for an entire day or night. Although they may get tired if they have a particularly busy shift, both nurses say this doesn't happen often enough to be a problem. In their opinion, the extended workday has only one real disadvantage. On working days they have a hard time fitting in such things as banking, personal appointments, and shopping. Sandra thinks the starting and finishing times of the shifts are more crucial than the length of the working day. If she works from 7 a.m. to 7 p.m., for example, she has enough time for evening outings. But if the shift ends at 8 p.m., she finishes work too late to attend most events.

Nurses Jane James and Cathy Fitzgerald used to work full time on extended shifts at the same hospital, but Jane has been working part time since she returned from maternity leave. Cathy also switched to part time after a car accident left her with a chronic back problem. She found working extended shifts on a full-time schedule too gruelling because she didn't have enough time off to get the rest she needed. For Jane and Cathy, the extended shift is acceptable because they only work part time. Even so, Jane says a twelve-hour shift doesn't leave her enough time to sleep during the day when there are small children in the home. On the other hand, working twelve hours at a time means she works fewer shifts for the same money.

For nurses the compressed workweek has been a mixed blessing. Those who have few home and family commitments regard the extended time off as a bonus. Those nurses with home responsibilities are discovering that the extended shift puts a strain on their energy for other activities.

▌ THE 3/38 COMPRESSED WORKWEEK (3/38 CWW)

The 3/38 CWW is a bit of a misnomer because the normal schedule of three 12.5-hour days actually totals 37.5 hours per week. There are two common variations on this model:

- A 36-hour workweek made up of three twelve-hour days;
- A 42-hour workweek that alternates between three twelve-hour shifts and four twelve-hour shifts.

The 3/38 CWW has the same advantages and disadvantages as the 4/40 CWW with two important differences:

- It is more suitable for continuously operating facilities;
- Fatigue is a more serious concern.

The 3/38 CWW is sometimes used to alleviate chronic overtime. Factories that operate around the clock six or seven days a week often run into problems of burnout and turnover among their employees. Replacing the three standard eight-hour shifts with four twelve-hour shifts means that factories can operate six days a week without overtime. On this system, the factories can run for seven days a week if the average workweek is 42 hours.

To eliminate excessive overtime at one of its Ontario plants, 3M Canada created an imaginative variation on the CWW. The company uses three standard eight-hour shifts from Monday to Friday. On Saturday and Sunday, two shifts work twelve hours a day. The weekend employees work a total of 24 hours a week, but they are paid for 40 hours. They also receive a full benefit package. This arrangement has the additional advantage of giving employees a choice between eight-hour and twelve-hour shifts.

▌ MODIFIED WORKWEEKS

The little-league version of the compressed workweek is the modified workweek, which has two common variations:

- The normal workday is extended by approximately 45 to 50 minutes, resulting in one extra day off every two weeks;

- The normal workday is extended by approximately 30 minutes, resulting in one extra day off every three weeks.

Modified workweeks can result in inadequate staffing on Mondays and Fridays unless mechanisms to ensure even coverage are included.

■ STAGGERED HOURS

Standard flextime programs do not work in factories, hospitals, fire stations, or other places that require continuous staffing. The best way to improve flexibility in these workplaces is to offer employees a choice of two or three possible starting times for each shift. For example, one-third of the day shift at a factory might start at 7 a.m., one-third at 8 a.m., and one-third at 9 a.m. Afternoon shifts would start at 3 p.m., 4 p.m., and 5 p.m. The evening shifts would begin at 11 p.m., midnight, and 1 a.m. This approach has several advantages:

- Employees have more flexibility and freedom of choice;
- Overlapping shifts provide the chance for workers to exchange information;
- Congestion is reduced in the lunch room, change room, parking lot, and at security check points;
- In large factories, staggered hours diffuse rush-hour congestion on roads leading to the work site.

In factories, businesses, and offices where the workload is lighter at the start and end of the day, staggered hours can also facilitate set-up or clean-up operations, or can be used to extend hours of service. They have one main disadvantage: shifts must be temporarily realigned every time the plant shuts down and starts up again.

Would a Compressed or Modified Workweek Suit Your Needs?

A compressed workweek will not reduce your workload. It won't solve your problems if you are burned out or overloaded. However, a compressed workweek can be an attractive option if:

- You want a regular three- or four-day weekend;
- You are able to work long hours without getting tired;
- You can't afford to work less in order to get more free time;
- Longer workdays will not interfere with your spouse's or children's schedules.

A compressed workweek is not recommended for older workers, for workers with health problems, or for parents of preschool children. In these situations, a modified workweek is better because it means working only slightly longer hours. Staggered hours may be the best option if your main problem is rush-hour traffic or a family responsibility that would be helped by a change in your starting or quitting time.

A flextime program with banked hours is more flexible than any form of compressed or modified workweek. Whenever possible, flextime is the recommended approach.

Would a Compressed or Modified Workweek Work in Your Job?

The compressed workweek seems most suited to workplaces where:

- The work is not physically demanding or stressful;
- The danger of accidents is small;
- The workforce is primarily young and few workers have parenting responsibilities;
- The normal workweek is less than 40 hours.

Just to review, the 4/40 compressed workweek is suitable for most single-shift factories and institutions. Single-shift factories and offices can both use the modified workweek. In factories, the schedule usually applies to all employees. In offices, the modified workweek is usually optional.

Telecommuting

Telecommuting is sometimes called *home work* because it means that you do all or part of your work at home.

Futurists like Alvin Toffler surround the idea of telecommuting with overtones of technology and romance. In their scenarios, everyone will one day live in "electronic cottages" connected to the office by telephone, computer, fax machine, and television. These images obscure the fact that telecommuting is neither new nor necessarily high-tech. For decades, millions of North Americans have been taking work home without elevating it to a science.

One thing has changed in recent years: instead of merely taking extra work home, many people are finding it practical and beneficial to spend some or all of their regular office hours at home. Computer modems and other electronic hardware make it possible to stay in contact with the office without having to be there in person. However, the change is only a matter of degree. If you recognize that telecommuting is quite an ordinary experience, it will be easier to think about doing it yourself and easier to sell the idea to your employer.

There are three ways to approach telecommuting.

Partial telecommuting is working at the office part of the time and working at home when you need undisturbed privacy for tasks such as report writing, planning, budgeting, and so on.

Full telecommuting means that you work from home exclusively or almost exclusively. Your work space at home may contain fairly extensive telephone and computer equipment for communicating with the office.

Satellite telecommuting involves working with three or four other people in a small neighbourhood office close to home. The satellite office is linked electronically to the main centre downtown. Strictly speaking, this does not qualify as working at home, but it offers some of the same benefits — less commuting time, for example, and the ability to have lunch with the kids.

Telecommuting sounds appealing, but it has drawbacks as well as advantages. The obvious advantages of working at home are:

- Less commuting time;
- A more pleasant work environment;
- Better integration of work and family life;
- Fewer distractions and interruptions;
- The freedom to work independently and at your own pace.

Some of the disadvantages of telecommuting are:

- A sense of social isolation and alienation from co-workers;
- A feeling that you are left out of the decision-making process;
- A possibility of being overlooked at promotion time;
- Vulnerability to abuse by your supervisor;
- Vulnerability to being laid off;
- Fuzzy boundaries between work and family life.

Both the advantages and disadvantages associated with telecommuting become stronger the more you move towards full telecommuting.

What Do Employers and Unions Think of Telecommuting?

Employers and unions have mixed attitudes about telecommuting. Employers fear losing control of telecommuting staff and worry about the difficulties of supervising and communicating with them. They may also have concerns about the extra costs associated with a work station at home, and may fear setting a precedent for other workers.

On the other hand, employers are often attracted to telecommuting by the promise of happier and more productive employees. Sometimes they welcome the opportunity to reduce overcrowding in the office.

A formal written proposal may not be the best way to raise the issue of telecommuting with your employer. Partial telecommuting often begins in a casual manner without involving anyone but the immediate supervisor: "I'm sure I could get the quarterly report done on time if I could stay at home tomorrow and work without interruptions." Full-time telecommuters may also start working at home in this short-term, casual way. Mini-trials like this give both you and your employer a better idea of what would be involved if you were to work at home.

Unions are under some pressure from members to expand telecommuting opportunities, but they have some serious and valid concerns. Their fear is that at-home workers will be hard to organize, that they will be vulnerable to pressure from their employers, that telecommuting will degenerate into a piecework, cottage industry like the garment trade, and that employers will try to invade employee privacy by monitoring their work via computer.

One way to deal with your union is to avoid theoretical discussions about telecommuting. These discussions tend to emphasize the problems rather than the benefits. Instead, focus on specific factors concerning your personal situation and your job.

Would Telecommuting Suit Your Needs?

Telecommuting may be the best option for you if:

- You spend a lot of time commuting;
- You have a physical disability that impedes your access to the office;
- You are recovering from a serious accident or illness;
- You work in a distracting environment at tasks that require a high level of concentration;

Home Work and Self-Employment

Freelancing and contract work are forms of self-employment. They fall outside the definition of telecommuting because they involve profound changes in the employer-employee relationship. However, they represent viable options for people who want to work at home.

Freelance work involves selling a product (such as a magazine article or a graphic design) rather than selling your time. The buyer and seller have no responsibilities to one another beyond the terms of the specific project in question. Freelancers are free to sell their services elsewhere and the client is free to buy from other suppliers. Freelancing has a high level of freedom and little or no job security. In both Canada and the United States, self-employed individuals tend to get somewhat better treatment at income tax time than do employees.

Contract work involves selling your time to an employer for a fixed duration. Contract employees often get a higher hourly wage than regular staff, but they have no job security beyond the end of the current contract.

Freelancers and contract workers usually have more latitude than regular staff about when and where they work, but they have less protection because the provisions of the labour code do not apply to self-employment. Self-employed workers are on their own in dealing with abuses by their clients.

Self-employment is often suitable for professional, technical, and service jobs such as woodworking, hairdressing, psychological counselling, massage therapy, small appliance repairs, engineering consultancy, and furniture refinishing. However, self-employment can be extremely insecure, and no one should change from a staff position to freelance or contract status without carefully assessing the risks involved. Consider self-employment only if working at home is important enough to justify the risk. Two useful resources are *Working at Home* by Carol Zetterberg and *The Work-at-Home Sourcebook* by Lynie Arden.

- You want to have some contact with your children during the workday.

Telecommuting can give you more control over your home and work life. You can do your errands in the time you used to spend commuting. You can have lunch with your children, or put dinner in the oven at three o'clock. Having a sick child at home does not mean losing a day of work. You have the freedom to smoke or to work in a smoke-free environment. You can arrange the lighting, the furniture, the sounds, and the colours of your work space to suit your preferences. You can work outside of office hours if you like. You are free to take breaks when you want to work in the garden, walk the dog, or have a short nap. You can dress more casually and will probably save money on clothes, transportation, and eating out.

Telecommuting may look like the ideal way to combine a job with childcare, but there are definite limits. In general, it does not suit people with preschoolers. They find themselves feeling frazzled because they cannot give enough attention to either their work or their children. People combining home work with school-age children or infants have mixed experiences; some rave about it, others rage against it. Much depends on the individual personalities of the telecommuting parents and their children. Some nursing mothers have found it easier to take their baby to work rather than to work at home. *Of Cradles and Careers* by Kaye Lowman has good examples of this option.

If telecommuting seems made-to-order for you, stop and consider the following questions before you become too enthusiastic.

? *Do you have enough self-discipline to keep working when no one is watching over you?*

Can you resist the temptations of watching TV, doing the laundry, digging in the garden, or taking the kids to the beach?

? *Will you be able to stop working at the appropriate time?*

If you are a workaholic, you might find it harder to leave work alone because you're not physically separated from your work environment.

? *Will there be many distractions?*

Do you have overly friendly neighbours? Will your spouse or other family members be wanting your attention while you are trying to work at home? How much quiet and privacy can you realistically expect?

? *Do you have adequate work space at home?*

Is it comfortable, well-lit, and relatively soundproof? Can you protect equipment and important files from break-ins and playful children?

? *Will you feel lonely working at home?*

This is less of a problem if you will be telecommuting only one or two days a week. If companionship is one of the things you like about work, you may feel too isolated working at home.

? *Will working at home interfere with your professional ambitions?*

The more you work at home, the more you will be excluded from office politics, and this could affect your prospects for promotion. If you foresee any problems in this area, try to arrange a temporary trial period before you lock yourself into a full-scale arrangement for working at home.

Would Telecommuting Work in Your Job?

Only a few jobs are suitable for full telecommuting. It will not work for most management positions. It will probably work well for sales reps and staff researchers. Most white-collar jobs involve some tasks that can be done at home. If the job requires concentration, you can often work more efficiently and creatively at home. The following tasks are well suited to the home environment: clerical work, report writing, designing graphics, legal work, correspondence, research, programming, writing, sales work, planning, telephoning, and data entry.

The following questions will help you decide how much of your work you could do from home.

Spotlight on Telecommuting

Sid Tafler became the news editor of *Monday* magazine, a news and events weekly in Victoria, B.C. after working as a freelancer and journalism instructor for the previous eight years. Sid had always worked at home, and had his own home office complete with personal computer, printer, modem, and electronic mailbox service.

Sid decided to take the job at *Monday* because he wanted to be involved in the production of a "total product." After the relative isolation of home work, he enjoys the close working contact with four editorial staff and another fifteen in the production department.

Sid does all his editing work in the office because he needs to be accessible to the magazine's other editors and writers. However, he prefers to do his actual writing at home one day a week. He finds that he can concentrate much better without the distractions of an office. With only four terminals and five staff members, it can also be difficult to get sufficient computer time on deadline day.

When he works at home Sid likes "not shaving, no tie, and working in the comfort of my own space." His boss doesn't object to his working at home, but the first time he failed to show up at the office the receptionist assumed he was taking time off, and his paycheque was docked a day by mistake. The incident made him realize that working at home is not a choice that most employees take for granted.

For Sid, computer technology increased the feasibility and efficiency of home work. He can either send his completed work directly to the office via his telephone modem or put it on a disk and transfer it to the system the next day. As a member of the Periodical Writers' Association of Canada, he uses his home computer to network with other writers across the country. He can also link up to a number of computer databases for research purposes.

Because his job as an editor involves supervising and training other staff, Sid has to spend much of his time in the office, but he appreciates the opportunity to do some of his work at home. Since he can write more efficiently that way, he has more time during his office hours to devote to other tasks.

? *What equipment do you need to do your job?*

Is the equipment expensive; does it take up a lot of room? Would two sets of equipment for home and office be required? How much of your job could you do at home without expensive equipment?

? *How much do you use hard-copy files?*

Information that is stored electronically transfers more easily between home and office.

? *How many face-to-face contacts do you need to make in your job?*

You can deal with telephone contacts and correspondence from home, but the home office is usually inconvenient or unsuitable for meetings with clients or other staff members.

? *How much time do you spend in front-line customer service?*

The more you are actively engaged in front-line service, the less likely it is that you will be able to work from home.

? *How many decisions can you handle by phone?*

Can someone else handle situations that come up when you are away? If you handle supervisory duties, do you have a responsible deputy who can take charge in your absence?

? *How fair is your employer?*

Telecommuting makes it somewhat easier for employers to take advantage of their employees. If you have any doubts about this, build safeguards into the design of your program.

... WELL, WHAT DID YOU EXPECT ?...YOU ONLY
WORKED PART TIME...

STEP THREE

CHOOSING YOUR TIME

Taking Stock
of Your Life

After surveying the options in Step Two, you may know exactly which option you want and how you can take full advantage of your new work schedule. In that case, you might as well skip to Step Four: Deciding About Money.

If you are still not sure which work option you like best, you may first have to decide how much free time you need and what you would do with it. Step Three is designed to help answer these questions. Step Four will help you decide how much free time you can afford.

Sometimes work is a problem only because we have not looked at the "big picture." We may think we want to work less when what we really need is to assess how much time we devote to other spheres and why. The exercise which follows is designed to help you determine what you want most out of life and what you would just as soon eliminate in order to make room for more important activities.

When you have completed the exercise, you will be able to see the extent to which your life contains the desired balance between work and activities in other areas, such as family, friends, recreation, travel, and so on. The exercise will also help you decide what changes you need to make in the way you use your time and whether a new work schedule should be part of those changes.

Instructions for Taking Stock

❶ Photocopy the following nine pages and use the copies to do your Taking Stock inventory.

❷ Use a pencil to do your inventory so that you can make changes easily. Have available red and green felt pens or pencil crayons.

❸ The inventory looks at eight major spheres of activity: work/career, housework/maintenance, spouse, family, social life, recreation, self-development, and spirituality. Some activities, such as taking the family to church, may show up in two or more spheres.

❹ Go through the exercise fairly quickly at first, without taking a lot of time to stop and think about your decisions, so that your inventory reflects your intuitive feelings. If you really want to think about some questions, go back to them later.

❺ Approach the exercise as an opportunity to explore possibilities rather than as a way of arriving at hard and fast decisions about your future.

❻ Look backward in your life as well as forward. Consider not only what you think might make you happy in the future but also what has brought you pleasure in the past.

❼ Put aside temporarily all questions of what you should do or must do. Don't be concerned about what other people think. For the moment, you are interested only in *your* needs and *your* feelings.

Work and Career

What aspects of your job(s) do you find most important or satisfying?

_____

_____

What aspects of your job(s) do you find least important or satisfying?

_____

_____

What work activities would you like to do more of?

_____

_____

What courses or training would enable you to do your job better or make your work more interesting?

_____

_____

Are you satisfied with your current job?
yes _____   *sort of* _____   *not at all* _____

What new kinds of work or career opportunities would engage your interest?

_____

_____

Including commuting time, how many hours per week do you now spend at paid employment? _____

Including commuting time, how many hours per week would you like to spend working for pay? _____

Housework and Maintenance

Housework and maintenance activities include such tasks as house cleaning, shopping, laundry, cooking, eating, banking, and so on.

Which of these tasks do you most enjoy?

_____

_____

_____

Which of these tasks would you like to eliminate or spend less time on?

_____

_____

_____

What housework and maintenance tasks would you like to spend more time on (for example, baking your own bread or redecorating your home)?

_____

_____

_____

In an average week, how many hours do you now spend on housework and maintenance activities? _____

How many hours per week would you *like* to spend on housework and maintenance activities? _____

Spouse or Partner

How close are you to your wife, husband, or partner? (Skip this page if you're unattached.) How often is your partner the main focus of your attention? As parents, for instance it's easy to get caught up in being "mommy" and "daddy" and to forget how to be friends and lovers. How important is your spousal relationship, as reflected in the way you spend your time together?

Which activities with your spouse do you enjoy the most?

_____

_____

Which activities would you like to do more often with your spouse?

_____

_____

Which activities with your spouse do you enjoy the least?

_____

_____

What would you like to do less often with your spouse?

_____

_____

In an average week, how many hours do you spend on activities with your spouse? _____

How many hours per week would you *like* to spend on activities with your spouse? _____

Family

Family structures in North America are becoming more diverse; answer the following questions according to your own sense of who your family is. If you think of a special friend as a member of your family, if you have in effect "adopted" this friend as a parent, sibling, or offspring, include that person in this sphere as well.

Which family activities are most important to you?

_____

_____

_____

What would you like to do more of with your family?

_____

_____

_____

What family activities would you prefer to cut back?

_____

_____

_____

In an average week, how many hours do you spend on family activities? _____

How many hours per week would you *like* to spend on family activities? _____

Social Life

This sphere concerns all those activities that bring you into close contact with people outside your family.

Which of your current social activities do you enjoy most?

_____

_____

Which of your current social activities would you like to do more often?

_____

_____

What additional social activities would you like to engage in?

_____

_____

Which of your current social activities would you like to drop or cut back?

_____

_____

Would you like to spend time with new friends or social groups? (specify)

_____

_____

In an average week, how many hours do you now spend on social activities? _____

How many hours per week would you *like* to spend on social activities? _____

Recreation

This sphere concerns all those activities that you do primarily for
fun, interest, or relaxation.

What do you do now for entertainment that is most enjoyable?

_____

_____

Which of your hobbies or sports activities bring you the greatest
satisfaction?

_____

_____

What are the most valuable or enjoyable experiences you have
had in the way of travel and vacation activities?

_____

_____

What entertainment activities, sports, hobbies, or travel
experiences would you like to add to your life?

_____

_____

What entertainments, sports, hobbies, or travel activities take
more time than they are worth?

_____

_____

In an average week, how many hours do you spend on entertainment, sports, hobbies, and travel? Consider each week of
vacation to be two hours per week. _____

How many hours per week would you *like* to spend on these
activities? _____

Spirit

This sphere concerns any activities that have to do with your relationship to the larger universe. Include private spiritual practices (prayer, meditation), group practices (religious services, study groups), and volunteer commitments or causes that you support.

Which of your present spiritual activities or practices are most important to you?

_____

_____

What causes or volunteer activities are most important or satisfying for you?

_____

_____

Which of your current spiritual activities or volunteer commitments would you like to drop or cut back?

_____

_____

What additional spiritual activities or volunteer commitments would you like to add to your life? (specify)

_____

_____

In an average week, how many hours do you now spend on volunteer commitments and spiritual activities or practices? _____

How many hours per week would you *like* to spend on these activities? _____

Self

Sometimes we need to relax, do nothing, and pay attention to our interior lives. We need time alone to empty our minds and take care of our feelings. In this sphere, include all those activities that you do for no other reason than to please yourself.

What do you do now to take care of yourself (the things that make you feel most relaxed and at ease)?

_____

_____

What do you do now that helps you feel centred and in touch with your emotions?

_____

_____

What activities do you do by and for yourself that aren't worth the time they take?

_____

_____

What new things would you like to do that would make you feel centred and at ease?

_____

_____

In an average week, how many hours do you now spend on these activities? _____

How many hours per week would you *like* to spend on these activities? _____

INVENTORY SUMMARY

HOURS YOU NOW SPEND PER WEEK	SPHERE	HOURS YOU WOULD LIKE TO SPEND
_____	Work/Career	_____
_____	Housework/Maintenance	_____
_____	Spouse	_____
_____	Family	_____
_____	Social Life	_____
_____	Recreation	_____
_____	Spirit	_____
_____	Self	_____

RANKING

LIST A	LIST B
	HOW I WOULD
HOW I ACTUALLY SPEND MY TIME	LIKE TO SPEND MY TIME
1._____	1._____
2._____	2._____
3._____	3._____
4._____	4._____
5._____	5._____
6._____	6._____
7._____	7._____
8._____	8._____

Inventory Summary

Now that you have completed the Taking Stock exercise, take a few moments to review your responses. Have you been honest with yourself about your likes and dislikes? Are there things you might like to do (or quit doing) that you are afraid to admit? Did you withhold honest answers fearing your responses were too selfish? If so, go back and revise your inventory so that it reflects your true feelings. Make sure your choices are really your own and not those which you feel would please others.

Take one final look at the overall picture. Are you surprised by any of your choices? Did you discover any aspects of your life that were once rich and exciting but have now become stressful and boring? Have any activities that used to be important to you lost their appeal? Did you become aware of new interests or values?

It would be wonderful if we had time to do everything we wanted to do, but for most of us that is not a possibility. Making choices is a necessary fact of life. In order to have sufficient time to accomplish those things that are really important to us, we must be willing to let go of activities that are attractive but less important. The Inventory Summary will help you decide which activities are more important to you than others.

Using your notes from the Taking Stock exercise, copy into the left-hand column of the Inventory Summary sheet the hours you now spend on each sphere. In the right-hand column enter the hours you would ideally like to spend on each sphere.

Next, make two new lists using the table that ranks the eight spheres in order of importance. In List A, rank the spheres according to the amount of time you now spend on them. In List B, rank the spheres according to their value and importance in your life.

Examine your two lists carefully. How do they differ? Look for spheres that rank higher on List B than on List A, and mark those spheres with stars. Choose one sphere where you feel the most urgent need to expand your activities. Circle this sphere with a green pencil or felt pen.

Next, look for spheres that rank higher on List A than on List B.

Mark those spheres with stars. Again, choose one sphere where you feel the most urgent need to cut back on your activities. Circle this sphere with a red pencil or felt pen.

Now you should have a much clearer picture of the differences between the way you would prefer to spend your time and the way you actually spend it. If there are big differences between your two lists, you may feel the urge to change everything at once. *Don't.* That approach is bound to fail because you will soon feel overwhelmed and give up altogether.

Instead you should cut back on activities in one sphere (the one you circled in red). Plan to use the extra time you gain here to expand your activities in another sphere (the one you circled in green). The next two chapters will help you create action plans based on this approach to change.

If you implement these plans according to schedule, within six months you will have made significant changes in the way you use your time. By focusing on new red and green spheres at six-month intervals, you can eventually establish the overall balance you want.

...WE'RE NOT SURE WHAT SHE REPRESENTS — BUT
WE SUSPECT SHE WAS A WORKING MOTHER...

Making More Time in Your Life

In the previous chapter you selected two life spheres in which you would like to make changes. You resolved to reduce the amount of time you spend in one sphere and to expand your activities in another. In the next two chapters you will learn some techniques for bringing those changes about.

In order to make time in your life for new activities, you need more than good resolutions. Resolutions make us feel virtuous, but on their own they change nothing. You need a plan of action. The following exercises on planning for change are designed to help you turn your resolutions into realities.

If you take time to complete the exercises according to the instructions, you will end up with a workable plan for rearranging your priorities. If you merely read this chapter without doing the exercises, you might end up with some interesting ideas, but likely nothing will come of it. Turning resolutions into realities is a process that requires action on three levels.

❶ Recognize and confront any emotional or practical factors that are blocking change.

❷ Develop a step-by-step plan for change. Make your plan specific, realistic, and workable.

❸ Start implementing your plan.

Let's take these steps one by one, starting with an action plan for making more time in your life, then creating an action plan for expanding your activities in another sphere.

Begin by looking more closely at the sphere you selected for pruning. Go back to the Taking Stock exercise sheet you drew up for that sphere and add any activities you might have left out. (Don't worry if the sheet is getting a little messy by now. That's probably a good sign.)

Looking at that exercise sheet, ask yourself the following questions:

? *What do I get from this part of my life that has positive value?*

Dig a little when you ask this question. Otherwise you might discover later that you have lost something you treasure.

? *Does spending so much time on this part of my life serve an indirect purpose?*

Does it allow you to avoid something scary, uncomfortable, or overwhelming elsewhere in your life? Does it help you to feel less guilty about some other part of your life?

? *Do I spend a lot of time on this part of my life by default or by design?*

If it is by default, maybe you should learn more about time management.

? *Is there a problem in this area of my life that I should address?*

For example, you may give many reasons for wanting to work less, but if the real one is that you hate your work or your boss, you would probably be better off finding another job.

? *Am I a perfectionist who makes unrealistic demands on myself in this part of my life?*

Maybe it is time to stop nagging yourself so much.

? *Does someone else (my boss, spouse, best friend) decide how much time I should spend on this part of my life?*

Are you being drawn into it by someone else's agenda or timetable?

Are you letting the demands of other people nickel and dime your life away?

? *What are the reasons why this part of my life takes up so much time?*

List all the important financial or practical constraints that come to mind. Save the list for the next chapter.

By now you should have a reasonably clear picture of the emotional and practical problems you face in cutting back on your activities in this particular sphere. Perhaps you need to read more on these issues. A list of resources for further reading is included at the end of the book.

Now move on to the next step — developing a plan for change. Start by creating a Priority Profile for the sphere in which you want to cut back. (Step Five shows you how to develop a plan to cut back on work and career. If that's what you want to do, you might now like to skip ahead to the chapter Getting More of What You Want.)

On a clean sheet of paper, draw five columns as shown below:

PRIORITY PROFILE

ACTIVITY	TIME	PRIORITY	ACTION	TIME SAVED

In the left-hand Activity column, list all the specific activities in this sphere, using the Taking Stock exercise sheet to jog your memory of what they are. In the second column calculate how much time you spend on each activity during an average week.

When you have done this for all the activities on your list, move to the third column and designate each item as "A," "B," or "C" according to its level of priority in your life. The activities marked with an "A" are the most important for either personal or practical reasons. They are the ones you cannot drop. The activities rated "B" are desirable for one reason or another, but they are not essential. Those rated "C" have the lowest priority; they may have some personal or practical value, but they are expendable. If you hate or strongly dislike any of the activities on your list, circle the letter you gave it in the priority column.

Add all the hours you spend on these activities in the Time col-

umn. Does the sum match the amount you spend in this sphere of
your life during an average week? If not, check to see whether you
have left out anything (frequent or unexpected emergencies, perhaps), or whether you need to revise any of the estimates up or down.

Now it is time to do some cutting. Look through all the activities
on your list, paying particular attention to the "C"s and the ones with
circled letters in the Priority column. Which activities can you eliminate altogether? Be ruthless with the "C"s and cautious about anything designated "B." Write "delete" next to these in the Action
column. Which activities can be cut back part way? Write "reduce"
next to them in the Action column. Which activities can someone else
handle as well as, or better than, you? Write "delegate" next to them
in the Action column. What activities could you do in a different way
that would require less time? Write "revise" next to these in the Action column.

Finally, in the Time Saved column, calculate the amount of time
you will save each week as a result of the changes you have decided
to make.

Total the amount of time in the right-hand column. Have you
saved enough time to make the changes you want to make? If not,
you may need to go over your list again.

When you are ready to go on to the next step, make up a Do List
on a separate sheet of paper and rule it into four columns. Your list
will look something like this:

Do List

Activity	Steps	Priority	Date

Now go through the Priority Profile list and copy into the first
column of your Do List all the activities you decided to delete, reduce, delegate, or revise, leaving about three lines between each
item.

Consider what steps you need to take to change the amount of
time you spend on each of these activities. The activities you intend
to delete may require no action at all. Delegating an activity will
probably require some negotiation with the person or persons involved.

For every change you intend to make, ask yourself whether there might be any indirect results which should be taken into account. Ask also whether you should communicate or consult with anyone else about the change. For example, if you've decided to stop reading the Sunday *New York Times*, you may want to cancel your subscription. If your spouse occasionally reads the paper too, he or she may want to be consulted about the proposed cancellation.

Next, go back over the Do List and assign priorities to each step, using the "A," "B" and "C" system to categorize your choices. The "A"s are urgent or very important; the "B"s of medium importance; the "C"s are expendable. If any of the steps you plan to take seem unmanageable, break them down into smaller steps.

Once your action plan has been completed, you are ready to move on to the final stage — implementing your plan.

Begin by setting approximate deadlines for the steps you intend to take, starting with the "A"s and working through to the "C"s. Do not try to do everything at once. Allow enough time to accomplish all the things you need to do without overloading yourself. If your overall goal is to make more time in your life, you will defeat the purpose by adding fifteen extra tasks to next week's list of things to do. Don't worry if it takes six months to make all the changes comfortably.

When you have finished setting deadlines, enter the various steps you intend to take in a daily planning diary. If you do not have a planning diary, buy one. It is crucial to the success of your plan.

One of the first items to mark in your diary is a date to review your progress in approximately a month's time. If you want to cut back on the time you spend in another sphere of your life, mark a date in your calendar six months down the road to begin looking at possibilities to do that. It's easy to lose track of good ideas and intentions if we don't find ways to jog our memories!

After all of this you have earned a break, but first enter one more item into your planning diary. Set aside a couple of hours to tackle the next chapter of this book, Getting More of What You Want. That is where you will start planning how to bring more of the activities that you really want and like into your life.

Getting More of What You Want

To begin creating an action plan for getting more of what you want, go back to your Taking Stock exercise sheets. Find the sphere in which you have decided to expand your activities and add any activities you may have left out, particularly those you like. Look it over for a minute then stop to think how it feels.

When we compare the way we would like to spend our time with the way we actually spend it, we often find that practical considerations are not the main issue. If this is true in your case, some soul-searching may be in order. The following questions may help clarify your thinking in relation to the life sphere you want to enhance. If any of these questions raise particularly potent issues for you, take some time to explore them further, perhaps in your journal, in a letter, or in conversation with a friend.

? *Do you really want what you think you want?*

You may believe that family is the most important thing in life, even though you actually feel more comfortable and useful at work. When there is a disparity between what we do and what we say, we should be asking whether our heads and our hearts are in agreement.

Take some time to sort out your real wants from your *shoulds*. Maybe you have made choices on the basis of what you think would be good for you instead of letting your heart speak for itself.

? *Do you refrain from doing something because you think it would be selfish or because you feel that you don't deserve to have what you want?*

Few people consider themselves as successful, loving, giving, or accomplished as they believe they could be or should be. We are always tempted to force ourselves to be better than we are. We give ourselves rewards for doing well and withhold rewards or punish ourselves for falling short of our own expectations. We treat ourselves as reluctant donkeys that need the carrot and stick in order to get anywhere in life.

The problem with this approach is that the donkey eventually gets tired of being pushed around, digs in its heels, and refuses to move. We retaliate by denying ourselves any more rewards. This creates a stalemate: because we are not doing what we think we should do, we refuse to give ourselves permission to do what we want to do.

Trying to force ourselves into a particular kind of behaviour never works. It only causes us to waste energy warring with ourselves. This takes the pleasure out of life and disrupts the natural process by which we grow and become more like our ideal selves.

? *Do you let fear rule your actions?*

Fear wears many disguises. What we call boredom, laziness, or procrastination may, in fact, be fear of starting something new. Even if we believe that the end result will be pleasurable, the unknown can be terrifying. And fear gets stronger the longer we let it control us. If fear is keeping you from doing what you really want to do, take a look at the section Overcoming Fear at the end of this chapter.

? *Are you too much of a perfectionist?*

We often put off starting a new activity because we make unreasonable demands on ourselves. If you take up running, for example, with the idea that you are going to win next year's marathon, that goal may seem so daunting that you never actually begin.

? *Have you taken full control of your self-image?*

We often deny ourselves the right to do something because it does not fit our image of ourselves or the image that others have of us. If we are male, we may think that an activity is too feminine, or if we are female, that the activity is too masculine. A man who considers himself liberated may decide that football is too macho. A feminist may decide that needlepoint too closely fits the stereotype of being domestic. We might consider an activity too shallow or immature. Maybe we are afraid our friends or family will tease us about it.

Whether such negative judgments originate in our own mind or from outside, they rob us of the freedom to be who we really are and discourage us from wanting what we really would like. When we deny or disown any part of ourselves in order to protect our image, we lose the motivation to make significant changes in our lives.

? *What financial or other practical concerns prevent you from doing what you want to do?*

If time were not an issue, could you afford to do what you want in this sphere of your life? How much more money would you need? Would your spouse object if you spent more time on this sphere?

Although practical problems often seem insurmountable, you always have a choice in dealing with them. You can see them as excuses for your inability to get what you want, or you can turn them into a "do list" of obstacles to overcome.

Now that you have clarified your feelings about what you want, it is time for some brass-tacks planning. Begin with a clean sheet of paper and draw four columns as shown.

WISH LIST

ACTIVITY	TIME NEEDED	PRIORITY	TIME ALLOTTED

In the left-hand column, list the activities you would like to expand. Again, use your Taking Stock exercise sheets to jog your memory. Next calculate the average number of hours you estimate each activity would require each week and mark it in the Time Needed column. If it is a one-time activity, mark it with an asterisk.

Choose the most important activities on your list and give them an "A" rating in the Priority column. Mark the least important activities "C"s, and the remainder "B"s. (You will have more success if you try for equal numbers of "A"s, "B"s, and "C"s.)

How many hours of free time will you gain by cutting back your present activities? Make an estimate if it's not clear from your Priority Profile. This is how much new time you will have each week for the activities on your Wish List. Enter this number at the bottom of the right-hand column, then allot time to each of your "A"-rated activities. If you have time left over after the "A"s are done, go on to the "B"s and "C"s. However, if the "A"s are important to you, do not sacrifice them by trying to squeeze in the "B"s and "C"s. New activities often consume more time and energy than we expect, so reserve some spare time in your week. One-shot activities are marked with an asterisk. If they are important, you can probably fit them in as extras.

Take a few minutes to review the overall picture. If it doesn't feel comfortable, play with it until it does.

Now rule a second sheet of paper into four columns as follows:

GROWTH ACTION PLAN

ACTIVITY	STEPS	TIME NEEDED	DATE

Look through your Wish List, pick out one activity to which you allotted time, and enter it in the first column of your Growth Action Plan. Divide the activity into steps that would be small enough to accomplish easily in a short space of time. Don't forget to list preparatory and/or follow-up steps. List all the steps and the estimated time needed for each one. Repeat the process for all the Wish List activities to which you allotted time.

Review the finished plan to make sure it is realistic. (The next section deals with money issues, but do what you can now to resolve other practical problems.) Remember, trying to change too much in too short a period of time can be stressful, even if you are having fun.

Next, decide when you can expect to see some concrete results from your earlier plan for making more time in your life. This is important. In order to set target dates for your Growth Action Plan, you must be able to predict when you will have more spare time available. If the answer is unclear, put the problem aside for awhile and concentrate on making progress with your plan to cut back on your present activities. Leave a reminder on your calendar to review your action plan at a later date.

When you are ready to begin implementing your Growth Action Plan, look over the steps you have outlined and enter some approximate dates in the far right-hand column. Give yourself time; don't try to start everything at once.

When you've finished setting target dates, enter each step in the appropriate place in your daily planning diary. If you need the company of a friend or some other support, make those arrangements now. Set time a month from now to spend an hour reviewing your progress, and mark the date in your calendar. Remind yourself that the process you have just completed will be useless unless you actually follow the plan outlined in your diary. As you incorporate the new activities into your daily habits, planning will become less and less important. Until that time a step-by-step plan will help strengthen your resolve.

Overcoming Fear

Fear restricts all of us more than we care to admit. In *Guiding Yourself Into a Spiritual Reality*, fire-walking instructor Tolly Burkan offers the following advice for overcoming fear.

Tell the truth about the situation. If fear is controlling your decisions, acknowledge the fact. You could be telling the truth when you say, "I'm just too lazy to sign up for the course." But if you are really afraid to sign up for the course, admit it — especially to yourself.

Feel your fear. Fear is a message from inside saying, "Pay attention." Rather than viewing fear as a dictator that tells you what you can't have, think of fear as an assistant that can help you identify all the obstacles and contingencies you must deal with in order to get what you want.

Recognize your wants. When you want something badly enough, you will find a way to get it, but if you continually find reasons for not wanting something ("The course would take too much of my time" or "I'm not sure the course would meet my needs"), you undermine your power to overcome obstacles.

See yourself doing what you want to do. If you want to become a dancer, visualize a detailed image of yourself in the dance studio. Picture the clothes you are wearing and the other people present. Hear the music and feel your body moving. Imagine yourself on your way home after class. Clear and specific images are powerful motivational tools. They block out negative thoughts and rationalizations for not doing what we need to do in order to get where we want to go.

Get support. Let someone you care about know what you want and what you fear. Ask this person to be your cheering section and sounding board.

Make a concrete, step-by-step plan. General or abstract goals often paralyse action because they seem unattainable. When a task seems too big to manage, it usually is. The more we divide a big job up into a number of smaller ones, and focus on taking one step at a time, the less daunting the task becomes.

Decide what is the worst thing that could happen if your plan goes wrong and accept it. Once we have prepared ourselves to face the worst possible consequences of our actions, fear loses a lot of its power.

Shaping Your Free Time to Fit Your Plan

Free time is only as useful as you make it. If you intend to work less because you want to get involved in new projects or activities, you need to structure your free time with those activities in mind. Will you be able to use small amounts of time productively, or do you need large blocks of time? Maybe you need some of each.

In structuring your time off, be realistic about your habits and your biological time clock. If you are slow to get going in the morning, do not schedule a writing project or some other creative activity for the first thing of the day. Use that time for activities you cannot avoid — such as going to your regular job. Getting up and going to work will force you to make productive use of your mornings.

Some activities are best suited to short, regular periods. They include:

- Spending time with the kids after school;
- Gardening;
- Strenuous physical activity or vigorous sports;
- Courses that require intense concentration;
- Writing (for some people).

A shorter workday is an appropriate way to make room for these activities. It has one distinct disadvantage, however. Unless you are telecommuting, a shorter day does not reduce the time you spend each week getting to and from work. This can be an important consideration if you live a long way from your workplace.

A shorter workweek reduces the time you spend commuting. It is also advantageous for activities that involve lengthy preparation or travel time. Making pottery or stained glass are not projects that can be easily picked up and put down; some people cannot develop the momentum for creative projects, such as writing, unless they have several free days.

For camping, sailing, or other excursions, it helps if you can extend the weekend by adding Friday or Monday. Recreational facilities are less crowded on weekdays. There will be less traffic on the road to the cottage if you leave Thursday evening rather than Friday.

Full days off can be useful for:

- Freelance work;
- Writing or painting (for some people);
- Reading and relaxing;
- Errands;
- Day trips;
- Medium-sized projects, such as wallpapering a bedroom.

Some activities require more extended blocks of time. If you plan to take longer trips or tackle big projects, you may need a whole week off every so often, or several weeks or months at a time. If you like fishing or downhill skiing, you may want to schedule your time off during the appropriate season.

Weeks or months off may be necessary for:

- Travel, particularly to other countries;
- Education or training;
- Large projects, such as building a house or starting a business;
- Extended mental and physical health breaks.

Large blocks of time have the advantage of enabling you to really get away from it all. Unfortunately, unless you can make special arrangements, they also involve extended periods of time without a paycheque.

It may be possible to reduce your hours of work in more than one way: for example, a shorter workweek plus extra vacation time. However, you will probably encounter less resistance from your employer if you ask for only one kind of schedule change. Unless you can demonstrate the advantages to your employer of a more complex arrangement, you and your employer will be better off if you choose the one kind of time off that has most benefits for you.

STEP FOUR

DECIDING ABOUT MONEY

What Can You Afford?

In Step Three you reviewed how you use your time now, and decided how you would prefer to use it in order to get what you want out of life. Getting what you want may require working less or changing the hours you work. However, some decisions about restructuring your worktime will depend in part upon your financial position.

In Step Four we will look more closely at the relationship between money and time, including the effect of reduced worktime on employment benefits.

The exercises in Step Four will help you decide how much or how little you need to work to stay afloat financially. If you want to rearrange, rather than reduce your work hours (flextime, compressed workweek, or telecommuting), your financial picture will be unchanged; in that case, skip ahead to Step Five.

When we look at the difference between how we would like to spend our time and what we actually do with it, we usually find that money is a large part of the problem. We want to go sailing, but spend most of our time trying to pay for the sailboat.

We need money to live, but the amount of money we need depends upon the lives we lead — the kind of home we live in, whether we own a car or even two cars, whether we vacation in a condo in Florida or in a tent at the nearest campground. Since most of us trade time for money in the form of a paycheque, the lifestyles we establish will determine how much time we spend working and how much we have left over for ourselves.

Monthly Budgeting

	Current Monthly Expenses	Minimum Monthly Expenses
Housing (rent or mortgage + taxes)		
Heat (average over twelve months)		
Electricity		
Telephone		
Transportation (fares or car payments)		
Food		
Furniture and appliances		
Clothing		
Medical and dental		
Entertainment and recreation		
Insurance (house + life + car)		
Vacation (averaged costs over 12 months)		
Loan and/or credit card payments		
Savings		
RRSPs (IRAs in the U.S.)		
Other		
Other		
Miscellaneous		
TOTAL		

One way to get more time for ourselves is to work less, but working less means making do with less money. If you want more time, there is no alternative but to cut expenses. That means changing the way you live, and a good place to start is by looking at how you spend your money now.

The first step is to go through your chequebook and calculate your average monthly expenses. Photocopy the Monthly Budgeting form on page 118 and enter current monthly expenses in the appropriate spaces. If the total is less than your current monthly income, check to make sure you have not forgotten anything.

Study each item on your list of current expenses to see where your paycheque goes each month. Are you spending money on anything that is not worth the time you have to work in order to pay for it? For example, how many hours do you have to work to buy lunch out every day? How much money could you save by taking buses and cabs instead of owning a car? Could you live without cablevision or weekly movies?

Take some time to brainstorm — perhaps with your spouse or a friend — all the ways you could live on less. If you have never before tried to budget your money, you will probably find plenty of room to cut your cost of living.

Next, draw up a new budget based on your minimum expenses. Here are some tips to help make your projections as realistic as possible.

- To cover unexpected items, set aside at least 10 percent of the total budget for miscellaneous expenses.
- Beware of "robbing Peter to pay Paul." Baking your own bread may save on food costs, but unless you love baking bread it may not be worth the time expended.
- If you plan to take up a new activity — painting, horseback riding, or a university course — be sure to include any extra costs in your budget.
- If you plan to buy a big-ticket item sometime in the future, such as a car, boat, dishwasher, or sofa, be sure to allow for it under savings.
- If you plan to reduce the hours or days you work, you will probably save money in some areas (income tax, childcare,

transportation) but spend more in other areas (higher self-paid costs to retain full employment benefits, or the cost of your new free-time activities). Include estimates of these changes in your budget.

When you have completed your new budget, you will know how much you need to earn in order to meet your expenses:

MINIMUM MONTHLY EXPENSES = MINIMUM TAKE-HOME PAY

To find out how many hours you need to work to cover your budget, divide the amount you need to earn by your current monthly take-home pay and multiply the result by the number of hours you now work each week. The answer is the minimum number of hours you need to work.

MINIMUM AMOUNT YOU MUST EARN FROM YOUR JOB	CURRENT MONTHLY TAKE-HOME PAY	CURRENT HOURS/WEEK	MINIMUM HOURS/WEEK
_____ ÷	_____ ×	_____ =	_____

How does this minimum workweek compare to the number of hours you want to work? If you want to work 32 hours a week and can afford to live on 28 hours a week, your problems are over. However, if you want to work 24 hours a week, yet need to work 28 hours to meet your expenses, you have some more thinking to do.

You can decide to accept the fact that you will have to work more to pay for the standard of living you want, or you can look for additional ways to cut your expenses. Another alternative is to find additional sources of income.

? *Do you have an extra room that you could rent to a student?*

If you own a cottage, you might consider putting it up for rent. Do you own a sailboat that you use only part of the time? If so, why not take on a partner?

? *Can you increase your income by bartering?*

Some communities have a Local Exchange Trading System (LETS) that makes bartering easier and more flexible. Information on the LETS system is available from Landsman Community Services, 1600 Embleton Cres., Courtenay, B.C. V9N 6N8. Since you will have more time at home, you might consider joining a babysitting co-operative.

? *Could you find work outside your regular job that would be more enjoyable or more remunerative?*

Many job sharers earn additional income from self-employment, freelance writing, private practice counselling, consulting services, handicrafts, and so on.

To find out how much you need to earn from other sources, divide the number of hours you want to work by the number of hours you are working now and multiply the result by your current income. The answer is the amount you will earn by working your preferred minimum hours.

PREFERRED HOURS PER WEEK	CURRENT HOURS PER WEEK	CURRENT MONTHLY TAKE-HOME PAY	MINIMUM MONTHLY TAKE-HOME PAY

_____ ÷ _____ × _____ = _____

Subtract your minimum monthly take-home pay from your minimum monthly expenses to find how much you need to earn from other sources.

MINIMUM MONTHLY EXPENSES

....

MONTHLY TAKE-HOME PAY FOR — PREFERRED HOURS

....

_____

INCOME FROM OTHER SOURCES =

....

As you go through this process of balancing income and expenses, remember that it is easy to get by on a little more money than you need, but quite stressful to live on less. To preserve your peace of mind, plan your budget with a safety margin of income over expenses. That way an unexpected rent increase won't sabotage your whole program.

The above exercise is designed for tinkering with your spending patterns in relatively modest ways. If you find yourself wanting to rethink your relationship with money more deeply, a highly recommended tool-kit is *Your Money or Your Life* by Joe Dominguez and Vicki Robin.

What Will Happen to Your Benefits?

One of the key issues in choosing a work option is its effect on employment benefits. Some work options have no effect on benefits; others can reduce them significantly. Generally speaking, your benefit package shrinks proportionately when you choose an option that involves working fewer hours. In job sharing or permanent part-time, a benefit package is usually prorated according to the percentage of time each job-sharing partner works. The options of flextime, compressed workweek, telecommuting, and banked overtime, which involve a rearrangement rather than a reduction of work hours, should not result in any loss of benefits.

If cuts in worktime are less than 25 percent, as in most V-Time programs, you can often negotiate to keep full benefits unless they are automatically prorated according to your salary. Most phased retirement programs and some leave arrangements also allow you to retain full benefits.

If you work 25 to 60 percent fewer hours, you can expect the reduction in benefits to be proportionate. If you cut your hours by 60 percent or more, you may lose a disproportionately large share of benefits.

As you look at the effect of reduced worktime on the benefits listed below, check off the benefits that are included in your current package. When considering options, you should ask yourself what will happen to those benefits if you significantly reduce your work hours.

Once you have identified the benefits that you want to keep and those you can do without, you are in a position to ask for a specific benefits package as part of your work option proposal. Negotiations may then go through several stages of offer and counter offer in which you agree to give up some benefits in order to get a more satisfactory outcome in areas that are of greater importance to you. If you and your employer can't reach a satisfactory agreement, you may decide to withdraw your work option proposal rather than lose valuable employment benefits.

Unemployment Insurance (UI). UI contributions and benefits are based on a percentage of income. If you reduce your income by moving out of a full-time position and then get laid off, you will receive a proportionately smaller UI benefit. Also, a person must work a certain number of weeks to claim benefits, so if you are working alternate weeks, for instance, it will take longer to accumulate the required number of weeks, which may affect your eligibility for benefits.

Canada Pension Plan (CPP). CPP contributions and benefits are also based on a percentage of income. **[AMERICAN READERS: Social Security Contributions are the U.S. equivalent of CPP.]** Reducing your income may reduce your pension benefits, but this is not always the case. As long as you continue to earn more than a specified annual income, your benefits will not be affected, even if you reduce your hours to half time. There is also provision for earning no income, or a low income, without loss of benefits, during childraising years. If you plan to work less for a prolonged period, for whatever reason, contact a Canada Pension Plan agent for an estimate of the effects on your pension.

Workers' Compensation. Workers' Compensation Board benefits are also based on a percentage of income. If you are injured or disabled while earning less income, your benefits will be reduced accordingly.

Vacation. In most work options, paid vacation benefits are based on the amount of time worked. For example, if you were entitled to twenty days of vacation per year working full time, you would get twelve days of vacation if you worked only three days a week. This is not as bad as it sounds: in both cases you would have four weeks off work each year.

Sick leave. Sick leave is usually prorated when you work less, but the overall effect is minimal since the less you work, the less likely you'll be sick on a work day.

Statutory holidays. Statutory holidays may or may not be prorated, depending upon your agreement with your employer. An arrangement may be negotiated that gives you the same paycheque every work period, regardless of when statutory holidays fall.

Registered Retirement Savings Plan (RRSP). Employer contributions are usually calculated as a percentage of income. Earning less reduces the speed at which your RRSP grows. **[AMERICAN READERS: Independent Retirement Accounts (IRA) are the U.S. equivalent of RRSPs, and are similiarly affected.]**

Company pension plans. Unless you make special arrangements with your employer, your company pension plan will likely be affected by a reduction in your income. This applies to some plans more than others. The effect should be minor if your pension is based on an annuity or an RRSP. For example, if you worked three days a week for five years and worked full time for the remainder of a 40-year working life, your eventual pension would decrease only about 5 percent.

Most salary-based plans are not seriously affected if you work less in the early or middle part of your working life. However, if you work less in the latter part of your working life, the effects could be severe. Some plans base benefits on the income earned in the last five years of work; usually, those last years are when you'll be earning your highest salary. For these reasons, older workers should always make any proposal to work less contingent upon full pension protection. Most employers will agree to special arrangements that make such protection possible.

In some cases, a reduction in worktime will exclude an employee from participating in a company pension plan. If staying in a plan is important to you, check to make sure that you will not be excluded before you propose reduced work hours. Always request a written assessment of how your work option will affect your pension, and postpone finalizing an agreement until satisfied that your benefits are protected.

Medical and dental plans. Although your eligibility for medical and dental plans will not change, you may have to pay a larger portion of the premiums out of your own pocket if you work fewer hours. Similar conditions apply to extended medical benefits. Sometimes permanent part-time employees are able to retain full employer-paid medical and dental coverage. [**AMERICAN READERS: Because U.S. medical plan premiums are higher than their Canadian counterparts, it is more likely that working less could exclude you from medical coverage — and it is that much more important that you negotiate for continued coverage if you aren't covered under a spouse's plan.**]

Group life and disability insurance. Coverage usually continues when you work less than full time, but benefits in the event of death or disability would be based on your reduced income. Policy rules sometimes exclude employees who work less than a specified minimum number of hours.

Short-term illness insurance. Benefits depend on the terms of the plan. Again, some plans exclude those who are not working full time. In other cases, premiums are based on reduced income and/or percentage of time worked.

Profit sharing. Most profit-sharing plans are based on a percentage of income or salary. Working fewer hours will reduce your share accordingly.

Other benefits. Check with your personnel department to find out how any other benefits might be affected.

The Politics of Benefits

Part-time employment occupies an interesting place in the history of labour/management relations. For years, some employers have tried to cut corners by withholding employment benefits from part-time workers, and have paid them disproportionately low wages.

Reacting to these practices, many unions have adopted the view that part-time work undermines conditions for all workers. Organized labour's solution has been to demand that employers give full benefits to all unionized employees, regardless of status.

Giving full benefits to all workers should help part-time employees, but this policy has created a negative side effect: it limits workplace flexibility by restricting the expansion of permanent part-time employment. In other words, many employers are unwilling to adopt job-sharing or permanent part-time work options that call for full benefits for all employees because they are unwilling or unable to pay the additional costs of the programs.

The result in such unionized workplaces is often a three-tiered wage structure:

- **Full-time** employees get full benefits, seniority protection, and predictable schedules.
- **Permanent part-time** staff also get full benefits, seniority protection, and predictable schedules.
- **Casual** employees have no benefits, little or no job security, and unpredictable work schedules.

The cost per hour for employers (not including hidden costs like worker burnout) looks like this:

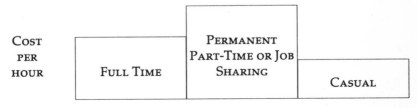

COST PER HOUR | FULL TIME | PERMANENT PART-TIME OR JOB SHARING | CASUAL

This means employers can save money by hiring casual workers instead of permanent part-time workers. The effect on the distribution of the three classes of workers is shown at the top of the next page.

Under this system, few employees get the opportunity to work on a permanent part-time basis with full benefits, job protection, and predictable schedules. Most employees wanting to work part time must settle for casual status at considerable cost to themselves. Failing this, they continue to work full time, regardless of their preferences, sometimes even when it causes undue stress at home or on

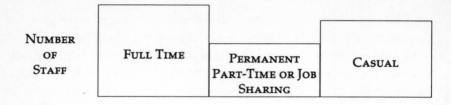

the job. When employees are under-employed or forced to stretch beyond their limits in this way, employers pay heavy indirect costs in absenteeism, staff turnover, and burnout; no one wins.

If the three-tiered system is replaced with one in which part-time and job-sharing employees receive prorated benefits, and casual staff get a prorated cash payment instead of benefits, the cost-per-hour to the employer becomes equal across the board. That system looks like this:

Cost Per Hour	Full Time	Permanent Part-Time or Job Sharing	Casual

This system is fair to everyone because a worker's total hourly remuneration, including benefits, is not affected by job status. Employers have no economic incentive to restrict part-time employment or to overuse casual staff. Distribution of the three employee categories is determined more by workers' needs and preferences. The result looks more like what is shown at the bottom of the page.

Most people who support workplace flexibility recommend prorated benefits for part-time staff and cash-in-lieu payments for casual staff because it means that workers are more often able to obtain the work schedule and the job status of their choice.

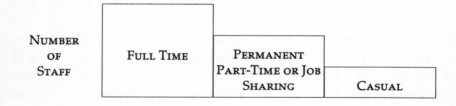

STEP FIVE

DESIGNING A PROGRAM

First Steps

This chapter is going to help you design a brand new work schedule — a work schedule that will accommodate your family, your lifestyle, and any other factors that are important to you. Before venturing into the design stage, however, check the following list to make sure that you are ready. Ask yourself if you have:

- Clarified your thinking about work;
- Examined the nine basic work options;
- Decided what you want to accomplish by changing your work schedule;
- Looked at your financial picture;
- Picked a work option that best suits your needs.

If you have not decided on a work option, go back to Step Two. After you have reviewed all nine options, consider carefully which one comes closest to fitting your needs. Maybe you will have to discuss your choice with a co-worker or your spouse to help clarify troublesome points. Remember, variations are possible, so do not feel defeated or frustrated because you have not found exactly what you want.

Before talking with supervisors and co-workers about the option you have chosen, become familiar with the information so that you will not need to refer to written material as you speak. This will help create the impression (and truthfully so) that you really do know what you are talking about, and what you want. Appearing confident and knowledgeable at this point is important because you are laying the groundwork for successfully presenting a proposal later on.

Designing your new work schedule and writing a proposal to present to your employer are parts of a step-by-step process. The design process is important because no work option is foolproof. Most work options are successful, but things can go wrong — for the employer or the employee or both. In this section we will discuss the conditions under which a particular option is not particularly successful and suggest how to avoid or overcome these limitations in the design stage.

Until now you have been primarily concerned with deciding what work schedule would best suit your needs. From here on, you will also be considering how your new schedule could be made to serve your employer's interests as well.

Making sure that your employer's needs are satisfied is important, otherwise the program you propose will probably be rejected right at the start or cancelled as soon as weaknesses become apparent. On the other hand, you should not be so preoccupied with accommodating your employer that you fail to look after yourself. There is no point in going through the disruption of changing your work schedule if the results do not meet your basic objectives.

Fortunately, it rarely comes to an either/or choice between satisfying your own needs and those of your employer. With a little ingenuity you should be able to design a program in which both you and your employer end up winners.

Another thing to keep in mind is that the guidelines for designing various work option programs are based on general principles, but your situation may be special. Most people have needs and wants that are unique to them. Every industry or profession has its own quirks or oddities. In real life, work option programs don't always fit neatly into one of the nine established categories.

You may find that you have to custom-design a schedule that will fit you and your job, using general principles as a starting point or outline. In the same way that it is easier to chop wood by splitting along the grain, it is also easier to create a schedule that works for you if you respect the nature and structure of your particular set of duties.

When you start to design a program, one of the first questions you must ask yourself is whether you are designing it for yourself only, or whether it would be open to others. In some situations, an employer may find it easier to meet the individual needs of one person than to accept a proposal that would affect the work scheduling of the entire staff. Sometimes, it is easier to get a program approved when a group of employees makes the proposal. Group programs often create a bigger benefit for the employer, and thus provide more incentive to make changes. (A case in point would be the initial implementation of flextime, which solved a German employer's problem of traffic congestion on the road to the factory.)

As you can see, there is no immediate answer to the question of whether it would be better to go it alone or to design a group program. The best solution is to design your own schedule first, attuning it to your particular objectives. If it turns out that others are interested in changing their hours of work, you may decide that you would all benefit by acting together. In that case, you could go on to design a collective program that would also give you the schedule you want.

Some programs (V-Time, flextime, and banked overtime) are almost always set up to provide options for several employees. However, thinking about how the program would work for your own job is a good way to prepare for the implementation of a group option. Individual and group proposals will be discussed in more detail in Step Six: Getting What You Want.

As you go through the questions in Step Five, make careful notes on your responses. These notes will be the raw material for your written proposal to your employer.

When you think you have resolved all the issues and have settled on a basic design, spend some time troubleshooting. What special circumstances might come up from time to time in your job, and how would you handle them? What kind of communication problems might result from the new arrangement? Will your new schedule cause problems for other people?

Describe your plan to a sympathetic co-worker and ask that person to play devil's advocate by trying to find the weaknesses in your design. At work, spend a week or so imagining how you would do your job with the new schedule in place. Can you see any problems?

When it comes time to present your ideas to your employer, you will probably have to respond to a number of "what if" questions.

Try to anticipate possible concerns and objections. You should be ready with suggestions for coping with problems, or else be able to identify good reasons why the problem will not come up.

The following are typical of the questions you are likely to encounter. Make sure you can answer them fully.

? *Who will be involved?*

This one is easy to answer if you are the only person applying for a work option, but if you are designing a program for a group of employees you will need to know who will be eligible and who will approve requests to participate.

? *What is the new schedule?*

For collective programs, the question is often "What range of schedules is allowable?" You will also have to know how the new schedule will influence attendance at staff meetings and staff training sessions. As well, consider how it will affect statutory holidays and the scheduling of vacations.

? *Who will look after your responsibilities when you're not at work?*

Will someone else be hired to fill in while you are away? Will an existing staff member cover for you? What will happen if emergencies come up?

? *How will you handle communication with your clients or co-workers?*

Examine the ways in which information is now transferred and consider whether procedures will have to be changed. New procedures should include a way for others to keep track of your schedule.

? *How will the new arrangement affect your seniority and your employment benefits, particularly your pension?*

The challenge here is to decide what you want in the way of job protection and benefits, while keeping the cost and/or inconvenience to your employer within an acceptable range.

? *How will your employer benefit from the change?*

Will the change you are proposing provide better coverage at peak

··· GREAT IDEA, FRED··· I KNEW THERE HAD TO BE
SOME WAY TO COMBINE WORK AND PARENTING···

hours, or extended hours of service? Will it bring new ideas and skills to the organization? Will replacement staff also be available as emergency relief staff?

? *How will the change in schedule be implemented?*

Perhaps you'll set a trial period to introduce your new schedule. If the program is open to all employees, a needs survey will make it easier to design a program that will meet most people's requirements. Who will monitor and supervise the program? What will happen if it doesn't work out? Legal factors, such as union contracts, should be considered, along with such things as whether there will be additional work for the payroll department because of the change. How can costs of the program be minimized?

Keep these questions in mind as you design your new work schedule. The following chapters on specific work options will deal with these issues in more detail.

Before you turn to the chapter on your chosen work option and actually begin the design process, remember these points. First, keep your design simple. Your new schedule will create less confusion for you, your supervisor, and your co-workers if the mechanics are simple and straightforward. The second rule is to use established systems whenever possible. If your workplace already has a committee that deals with hours of work, use that committee to implement the work option rather than setting up a new flextime or V-Time committee. Do not invent a new system for recording hours if existing time sheets will work with minor modifications.

Study Your Job Before You Start

Before making any changes to your work hours, you need to understand the structure and demands of your job as it is now. The first step is to analyze your job in terms of its individual tasks. Then look at the way your worktime is organized. For now, concentrate on identifying the areas that may give you trouble and on the aspects of your job that will make it easier to design a work option program.

Don't worry about solving any problems at this point; that comes later when you write your proposal.

Once you have answered the following questions, turn to the chapter on your chosen option. Again, make notes as you read; these notes will be useful when you move on to the next step.

? *What are the sub-tasks that make up your job?*

We tend to think of our job as one continuous stream of activity when, in reality, it is usually a matrix of related but different responsibilities and tasks. Try to see the individual parts of your job that make up the whole.

To do this, it helps to think about the ways in which you divide your work so that it is manageable. If you were writing a book, for example, you would write one chapter or subsection at a time. Writing each chapter would involve a number of smaller tasks: researching the material, creating an outline, writing a first draft, editing and rewriting the second draft, and so on.

When you have dissected your job into its component parts, mentally put them into some kind of map that illustrates their relationship to one another. Maybe they are not related. Some jobs consist of three or four unrelated tasks that have been linked together to fill a 40-hour workweek.

Now try to identify one or more tasks that someone else could do. Does this task, in turn, consist of a set of smaller tasks? Could someone else do any of these?

? *How many of your tasks are time dependent?*

External factors govern the time and scheduling required for tasks such as answering the telephone, giving medication to patients, attending regularly scheduled meetings, or tightening a screw on the next widget as the assembly line delivers it to your station. Other tasks can be classified as *time independent*. Within limits you can choose when to write reports, answer letters, schedule appointments, clean up, etc. Most jobs are a mixture of time-dependent and time-independent tasks.

Determine for yourself how much of the timing of what you do at work depends on what others are doing, and how much you are free to do at a time of your own choosing. This information will be important in redesigning your job.

? *What are the natural breaks in your job?*

For teachers, work falls neatly into terms and classroom periods. Accountants can separate their work into monthly, quarterly, and annual statement periods. Every hour in the day constitutes a separate work period for marriage counsellors and massage therapists. Assembly line workers and nurses divide their work into shifts.

The above examples should lead you to wonder if there are natural breaks within your workday. Can you complete a given task or set of tasks by the end of a shift or the end of a week? Can you identify certain times of the year as natural starting and finishing points? Are there slow times during the day, week, or year when it would be relatively easy to work less?

You may be able to use the process of attrition to reduce your workload. If you work as a family therapist or a graphic artist it would be difficult to reduce the number of hours you spend with each client. However, you could easily reduce your workload by taking on fewer new clients as old clients leave.

? *How do you handle information in your job?*

How many people do you trade information with each day? How much of the information you deal with is written down? How much information do you carry in your head from day to day? If someone were to begin your job tomorrow, what would you need to write down that is now committed to memory?

? *Who would be affected by a change in your work hours?*

Make a list of the people who would be affected by your absence from work—supervisors, co-workers, support staff, and clients. Ask yourself whether your boss would be able to find files if you were not there. Would your co-workers have to take extra telephone calls? If you are a supervisor, would your subordinates get adequate supervision? In what ways would your clients be inconvenienced? Begin thinking of ways to minimize the disruptions others may experience if you change your hours.

? *How easy would it be to replace you?*

Most of us like to think of ourselves as indispensable, and we don't mind at all when the boss says the firm couldn't get along without us. In fact, few people are truly irreplaceable. Chances are that if you weren't around, your boss would find other ways to get your work done. He might use co-workers who are trained to do some part of your job, or he may call on the person who does your work while you are on vacation. How would your work get done if you had a serious accident tomorrow and had to spend six weeks in hospital?

You may need to look outside your workplace for a capable part-time replacement. Is there anyone in your circle of acquaintances who is looking for work and could handle your job? Former employees who have retired or have been laid off are also good prospects.

Job Sharing

Designing a job-sharing program involves finding workable answers to the following questions.

■ HOW WILL THE WORK BE DIVIDED?

Make a list of all the tasks you do in the course of performing your job. Then determine which ones could be shared with a partner and which ones should be designated to one person. Duties requiring prompt action should be shared unless partners work half days or alternate days.

How many tasks carry over from day to day or week to week? Would it be easy to divide your job into separate sets of tasks? Sometimes it works better to split a job rather than share it if the job involves distinct task areas and little carry over. If you do decide to split your job, make sure that both partners have enough time-independent tasks to keep busy during slack periods.

Sometimes it makes sense to divide the duties of a full-time position on the basis of work schedules. For example, in a job-shared clerical position, the partner working the morning shift could open and distribute all incoming mail. The partner working afternoons could collect and post the outgoing mail. Both partners could be responsible for sending or delivering fax messages as the need arose.

■ HOW WILL TIME BE SHARED?

You can decide to split your job 50-50, 60-40, 75-25, or in any other proportion. However, a 50-50 split is best if you are sharing duties rather than dividing them, particularly if your job involves broad areas of responsibility or the supervision of other employees. When people share the same duties, they get on better if both partners have equal responsibility.

There are many ways to share time: mornings/afternoons, half weeks, alternate weeks, alternate months, or even six months on/six months off.

The charts at the bottom of this page show how partners A and B can divide the workweek equally using a split-week rotation or a full-week rotation.

When designing a time schedule, you should consider the practical demands of the job as well as your needs and those of your partner. In some cases, partners must take small blocks of time off (such as half days or alternate days) to minimize disruption. In other situations, life is simpler if the partners work alternate weeks or months.

Mentally road test your preferred schedule while you are still working full time. Imagine that you are doing your partner's work; at the appropriate time, switch over and imagine doing your own share of the work. What information would you need to transfer at changeover time? What aspects of the job will be disrupted by the changeover (meetings or consultations, for example)? Should you

	SPLIT-WEEK ROTATION				
	MONDAY	TUESDAY	WEDNESDAY	THURSDAY	FRIDAY
Week 1	A	A	B	B	B
Week 2	A	A	A	B	B

	FULL-WEEK ROTATION				
	MONDAY	TUESDAY	WEDNESDAY	THURSDAY	FRIDAY
Week 1	B	B	B	A	A
Week 2	A	A	A	B	B

plan your job-sharing program to include an overlap of schedules so that you and your partner can plan common strategies or exchange information? Try to find the problems before they find you.

■ HOW WILL YOU COMMUNICATE WITH YOUR PARTNER?

Whether your job-sharing program succeeds or fails depends a lot on the schemes you develop for passing on important information about your schedules and the work you are sharing. The information you need to relay to your partner could include details of conversations with clients, co-workers, or supervisors; particulars about what came out of staff meetings; changes in appointments, contacts, and resource people. Your supervisor and co-workers will need to know when you are available and be told about any changes in schedule.

Once you start thinking about it, you will discover a variety of effective ways to keep in touch with your partner. Overlapping schedules, once-a-week meetings, or occasional coffee breaks together all provide good opportunities for face-to-face contact. Tape recorders, the telephone, and computer message boards are excellent devices for relaying information. You might also consider having a changeover file.

To simplify matters for other staff, plan to post a copy of your work schedule by your desk and also leave a copy with your supervisor. Train your co-workers to develop the habit of seeing you and your partner as a team, and to communicate with the partner on duty. Emphasize the fact that you and your partner will be responsible for keeping each other informed. If you check in with important clients before you go off shift, you will minimize the number of times people miss you.

Finally, you will have to decide to what extent and under what circumstances you and your partner can contact each other at home. If you don't want your work to intrude on your private life, it is important that your partner and supervisor know this. On the other hand, if you're the kind of person who likes to be consulted when important issues come up unexpectedly, your partner should be encouraged to include you.

■ HOW WILL EMPLOYMENT BENEFITS BE SHARED?

As a general rule, people who share a job must also find a way to share one set of employment benefits. Statutory benefits (Unemployment Insurance, Canada Pension Plan, Workers' Compensation) are automatically prorated. [**AMERICAN READERS: Social Security contributions are also automatically prorated.**] Compensatory benefits can also be prorated with each partner taking his or her share of statutory holidays, allowable sick leave, and paid vacation time.

You will have to make some decisions about supplementary benefits, such as the medical, dental, and pension plans. If one partner is covered by a spouse's medical and dental plan, the other partner can keep both benefits. Sometimes partners trade benefits: "You take the medical plan; I'll take the dental plan." Sometimes, each partner pays half the cost of medical or dental plan premiums so they are both on the company plan.

With pensions, the most common solution is to prorate accumulated years of service: each year of half time is equivalent to six months of full time. However, because private pension plans differ so greatly, it is important that you discuss your particular situation with a personnel officer in your organization before submitting a proposal.

■ HOW WILL JOB SHARING BENEFIT YOUR EMPLOYER?

The results of many case studies show that job sharing can lead to increased productivity and to lower rates of absenteeism, tardiness, and staff turnover. These advantages are often hard to measure, however, and there's no guarantee they will occur. Can you design a program in a way that it offers your employer tangible and clear-cut advantages? For example, two secretaries split the workday so that one partner is always available during lunch hour. In another case, an employer advertises for one person to fill a full-time warehouse position, but he also needs an extra person on Mondays. Two job sharers apply, each offering to work three days every week, which solves the employer's staffing requirements nicely.

Some job sharers agree to cover for each other when one is ill or on vacation. Some partners will agree to work full time during seasonal peaks or emergencies, welcoming the extra income earned.

Does your partner have skills, contacts, or resources that would be advantageous to your employer? If so, emphasize that in your proposal.

■ HOW CAN COSTS TO YOUR EMPLOYER BE MINIMIZED?

Having another person on the payroll costs an employer about $100 per year in extra paperwork. Most employers will accept this expense, but would-be job sharers should avoid other added costs where possible.

To avoid extra benefit costs, partners can agree to share the same package of benefits. If partners work complementary schedules, they can share the same work space and equipment. Training costs will often be minimal if the new partner is a former employee.

■ HOW WILL YOU FIND A PARTNER?

There are good reasons why you should try to find your own partner instead of leaving this step to your employer. First, selecting your own candidate improves your chances of being paired with someone you find compatible. Second, it reduces the amount of work your employer must do if your proposal is accepted. Finally, it usually works best if both partners participate in the design of a job-sharing arrangement.

Working together on a co-operative proposal is an opportunity to test your abilities to work together on the job. It will help establish an equal partnership. Your partner can also offer moral support throughout the approval process.

Before taking steps to select a partner, it is important to identify your own needs so that you can look for someone whose needs and skills complement your own. If there's one part of your job that you dislike, select a partner who would enjoy it. If you prefer to work mornings, find a partner who wants to work afternoons. Before seeking a partner, it may also be necessary to check with your union or employee association about rulings on seniority which could affect your freedom of choice.

Here are some questions to consider.

?   *Will you and your partner share the same duties or will you each have different tasks?*

If you intend to share the same duties, you will want a partner whose qualifications are roughly equal to yours. You may also decide to look for someone who is strong in areas where you are weak.

?   *If you intend to split the duties of the job, what tasks will you give up?*

If your partner is to have sole responsibility for some tasks, make sure that he or she is fully qualified in those areas.

?   *What work schedule do you want? What do you consider essential, and what are you prepared to negotiate?*

?   *Are you willing and able to cover for your partner in case of illness? Should your partner be willing or able to cover for you?*

?   *Do you want a partner who would be willing to trade blocks of worktime in exchange for a longer vacation?*

?   *Do you want a partner with whom you can trade childcare, or someone already covered on a spouse's medical plan?*

You may have someone in mind who would make a suitable partner to share your job. If not, here are some places to look.

Co-workers: Very often the best job-sharing partner is someone who already knows something about the work you do. That could be a co-worker, a former employee, or a person who fills in on a casual or relief basis. Women who have left employment to raise children are excellent candidates for flexible or part-time employment.

Unions: Let your union or professional association know that you are looking for a job-sharing partner. Some employee organizations have job-placement services, and most have newsletters where you may be able to advertise the position.

Work option resource centres: The growing interest in work options has led to the creation of agencies that specialize in work option information. These agencies usually maintain lists of potential job sharers. Work Well or San Francisco's New Ways to Work can let you know if such a resource exists near you. (See the Resources Section for addresses and phone numbers.)

Classified ads: Advertising in newspapers and trade journals usually produces good results, although it does involve some expense and time spent in screening replies. The following example might serve as a model for writing your own advertisement.

Writer/Researcher

Exciting opportunity for experienced writer/researcher to work less than full time. I am seeking a partner to share my position at a well-established firm producing periodicals for national distribution. I need someone who can write, edit, and co-ordinate research material on innovative human potential subjects. Some travel required. Send resumé, Box 77, care of this newspaper.

Once you have received responses, you will have to select the most suitable candidates and arrange to interview them. Make the selection process more effective by preparing a set of questions that all applicants will answer.

Here are some issues you may wish to deal with when interviewing candidates:

- The type of work the job entails;
- The salary and benefits;
- The applicant's work habits and how they are likely to mesh with yours. Consider particularly the applicant's apparent flexibility, ability to cooperate, organizational skills, need for recognition, and communication skills;
- The applicant's work history and educational background;
- The reasons for wanting to work less than full time;
- The applicant's long-term employment goals. What would this person like to be doing in three years time?

Your own emotional reaction to the applicant is important. Did you feel comfortable talking with this person? Compatibility bears as much weight as professional qualifications. Although one candidate might have exceptional skills and experience, another less-qualified candidate might be easier for you to work with. When faced with such a choice, remember that an agreeable personality, steady work habits, a sense of fairness, and the ability to communicate well are crucial to a successful job-sharing partnership. The most highly qualified people will not make suitable partners if they are lacking in these areas.

■ HOW WILL YOU IMPLEMENT YOUR JOB-SHARING OPTION?

Before setting a plan in motion, questions have to be settled relating to the more pragmatic aspects of start-up. For instance:

? *What will be the start-up date?*

? *Will there be a trial period, and if so, for how long?*

? *What happens if one of the partners drops out? Will the remaining partner work full time until a replacement is found? Who will be responsible for finding a replacement?*

? *What happens if the original job holder wants to return to full time?*

? *Will the job-sharing partners be evaluated individually or as a team?*

Some of these issues will be resolved during negotiations with your employer, but the negotiation process will probably proceed more smoothly if you know what you want ahead of time.

Permanent Part-Time

Designing a permanent part-time schedule involves coming up with workable answers to the following questions. An additional suggested resource is *Part-time Professional* by Diane Rothburg and Barbara Cook.

■ WHAT WILL HAPPEN TO YOUR WORK WHEN YOU'RE NOT THERE?

If you plan to work fewer hours, someone will probably have to take over part of your job. There are several ways to arrange this.

Job splitting: To create two permanent part-time positions from one full-time job, either divide it into two separate jobs with two different sets of tasks, or create two shifts to deal with the same set of tasks.

When creating two separate jobs, it is possible to make them equal or unequal in size. If the type of work calls for splitting duties rather than dividing the duration of the work period, consider which tasks you should keep and which ones are best designated to the new position. In deciding this, you might look at your own strengths and weaknesses, and at what you are trying to accomplish by changing your work schedule. For instance, if a particular task must be performed at a certain time of day, which happens to be when you expect not to be working, then this task should be relegated to the new position. Similarly, if one aspect of your job is making your life miserable, it is an obvious selection for the newly created position.

Job sharing: If you can't divide your job neatly into two independent parts, you may need to consider a job-sharing arrangement. In some organizations it may be easier to classify a shared position as two permanent part-time jobs than to create a new job classification for shared jobs. For design guidelines, consult the chapter on job sharing.

Relief staffing: If you plan to make only a small reduction in worktime, a member of the regular relief staff may be able to assume your duties when you are off. If your organization does not have trained relief staff on call, you may want to suggest that your employer create such a position. A good point to make is that relief staff can cover for other employees on vacation or sick leave.

The best candidates for relief staff are people with flexible schedules who do not want full-time work: parents of school-age children, students, retirees, and artists, for example.

Cross training: If you are a supervisor or someone in a senior position, you may be able to train a co-worker to perform your duties on an acting basis while you are away. Such an arrangement is probably not suitable where the worktime reduction is more than 20 percent of full-time hours.

Training a junior employee to do your job has other advantages, too. It will minimize disruption if you should get sick, go on vacation, or get promoted.

Streamlining duties: Sometimes there is no need to bring in new staff to take over part of your job. You may be underutilized anyway; in that case, reducing your hours will improve your efficiency. Alternatively, try to find out if someone else in the organization is underutilized; that person may be able to assume some of your duties. Sometimes you can streamline your job by identifying duties that have become redundant and eliminating them from your job description.

Be careful about streamlining your job, however. It can happen that the old duties are neither eliminated nor passed on, and you'll end up trying to do the same amount of work in less time. A few hours per week can sometimes make the difference between feeling underused and overburdened. Don't set yourself up for burnout.

There is another danger in streamlining your job. Suppose your financial situation changes and you need more work. If your employer is saving money because you're working part time, it will be harder to return to full-time hours should you wish to do so.

■ WHO WILL FIND SOMEONE TO FILL THE SECOND PART-TIME POSITION?

If your employer might be discouraged from accepting a proposal because of the extra work associated with filling the new position, you'd be well advised to find the fill-in employee yourself.

If you assume this task, approach former employees and employees on maternity leave, retirees, or friends and professional associates who are currently unemployed. In particular, look for someone who has good reason for wanting to work part time and who would be comfortable with a schedule that is complementary to your own.

A good prospect is someone who would accept the job on a permanent basis. With a person who is primarily interested in temporary work, you may have to spend time and energy seeking a replacement sooner than expected, or find yourself feeling pressured to return to full-time work. However, if you are switching to part time as a way to phase into retirement, the most suitable person would be someone wanting to ease into a full-time position: a student about to graduate, for example, or a parent whose youngest child will soon be entering school.

■ WHAT WILL YOU DO TO MINIMIZE THE DISRUPTION CAUSED BY YOUR DECISION TO WORK PART TIME?

Your absence is bound to affect others at your workplace. At times you will not be available to take telephone calls, answer questions, or cope with unexpected problems. You will miss some staff meetings. Consider the following ways to minimize such disruptions.

Choose a reasonable schedule. You can make life easier for your supervisor and co-workers if you set working hours to coincide with peak workloads, regular staff meetings, or with natural breaks in workflow. The less complicated your schedule, the easier it will be for others to follow and the less likely they will be confused as to when you are in or out.

Define your duties carefully. If your job has been split to create two new part-time positions, make sure everyone knows exactly which are your duties and which belong to the other part-time person, or, in other words, where each job begins and ends. This means taking pains to define duties as clearly and specifically as possible.

Establish and maintain good communications. When you work part time, you can't rely on keeping information in your head. You have to put more information on paper (or into the computer) so other people can find it when you're not around. Also, when there are longer lapses between working periods your recall of aspects of the job may be less accurate. To avoid communication problems, designate one person to take your messages when you are away, and consider using an answering machine or voicemail. Keep a copy of your schedule on your desk and make certain other key people, such as your supervisor and the office receptionist, have an up-to-date copy. If you are a supervisor, let subordinates know what kind of problems justify calling you at home. Avoid causing others problems or delays by making sure you complete tasks, return files, and answer all messages before you leave for your scheduled time off. Also, check with co-workers and supervisors before leaving in case there are last-minute details to discuss.

Cross train a substitute. If you are the only one who is proficient at certain tasks, business will slow down when you're not at work. To avoid delays and frustration, train a co-worker to perform these duties.

Use resources efficiently. When a job is split, consideration must be given to where the other person will work. Scheduling different hours means equipment and work stations can be shared instead of duplicated. Working alternate schedules also makes it easier to take each other's messages.

Look for countervailing advantages. Working part time usually causes some inconveniences, even if only minor ones, but there may also be some built-in advantages for your employer. Two people splitting a job might be able to cover for each other during vacations or sick leave. Two part-time people on staff might mean that your employer need not hire extra help for peak periods or emergencies.

■ HOW WILL YOU IMPLEMENT PERMANENT PART-TIME?

In many organizations a structure for part-time work already exists, and questions of benefits, contract language, and so on have already been handled. Just fit yourself into the existing system if it's fair. If your employer does not have such a system in place, refer to pages 208 to 240 for ideas on how to write up your proposal.

Leaves of Absence

Compensatory and discretionary leaves are structured quite differently. Compensatory leave is paid leave that is part of an organization's standard benefit package. It is available to all employees in the form of sick leave, vacation time, statutory holidays, etc. Provisions of compensatory leave should be negotiated by your union or, in the absence of a union, by a representative group of employees. (See also the information on Compensatory Benefit Leaves on page 262.)

Discretionary leave is available to individual employees upon request. It is usually dependent on the goodwill of the employer or supervisor, and is often leave without pay. It covers the categories of personal leave, educational leave, sabbaticals, deferred earning plans, and extended leave. Such leaves are one-time events and are granted by an employer in response to one employee's unique circumstances. They do not set a precedent for other employees. Personal leave, or leave without pay as it is also called, can include extended vacations, compassionate or bereavement leave, extended maternity leave, paternity, parental, and adoptive parent leaves.

Smaller organizations sometimes allow exceptions to the general pattern outlined above.

- Employees can sometimes take compassionate leave as part of their normal sick leave;
- Employers will sometimes consider adoptive parent leave equivalent to maternity leave;
- Individuals can sometimes trade salary increases for addi-

tional vacation time. For example, a 4 percent raise would be equivalent to two extra weeks of paid vacation.

In some cases, a union or employee association will bargain to make a particular discretionary leave available as an employee right. For example, the Canadian Auto Workers union has a collective agreement that includes a provision for paid educational leave. University teachers are entitled to a paid sabbatical every seven years. More often, however, individual employees must negotiate a discretionary leave on their own.

Before requesting a discretionary leave, you need to decide on the kind of leave you want, who will replace you, how to transfer your responsibilities, costs and conditions of the leave, and the countervailing advantages to your employer.

■ WHAT KIND OF LEAVE DO YOU WANT?

Leaves generally fall into one of three classifications, depending on how wages, benefits, and seniority are affected:

- **Sabbaticals** — paid leave with benefits and seniority maintained;
- **Personal leave** — unpaid leave with benefits and seniority maintained;
- **Extended leave** — unpaid leave with seniority maintained, but no benefits.

When asking for leave, the general rule is to request the best conditions you can realistically expect and negotiate downward if necessary. When requesting a leave, find out how your employer defines each category and use the same terminology to avoid misunderstandings.

Sabbaticals: Paid leave may also be called social service leave, paid educational leave, or leave with pay. Sometimes an employee's request for social service leave is granted indirectly by redefining the employee's role within the organization. Employees who want time off for community work may be "seconded" — or placed on special assignment — to a non-profit organization.

In some organizations, employees get paid educational leave for advanced training or professional development. Employees who need rest and therapy for drug, alcohol, family, or emotional problems sometimes get paid leave under the catch-all title of "employee training and development."

If your immediate supervisor is likely to be supportive, your best bet may be a quiet request for redeployment or special assignment. If you are working for an organization that views itself as having innovative personnel policies, a formal proposal along these lines might meet with equal or greater success.

In either case, a request for paid leave must be backed by a solid rationale. If you can't demonstrate how the leave arrangement will benefit your employer, you will probably have to settle for leave without pay.

Personal leave: All personal leave is without pay. It may be called leave of absence or simply leave. If you take a short personal leave — up to 90 days — you can probably retain your benefits without much trouble. The stronger your justification for taking leave, the longer your employer will be willing to continue your benefits. Personal leave is a catch-all category for all kinds of unpaid time off including:

- Extended vacation or travel time;
- Religious holidays;
- Therapy or recovery from illness;
- Drug or alcohol rehabilitation;
- Rest and relaxation;
- Extended maternity, new father, and adoptive leaves;
- Schooling or community service;
- Adjusting to a bereavement, or to attend a funeral;
- Care of sick children or other family members.

Extended leave: Common names for extended leave are inactive status, leave without pay, furlough, and care and nurturing leave. The duration of extended leaves may be from 90 days to a year or more. If your employer values your service sufficiently you may be able to retain your seniority, but in all likelihood you will not be entitled to continue your benefits. Time-buyer plans are usually classified as extended leave, but sometimes an employer can be convinced to maintain some or all employee benefits. See Don Abrams' book *The Time Buyer* for more details.

■ WHO WILL REPLACE YOU?

Finding someone to fill your shoes depends on several factors.

? *How long will you be gone?*

The longer the leave, the more qualified your replacement should be.

? *Do you have a choice about when to take the leave?*

Your replacement will have less difficulty handling your job if you take leave during a slack period.

? *Do you know when you'll be returning to work?*

If you know the date of your return, your employer can offer your replacement a contract for a fixed period of time. Otherwise you will have to find someone who is willing to accept an open-ended arrangement.

? *Will you be available to consult?*

If you are taking a leave to sail around the world, you won't be available for telephone consultations. In such circumstances your replacement needs to be fully briefed in advance, and must be capable of doing the job without your help.

When making a leave proposal, suggest practical ways of finding a suitable replacement. There are a number of ways to find someone who can handle your job on a temporary basis.

Rehire a former employee. Your predecessor or a recent retiree might welcome the opportunity for temporary employment. Check with your personnel department for the names of employees who quit to raise children or to go back to school. Contact the person who covers for you during sick leave or vacation.

Bring in a professional associate. Conferences, union meetings, and workshops bring us into contact with people who have skills similar to our own. Ask yourself if there is anyone in your circle of work-related acquaintances who might like to take over for you.

Have a co-worker, or co-workers, cover for you. Do you have an assistant or associate with a less demanding job who could take over while you're away? It may be easier to find a temporary replacement for that person's position than your own. Your co-worker might also welcome such a change, even if it's only temporary. If you plan to take leave during a period when the workload is lighter than usual, a number of co-workers may be able to share your duties.

Use relief staff. Relief, casual, and on-call staff can make good replacement staff since they usually require little orientation and training, and are known quantities to the organization. If your organization currently does not have relief staff and you can find a replacement who would be willing to fill this role after your return, it would mitigate your employer's cost of training such a person.

Advertise. You could leave it to the personnel department to find a replacement. However, they may bring in the wrong person—who could leave your job a mess—or deny your request for leave because of the difficulties of finding a replacement. Or you could advertise your position in the Help Wanted section of the newspaper and find the right person yourself. (Have replies sent to a post box at the newspaper in order to protect your privacy.)

Leave your work until you get back. Some jobs are built around projects that can be delayed for a period of time. If you can't afford an unpaid leave and you are willing to work overtime when you get back, you may be able to get a paid leave on the understanding that you will be responsible for catching up on accumulated work. This is not a recommended strategy, but it can work out where the leave is short and not health related.

■ HOW CAN YOU TRANSFER YOUR RESPONSIBILITIES WITH MINIMAL DISRUPTION?

When someone is taking over for you, there are many things your replacement will need to know. When you return, you will have to learn what happened while you were away. How will this information be exchanged?

In a profession like nursing, most duties are standardized. In institutional settings there are usually orientation programs for new staff members. Changeover requires minimal planning in these jobs. In other positions — a live-in houseparent in a group home for disturbed adolescents, for example — an elaborate changeover system may be needed. This is often true for highly specialized jobs, and for jobs that involve ongoing projects, strong personal relationships, or quick responses to a crisis.

The longer you plan to be away, the more complex your job, and the more inexperienced your replacement, the more attention you should give to developing a changeover plan. Here are some suggestions to facilitate this process.

Time your leave carefully. Most jobs have natural completion or transition points. An accountant, for instance, would not take leave just before the end of a fiscal period if it were possible to avoid it. In other jobs there are slack periods when it would be easier for a new person to fit in. If you can, capitalize on timing factors.

Allow for adequate overlap. The more complex and responsible your job, the more time and care are needed to brief your replacement and for you to be debriefed at the end of the leave period.

Complete outstanding tasks before you go on leave. Finish uncompleted tasks and, if possible, put new tasks on hold at the beginning and end of the changeover period. This will simplify the transfer process. Make sure all files are kept scrupulously up to date.

Create a changeover file. You can minimize confusion by leaving a good set of briefing notes. Reminders in the desk calendar ("March 15 — time sheets due") and instructions next to infrequently used equipment can also help.

Cross train your co-workers. Before you go on leave, teach one or more of your co-workers specific parts of your job. They can help your replacement with problems that arise while you are away.

Check in occasionally. If you can, set aside a time to call in each week during the first couple of weeks of your absence. This will give your replacement a chance to ask questions while learning the ropes.

Lighten the load for your replacement. If your job is particularly demanding, try to arrange for a co-worker to take over some of your duties, at least during the initial period of your absence. This will ease the transition for your replacement.

Leave some tasks until you return. Sometimes the parts of your job that would be most difficult for a replacement to learn can wait until you get back. If you use this approach, make arrangements to keep your workload manageable after you return. Perhaps a co-worker can take over some of your day-to-day responsibilities until you've cleared up the backlog.

■ ARE YOU PREPARED TO NEGOTIATE?

Your leave will create some expenses and inconvenience for your employer: the cost of training a replacement, any wages you receive while on leave, and the cost of any benefits you retain.

Designing a formal request for leave is a difficult balancing act. You must establish conditions that are affordable for you and yet keep costs low enough that your employer will grant the leave. Since the conditions of discretionary leave are negotiable, you must be sure of what you want and what you can afford to accept.

■ HOW WILL THE ARRANGEMENT BENEFIT YOUR EMPLOYER?

You are unlikely to get a leave unless you can design your request in such a way that it offers benefits to your employer. Sometimes advantages occur naturally. For example, if a senior employee takes six months off and is replaced by someone with fewer qualifications, the salary differential might represent a sizable saving to the employer. Where staff cutbacks are in the offing, an extended leave can sometimes help an employer prevent a layoff.

If you are planning to go to Europe for a year and could do a certain amount of work-related research for your employer while you are there, your employer might be induced to maintain your benefit package while you are away, or help with expenses. If you take time off to fulfil a major community service commitment — perhaps to lead a major fund-raising campaign — you may be able to convince your employer to keep you on the payroll as a public relations gesture.

V-Time

V-Time, or voluntary reduced worktime, is a comprehensive personnel program available to all employees within an organization who
want to participate. That means two levels of design are involved:
the design of on overall system and the design of individual work
schedules.

To design an individual work schedule under V-Time, use the
guidelines for permanent part-time if you plan to take your time off
in short blocks. If you plan to take longer periods of time off, consult
the guidelines for designing a leave of absence.

There are a number of design options for the overall V-Time system. Some design choices will be arbitrary while others will be necessary to help the program meet specific goals.

■ HOW MANY TIME-OFF OPTIONS WILL BE AVAILABLE?

The fewer the options, the easier V-Time is to administer. More
options increase the chances that the system will meet everyone's
needs and wants. Most programs offer between six and twelve
options.

■ WHAT TIME-OFF OPTIONS WILL BE AVAILABLE?

The best way to meet people's needs is to ask them what they want.
A needs survey will help determine what time-off patterns appeal

... IT FEELS GREAT ... WHAT USED TO BE MY 'OFF' DAY
IS NOW MY DAY OFF ...

most to the employees of your organization. A needs survey also helps locate support for the program.

If the needs survey is the first step in the design process, the written proposal can include suggestions for specific options. If a needs survey isn't available, the proposal can suggest a sample range of options with the understanding that the final range of options would be based on a future needs survey. A standard range of options would include 2.5, 5, 10, 20, 25, and 40 percent time off. Job sharing can be included within a V-Time framework if the available options include 50 percent time off.

■ WHAT ARE THE MOST CONVENIENT PERCENTAGES?

If the normal workweek is 40 hours, any multiple of 2.5 percent will result in an even number of hours off per week. If the normal workweek is 35 hours, steps of 2.875 percent will result in an even number of hours off per week.

If the needs survey shows that some forms of time off are very popular, these should be included in the range of options. If, for example, there is widespread interest in a workday that is an hour shorter, and also in a day off every other week, time-off options of 12.5 and 10 percent would accommodate these needs.

■ HOW FREQUENTLY WILL PARTICIPANTS BE ABLE TO SIGN ON?

Most programs allow participants to sign on at six- or twelve-month intervals. The shorter interval is more responsive to individual needs, but the longer time frame is easier for organizations to administer.

■ WHEN WILL PARTICIPANTS BE ABLE TO SIGN ON?

Some programs allow entry at the beginning of every quarter; others offer continuous entry. Continuous entry means you can sign on for a six- or twelve-month cycle at any point in the year.

Specified entry dates make it easier to coordinate relief staffing. For example, if the personnel manager knows on March 1 that she

Sample V-Time Benefit Chart (Part 1)

Time-off Option	UIC, CPP, Workers' Comp	Statutory Holidays	Sick Leave	Vacation Time	Seniority
Full Time	Full	8 hours each	100 hours/year	120 hours/year	Full
2.5%	Prorated 2.5%	8 hours each	100 hours/year	120 hours/year	Full
5%	Prorated 5%	8 hours each	100 hours/year	120 hours/year	Full
10%	Prorated 10%	7.25 hours each	90 hours/year	108 hours/year	Full
20%	Prorated 20%	6.50 hours each	80 hours/year	96 hours/year	Full
50%	Prorated 50%	4 hours each	50 hours/year	60 hours/year	Full

will have fifteen data entry staff working 10 percent less from April 1 to October 1, she knows that she will need to hire one full-time and one half-time relief worker for that period.

Continuous entry is more responsive to changing conditions. If an employee's physical health or mental state changes suddenly, continuous entry allows that employee to get immediate relief from stress.

■ HOW DOES V-TIME ALTER BENEFIT PACKAGES?

Usually benefits are prorated. The ways this can be done are discussed in Steps Four and Six.

Before deciding how to deal with benefits, any group designing a V-Time program should check with external agencies that administer its benefits — the group life insurance plan, the dental plan, the pension plan, and so on — to see if they have in place any restrictions on hours of work. (If any of these outside agencies prove inflexible,

SAMPLE V-TIME BENEFIT CHART (PART 2)

TIME-OFF OPTION	PENSION PLAN CON- TRIBUTION*	MEDICAL PLAN	DENTAL PLAN	EXTENDED MEDICAL
Full Time	Full	Full	Full	Full
2.5%	Prorated 2.5%	Full	Full	Full
5%	Prorated 5%	Full	Full	Full
10%	Prorated 10%	Full	Full	Employee pays
20%	Prorated 20%	Employee pays half	Full	Employee pays
50%	Prorated 50%	Employee pays half	Full	Employee pays

* Contributions for employees over age 55 will remain at the full-time rate

remember that your company can shop around to find a more responsive supplier.) Also find out whether the current payroll system is designed to handle non-standard benefit packages, and whether employee contributions or cash-in-lieu payments are possible.

When you have established an overall framework, give each participant information that clearly outlines the effect on benefits, like the charts at the top of this page and the previous one. These charts should be accompanied by notes that explain exactly what the changes mean, particularly those which affect pensions and statutory holidays.

The sample charts above are typical of most V-Time programs in that cuts of less than 10 percent have only a minimal impact on benefits, and pensions of older workers are protected.

In most programs, all participants earn seniority as if they were working full time. This is especially important if V-Time is offered as an alternative to layoffs. (Employees can hardly be expected to work less to help avoid layoffs if, by doing so, they slide down the seniority list and increase their own risk of eventually being laid off.)

■ CAN THE PROGRAM ACCOMMODATE OTHER WORK OPTIONS?

If the payroll structure for V-Time is well designed, it will be able to accommodate job sharing, permanent part-time, phased retirement, and short-term leaves of absence. A payroll system adjusted to fit this model can streamline personnel procedures and offer substantial flexibility in payroll management.

■ WHAT WILL HAPPEN IF THERE ARE DISAGREEMENTS?

Sometimes a particular supervisor will refuse requests to participate in V-Time. Or perhaps a supervisor and an employee will not be able to agree on a schedule for the employee's time off. Supervisors and the people working under them may disagree on the interpretation of rules governing such matters as statutory holidays or sick leave. To ensure that such conflicts are resolved cleanly, it is useful to designate an "umpire" who will arbitrate and mediate these disagreements. The umpire or arbitrator should be completely conversant with the rules of the program, a competent mediator, and someone neither side can accuse of favouring the other.

■ HOW WILL THE SYSTEM KEEP TRACK OF TIME OFF?

It is easy to keep track of simple schedules that involve one hour off every day or one day off every week. More complicated schedules can present problems. However, it is still fairly easy to set up a good system for tracking V-Time hours by creating a new category or column on every employee's time sheet. In this way, V-Time hours can be recorded in the same way as sick leave, by keeping a running balance of hours earned and used during each pay period.

■ WHO WILL BE ELIGIBLE FOR THE PROGRAM?

In some programs V-Time is available to all employees. In others access is restricted to non-managerial staff, or to staff who have completed a certain service requirement. In order to avoid resentment, criteria for eligibility should be as broad as possible.

■ HOW DO EMPLOYEES APPLY TO PARTICIPATE IN THE PROGRAM?

Most programs use a standard application form which is submitted to a supervisor or the personnel department. A simpler form is used for renewals unless the employee wants to change the previous schedule. Changes are treated as though they were first-time applications. Depending on the terms of the particular program, an application may or may not need the approval of the V-Time arbitrator, the personnel department, or the supervisor's superior.

■ WHAT RULES WILL GOVERN ROTATION OF RELIEF STAFF?

If ten assembly line workers each want a half day off every week, only one relief worker would appear necessary. But what if all ten workers want Friday afternoons off? Will V-Time participants share relief staff on a first-come, first-served basis, on the basis of seniority, or on the basis of some other system? To avoid conflicts, the rules governing the use of relief staff should be clearly spelled out, and copies of these rules given to all participating employees and their supervisors.

■ WHAT RULES WILL GOVERN THE DESIGN OF INDIVIDUAL SCHEDULES?

Employees and their supervisors are responsible for negotiating individual V-Time schedules. However, some rules should apply in order to prevent abuse and avoid unrealistic requests. The following mechanisms can help you arrive at workable schedules.

Personnel budgeting by department. Wages saved as a result of V-Time should remain within the branch or department to be used for relief staff, except when the program has been designed to avoid layoffs associated with lack of work.

Full briefing packages. All applicants should receive a complete briefing package to assist them in drawing up workable V-Time programs.

A comprehensive sign-on procedure. The V-Time application form should include questions about the exact terms of the proposed schedule, arrangements for sick leave, statutory holidays, and attending staff meetings, plans for minimizing disruption caused by the employee's absence from the workplace, and a plan for reassigning or eliminating the appropriate percentage of the employee's regular work.

A review process. All V-Time applications should be approved by the V-Time umpire. The umpire must be satisfied that neither the employee nor the employee's co-workers will be expected to do more work in less time. The umpire should also ensure that appropriate steps have been taken to avoid disruption in the workflow. If employees and their supervisors are having difficulty reaching agreement, the umpire can be requested to help with the design process. (With time, the umpire will develop an expertise in knowing how individual V-Time plans can be set up to work smoothly, and would-be participants and their supervisors may seek the umpire's help as a matter of course.)

Clearly spelled-out rules. Briefing materials should be absolutely clear about any restrictions on time-off options for particular groups of employees. Some restrictions may be justified by operational considerations. For example, a hospital may be able to accommodate a nurse's request for a full day off every week, but not a request for shorter shifts. A university may consider it unworkable to have support staff on vacation during the first month of a term, but be willing to approve extended vacations during the rest of the year.

For more comprehensive technical information on this work option see *V-Time: A Matter of Time* from New Ways to Work. Barney Olmsted and Suzanne Smith's *Creating a Flexible Workplace* also has a detailed chapter on the mechanics of setting up a V-Time program.

Banked Overtime

Banked overtime programs are usually designed for groups of employees who hold relatively interchangeable positions in factories, institutions, or businesses that operate almost continuously. If you have a one-of-a-kind job you may be excluded from the formal banked overtime program in your workplace. Occasionally, however, a single individual can negotiate an informal banking arrangement with the immediate supervisor. You are more likely to be able to arrange some sort of low-key hours banking agreement if:

- You have visible health or burnout problems;
- You are a particularly valuable or indispensable employee;
- You are a long-term employee with a good work record;
- You have a good relationship with your supervisor.

Any of these conditions would provide reasonable grounds for submitting a proposal. Devising a practical plan for having your work covered when you are off will enhance your chances further. Finesse is usually more effective than trying to force the issue.

Individual agreements should cover the same issues as a company-wide hours banking program, but in as simple and uncomplicated a way as possible.

Whether the banked overtime arrangement is geared for an individual or a group, every system must address five basic issues.

■ HOW WILL THE PROGRAM ADDRESS THE NEED FOR RELIEF STAFF?

Adequate relief staffing is the key to a successful banked overtime program. If relief staffing is inadequate, either you will never get the opportunity to collect your banked time, or your co-workers will have to carry an extra load in order for you to take time off.

The most common solution is to hire full-time relief staff who can be booked on a rotation basis. Relief staff are usually trained to fill several different positions. Often they work weekends as well, in order to reduce overtime for regular employees. In most cases the relief pool is large enough to cover for regular employees taking sick leave, statutory holidays, or vacations. The same pool can also cover for staff on V-Time.

In some programs, relief staff are guaranteed a minimum number of days each week, and receive a full benefit package regardless of the number of hours worked. In other programs they may have the option of working less than full time, with benefits prorated accordingly. Sometimes regular employees prefer to work only two, three, or four days a week because of other commitments, or as a means of phasing into retirement. For them, permanent part-time relief work might provide a suitable alternative to a full-time position.

Because full-time relief staff must be both flexible in skills and well trained, they are usually recruited from senior employee ranks. If an organization's overtime levels are unpredictable, it will be necessary to have some staff on temporary or auxiliary status. Usually these people are hired for entry-level positions, rather than as relief staff.

When designing a plan for relief staffing, seek to recruit people who need only minimal training and orientation. This could include employees who have been laid off, early retirees, student summer replacements, and employees who have left work to fulfil parenting responsibilities.

Not all companies have to hire relief staff to operate their banked overtime programs. Some businesses have predictable peaks in workload, and employees are willing to work overtime so long as they can convert it into extra vacation time. For example, an accounting firm that needs only five tax accountants most of the year may have enough work for eight such staff from the beginning of January to the end of April. The firm keeps six tax accountants on the payroll. All six bank overtime during the first four months of the year, and take turns collecting their banked hours in the form of extended vacations throughout the remainder of the year.

This approach involves setting staff levels somewhere between peak and minimum needs. It has the advantage of creating a stronger sense of equality and team spirit than a system which uses special relief staff. However, it may require more work stations.

■ WILL RELIEF STAFF BE AVAILABLE FOR ALL JOBS?

Trained relief staff in nursing, police work, and most factory jobs can move in and out of positions fairly easily. Mechanisms for covering other types of work, such as management, social work, and serving clients on an ongoing basis, are more complicated and require careful planning. People in these positions often have a difficult time getting time off, even though they may need a break as much as — if not more than — other workers. As a result, those who are excluded from a banked overtime program (particularly managers) may feel envious or resentful. Support for the program and employee morale will be higher if everyone is given the opportunity to participate.

The following strategies can be used to design a plan for relief coverage of positions with complex duties.

Cross training. A line employee can be cross trained to serve as acting manager. (The line staff's regular duties can more easily be covered by someone from the relief pool.) Cross training also provides back-up for vacations and sick leave.

Extending vacations. Regular vacations can often be extended without the need to hire relief staff, particularly when vacations are taken at off-peak periods.

Soft loading. Most staff members have peaks and valleys in their workflow. Many organizations assign staff additional responsibilities until they are busy even during the organization's slack times. If duties are assigned based on the staff member's *average* workload, then an employee can take occasional days off during slow periods.

Delegating. By temporarily delegating more minor tasks, employees may be able to reduce their workloads to the extent that they are able to take some time off.

Temporarily hiring retirees or ex-employees. Sometimes an employee's predecessor or someone who has retired from the company can be called in to provide relief staffing.

■ HOW WILL RELIEF STAFF AND REGULAR STAFF EXCHANGE INFORMATION?

Without adequate mechanisms for communication, important information may be lost, forgotten, or delayed. To prevent this, relief and regular staff should leave messages and reminders for each other, and keep written notes. They should make sure their counterpart is up to date on the status of important projects. Full-time employees should receive copies of all communiqués and attend staff meetings if possible. Where a relief staffer takes over for an extended period, efforts should be made to finish old tasks and put new tasks on hold at both the beginning and end of the relief period.

■ WHAT RULES WILL GOVERN THE ALLOCATION OF TIME OFF?

A banked overtime program needs a fair and efficient system for allocating time off. Allocation systems are always somewhat arbitrary, and often have built-in pitfalls. It is particularly useful to ask participants for their input on this part of the plan. Incorporate the following key questions into any survey you undertake.

? *Can employees take time off before they have earned it?*

This is usually called *anticipatory time off.* Sometimes employers are agreeable to this because it helps to level out maximum/minimum staffing needs.

? *Is it mandatory to bank overtime or can employees request compensation in cash?*

Many programs allow a choice. However, mandatory hours banking may be necessary to simplify the use of relief staff. Optional cash payments are not a feature of programs designed to avoid layoffs.

? *Is there a limit to the number of hours an employee can bank?*

? *Which employees will have first choice for time off?*

To ensure adequate staff coverage, employees are usually required to book their time off on a roster. If a company employs five full-time relief staff, for example, five relief slots will be available each working day. In many programs the time-off roster also serves as the duty assignment sheet for the relief staff. The same roster is often used to allocate vacation time.

Rules governing the order of signing up are essential because the last people on the roster will have more limited choices than those who sign up first. Rules should be fair and simple to administer. It also helps if people can book time off far enough in advance to make plans. Some organizations allocate time off on a first-come/first-served basis; some by seniority. Others give priority to employees who have accumulated the most banked time.

Another question concerns the length of time off. Will employees be able to take a day at a time or must they take consecutive days? If someone books five Fridays off, for instance, that blocks one relief slot for five weeks and limits the options for others. Some programs are designed to prevent this by restricting time off to one-week blocks. Others restrict the choice to single days.

■ HOW WILL YOUR EMPLOYER BENEFIT FROM THE PROGRAM?

A banked overtime program is not cost free, so it must be made to offer some advantages to the employer. Banked overtime is more expensive than regular overtime, but more manageable than trying to cover extra hours with casual workers. For instance, in order to keep a 200-employee pulp mill open on Saturdays, an employer would have to hire 200 casual workers, but a banked overtime program could do this with 40 full-time relief staff.

Banked overtime often improves morale and reduces rates of absenteeism, accidents, and turnover. It may also improve efficiency if the same relief staff can be used to cover for sick leave and vacation.

■ WHAT VALUE WILL BE GIVEN TO BANKED OVERTIME HOURS?

Where possible, overtime which is banked should earn a premium rate of pay so as to discourage the employer's excessive use of overtime. (Sometimes this premium is paid out as cash. Other times it may be converted to additional banked hours.) Because salaried employees rarely receive compensation for overtime, they may have to settle for a time trade-off with no premium — not perfect, but a big improvement on no compensation at all.

■ WILL RELIEF WORKERS BELONG TO THE UNION OR THE EMPLOYEE ASSOCIATION?

Relief workers should always be members of the union and get the same wages and benefits as regular employees.

Phased Retirement

The first step in designing a phased retirement program is to choose the type of phased retirement you want.

- If you cannot afford a cut in income, you will need a *company-paid program*. Company-paid programs offer only short-term reductions in worktime (six to twelve months).
- If you want maximum flexibility and the option of reducing your worktime over a period of up to twenty years, you will have to accept an *employee-paid program*. Employee-paid programs involve a significant loss of income.
- If you can only afford a small cut in income, and want to reduce your worktime gradually over a period of one to five years, a *partial pension scheme* is your best choice.
- If the work schedule you want is available through V-Time, permanent part-time, leave of absence, or job sharing, you can choose the *integrated option* approach.
- If you want to do temporary or part-time work after you retire, a *post-retirement work pool* is your best option.

■ COMPANY-PAID PROGRAMS

Company-paid programs are rarely established in response to an individual proposal, as employers are reluctant to create a precedent for other employees. If you are determined to have a company-paid program, you'll need strong support from your union or co-workers.

Company-paid programs are characterized by the following conditions.

- The benefits are short-term — usually six months to a year;
- Cuts in worktime are relatively small, rarely more than 10 to 20 percent;
- Time off can take the form of a shorter workweek or extended vacation;
- Employees receive full salary;
- Pensions and other benefits remain unchanged;
- The option is available to all employees who have reached the required age and/or years of service;
- Participants can attend pre-retirement planning courses on company time;
- Most programs include provisions for training the retiring employee's successor during the phasing-out period;
- Eligible employees and their supervisors receive information packages outlining the terms of the program.

Employers can be encouraged to establish company-paid programs as a gesture of goodwill to retiring employees. These programs can be touted as rewards for loyalty to the organization or can be used to expedite successor training. Because such plans are costly for employers, they are usually only won through hard bargaining by unions.

■ EMPLOYEE-PAID PROGRAMS

An employee-paid program can be a job benefit negotiated by the union or a group of employees. In that case, the structure would be the same as for a partial pension scheme but without the pension.

An employee-paid program can also be designed for a single individual. This is essentially the same as a permanent part-time arrangement, except that the employee and the employer both continue contributing to the pension plan as though the employee were working full time. (The terms of the pension plan must be adjusted to permit payments based on contributions, not salary.)

Companies may initially resist changing the pension plan for a single individual. If you run into opposition, you can point out that a flexible pension system will become increasingly necessary as more and more employees start working non-standard hours.

Overall, employee-paid plans are relatively inexpensive for employers to administer.

■ PARTIAL PENSION SCHEMES

Partial pension schemes are also a benefit provided by the employer in response to a negotiated settlement or a proposal from a group of employees. Because partial pension programs are relatively inexpensive for the employer, they are easier to negotiate than company-paid programs.

Partial pension schemes are usually characterized by the following conditions.

- The option is open to any employee within five years of retirement age;
- Options usually include a four-day week, a three-day week, and half time;
- Benefit packages remain unchanged;
- The employer and the employee both contribute to the pension plan as though the employee were working full time. The terms of the plan are adjusted to base pension payouts on contributions rather than salary;
- Employees are paid according to hours worked. This income is supplemented by a partial pension. The partial pension is usually calculated by multiplying the percentage of reduced time by the percentage of full-time pay expected at retirement. (For example, a person working 40 percent less and eligible for a 60 percent pension on retirement would receive a partial pension equal to 24 percent of full-time salary, bringing his or her income up to 84 percent of full-time pay);
- The partial pension is sometimes paid out of pension fund surpluses, sometimes through a separate pension fund, and sometimes out of the employee's individual pension account. Since this latter approach will reduce the employee's final pension figure by 5 to 15 percent, participants should be clearly informed of the terms of the scheme;

- Partial pension programs usually provide pre-retirement planning courses, successor training programs, and information packages for participants.

▉ INTEGRATED OPTION PLANS

If your firm already offers job sharing, permanent part-time, V-Time, or various kinds of leave programs, you can try to work out a phased retirement by requesting a change in the pension plan. You can make the request yourself or through your union.

Individuals on reduced work schedules should have the option of contributing to the pension plan as though they were working full time. When pension payments are based on contributions rather than on earnings, an individual could work part time for any number of years and still collect a full pension.

▉ POST-RETIREMENT WORK POOLS

Many Canadian companies offer part-time or temporary jobs to retired employees. To initiate such an arrangement, write a letter to the personnel department outlining your qualifications, areas of expertise, and the kind of work schedule you want (temporary, part time, special projects, etc).

Unions and employee associations can also be effective in persuading employers to establish post-retirement work pools. These programs require little administration — often nothing more than an information package and an application form for candidates. Many employers are beginning to see the advantages of having a pool of experienced and stable back-up staff available.

Designing a phased retirement plan raises issues similar to those for permanent part-time. Once you have selected the type of phased retirement you want, go back to the design guidelines for Permanent Part-Time, pages 149 to 153, to work out the details of your program.

Flextime

Flextime is most often established for an entire workplace, or for specific classes of employees. For this reason our design discussion will focus on group programs. In rare cases, a highly valued or long-standing employee, or someone who works independently of other staff, will be able to negotiate an individual flextime schedule. While the mechanisms for setting up an individual program are usually simpler than for a group, the design questions remain the same.

■ WHAT RULES WILL GOVERN PARTICIPATION IN THE PROGRAM?

Sometimes it is possible to divide a workforce into three groups: *automatically eligible, eligible-with-permission,* and *ineligible.* The first group would include only those whose job classifications are clearly amenable to flexing. The second group would include those with jobs where flexing might create problems, and the third group would include people with jobs where flextime would clearly be unworkable.

Many organizations deem all management jobs automatically ineligible, which can cause unnecessary resentment and undermine support for the program. Management eligibility for flextime should be decided on a case-by-case basis.

■ HOW WILL EMPLOYEES APPLY TO PARTICIPATE AND WHO WILL RULE ON ELIGIBILITY?

In most arrangements, employees who are automatically eligible do not have to apply; they can begin flexing as soon as the program is operational. Employees in the eligible-with-permission category usually apply to an hours-of-work committee made up of management and non-management staff. The committee, along with the applicant, reviews the duties of the position and decides on a suitable schedule. Most committees operate according to a set of guidelines.

- The schedule must meet the needs of the job;
- Any necessary relief coverage must be arranged;
- The work of the unit or department must not suffer;
- The program must be approved by the employee's supervisor and/or unit manager.

The hours-of-work committee may be given authority to alter flextime rules on an individual basis. For instance, it may offer flextime without the normal hours-banking privileges, or with a smaller bandwidth. This is a useful provision because it allows the committee more flexibility than if it were restricted to a simple yes or no.

■ WHAT BANDWIDTH WILL APPLY?

Bandwidth refers to the morning and evening limits on working hours. A common bandwidth is 7 a.m. to 6 p.m., which means that an employee working an eight-hour shift could come in to work as early as 7 a.m. or stay as late as 6 p.m. Determining an appropriate bandwidth often involves striking a balance between conflicting gains and losses.

The advantages of a longer bandwidth are:

- Longer hours of service to the public;
- Fewer difficulties with access to scarce equipment;
- Less crowding of the office;
- Better accommodation to the needs and preferences of employees;

- Savings on long-distance telephone calls.

The disadvantages associated with a longer bandwidth are:

- Increased costs for support staff, such as switchboard operators;
- Greater difficulty coordinating team activities;
- Slightly higher costs for utilities, such as heat and lights;
- Staff is harder to supervise.

■ WHAT CORE HOURS WILL APPLY?

Core time refers to a period every working day when all employees of the organization will be on hand. Core time enables the organization to function at full strength when workloads are heaviest. It also ensures sufficient overlap of schedules so that all employees can attend seminars, meetings and other communication sessions.

Popular core times are 10 a.m. to 2 p.m., or 10:30 a.m. to 3 p.m. Some flextime programs do not have a core time, but this approach is suitable only when work is self-directed and independent of clients and other staff.

As with bandwidth, the choice of core hours is often a trade-off between gains and losses. The advantages associated with a longer core time are:

- Greater ease of communication between staff members;
- A longer period of peak work coverage.

The disadvantages are:

- Less accommodation to the needs and preferences of employees;
- Increased need to buy extra equipment, such as photocopiers and computers.

■ WILL FLEXIBILITY BE PERMITTED AT MIDDAY?

A common midday flextime is noon to 2 p.m. Many organizations omit midday flexibility, considering it an unnecessary complication which adds to the difficulty of having enough staff to cover the lunch period. Where midday flex is present, core hours need to be wide enough to allow both morning and afternoon meetings. Organizations which experience heavy customer service demands in the middle of the day may offer a midday flex, with the proviso that employees must arrange among themselves to stagger their lunch breaks so as to maintain adequate staff coverage.

■ HOW WILL SETTLEMENT PERIODS BE DEFINED?

Employees on flextime often work more, or fewer, than their scheduled hours. Every so often this discrepancy must be adjusted. The time between adjustments is a *settlement period*.

Longer settlement periods give employees greater flexibility in setting their own work schedules, but reduce management's control over staff schedules. When a program allows time debits or credits to be carried over from one settlement period to the next, a shorter settlement period can give employees the flexibility they want and still provide sufficient control for management.

The usual practice is to make the settlement period equivalent to one pay period. The choices include the following.

- **Flex-day:** A one-day settlement period ensures tight control but imposes severe limitations on an employee's participation in the flextime concept.
- **Flex-week:** Extending the settlement period over one week allows employees more flexibility to cope with fluctuating workloads and personal responsibilities.
- **Flex-month:** A monthly accounting period provides a good deal of flexibility, particularly when debits and credits in work hours can be carried over from one period to the next.
- **Flex-year:** This scheme allows employees to work different hours at certain times of the year. In winter, for example, staff might work more hours, and fewer hours in the summer. The actual settlement period need not be as long as a year if there is adequate provision for banking hours or for carrying hours over from one period to the next.

■ WILL EMPLOYEES BE ABLE TO BANK EXTRA HOURS?

In most programs the employee's time sheet contains a running balance of surplus or deficit hours. There may be limits on how far employees can work ahead or fall behind in their salaried hours.

■ WILL EMPLOYEES BE ABLE TO TAKE A FULL DAY OFF?

Most flextime participants see the ability to take an occasional day off as a big attraction of the program. However, this is also the area that causes grief for employers. The most common problem is that staff tend to want Mondays or Fridays off, creating gaps in coverage on those days. Difficulties can also arise when employees do not give adequate warning of their intentions to take a flexday. It may also be hard to get all staff together for meetings.

These problems can be avoided in a number of ways. Employees can be required to sign up with their supervisors in advance for days off. The number of employees who can be away on any given day may be restricted. Such rules make it easier for supervisors to keep track of employee schedules and ensure that there are enough people available to handle peak workloads.

Some organizations reserve a specific day of the week for meetings, and no time off is allowed on that day. In organizations where internal communication is more important than daily interaction with clients (some engineering or architectural firms for instance), the opposite approach may apply: one day a fortnight may be set aside as a flexday. Allocating a few days a month for flexdays makes it easier for complete teams to get together on the remaining days.

Any of these mechanisms can be successful; the important thing is to organize days off in a way that will minimize disruption.

■ HOW CAN COMMUNICATION BETWEEN STAFF MEMBERS BE IMPROVED?

Staff meetings should always be scheduled during core hours. It is best to hold them on a specific day of the week. Employees should observe certain courtesies, such as informing co-workers of their intentions to take a day off, and consulting with them before making any significant schedule changes.

■ HOW WILL EMPLOYEES MAINTAIN CONTINUITY WITH CLIENTS?

New work habits can help keep disruption to a minimum. One way is to give clients an alternative contact person: "If you call back after 3 p.m. I won't be here, but Dwayne will be able to help you." Regular clients also deserve a courtesy call when any major schedule changes are planned. Other techniques for maintaining continuity with clients will develop spontaneously once flextime is in place.

■ HOW WILL SUPERVISORS MAINTAIN CONTROL?

Managers may be concerned that employees on flextime will be working without adequate supervision some of the time. How can a flextime program be designed so that managers do not feel they have lost control?

One solution is to arrange for every manager to designate a stand-in. Usually this is someone who works later or earlier than the manager. The stand-in is cross trained to do all or part of the manager's duties and is kept up to date on all policies and issues affecting employees and management. Besides providing coverage for vacations and sick leave, this type of backup is valuable insurance against the sudden loss of a manager, and is a good way to train future managers.

■ WHAT RULES WILL ENSURE ADEQUATE STAFF COVERAGE?

Flextime can enable a company to offer extended hours of service and will help an organization attract customers, particularly in sales and service departments. However, some mechanisms are required to insure that coverage is always available early and late in the day.

Some organizations designate a few people for the early and late hours in order to insure that at least a skeleton staff is always on duty. Other companies will rotate responsibility for early and late coverage, and for opening and closing the premises. Some organizations set their public hours shorter than their bandwidth. An insurance office, for instance, may accept clients from 8 a.m. to 5 p.m., though some employees might start as early as 7 a.m. and others work as late as 6 p.m.

◼ HOW WILL YOUR EMPLOYER BENEFIT FROM FLEXTIME?

Flextime can enable a company to extend its business hours. Flextime may help your company make more efficient use of equipment, and it could help to reduce lateness and absenteeism. Sometimes flextime makes it possible to stagger employees' lunch breaks over a longer period, thereby improving midday service. It is often an ideal solution for problems associated with peaks and valleys in the workload. Design your program to maximize such benefits.

◼ HOW WILL THE PROGRAM BE IMPLEMENTED?

The following mechanisms can assist in setting up a program.

Hours-of-work committee. This committee, made up of staff and management representatives, decides who is eligible for the program, develops operating policies, and conducts ongoing evaluations.

Flextime umpire. The flextime umpire should be someone with good mediation skills, who is respected by both labour and management. He or she may be called upon in any number of situations where there is conflict over application of the rules or interpretation of policy.

Trial period. Agreeing to a trial period, or to a trial program, may help gain approval from management for implementing flextime.

Recording system. Besides keeping track of hours, it is necessary to record debits and credits of worktime. A *flextime machine* has been developed which records employees' accumulated hours rather than specific starting and quitting times. Employees can also sign in and out, punch a time clock, or maintain personal time logs.

Overtime policy. Flextime can sometimes run afoul of overtime legislation. An employee who chooses to work nine hours on Mon-

... I TAKE IT YOUR NEW HOURS ARE WORKING OUT WELL, SANDUSKY...

day and Tuesday in order to leave early on Wednesday is not working overtime. On the other hand, suppose an employee starts work at 7 a.m. and plans to leave at 3 p.m. What happens if the boss shows up at 2 o'clock with three hours worth of urgent tasks? Should this employee be paid straight time or overtime rates between 3 p.m. and 5 p.m.?

Most provinces have provisions to allow overtime rules to be adjusted when requested by both labour and management. The Labour Standards Branch of your provincial ministry of labour has information about overtime rules in your province. **[AMERICAN READERS: The U.S. Department of Labor has legislation on overtime; some states have regulations as well.]**

Policies must be determined as to what constitutes overtime and how overtime should be compensated. The hours-of-work committee or the flextime umpire can be empowered to arbitrate disputes and set limits within which a supervisor can ask for overtime or a change of an employee's schedule.

Adequate information. Briefing materials that clearly define all aspects of a flextime program will reduce confusion and ease the implementation process.

Compressed and Modified Workweeks

Any design for a compressed or modified workweek should address the following issues.

■ WHO WILL BE ELIGIBLE FOR THE PROGRAM?

Who is allowed to participate in the program? Who *must* participate? Who is excluded?

In a factory or institutional situation, the compressed workweek is likely to disrupt operations unless all line staff and their supervisors take part in the program. However, participation of support staff such as janitors, personnel managers, shipping clerks, switchboard operators, marketing people, security officers, and accountants may need to be decided on a case-by-case basis. Some support staff may be required to participate in the program if their workflow mirrors that of line staff. Some staff may need to remain on a standard schedule to better mesh with clients or outside suppliers. Other staff may be free to choose.

In office settings, programs can be designed so that most staff can choose whether or not to participate, within certain limits. Work teams are advised to harmonize schedules. As in factories, participation may be contingent on workflow within the organization, or the need to interface smoothly with clients or agencies outside the organization.

■ HOW LONG WILL THE WORKDAY LAST?

Several factors go into deciding the length of the workday. Employee preferences are obviously important. As well, a shorter workday is better than a long one in situations where tasks are strenuous or concentration is intense.

The length of a shift should take into account peaks in workloads, and shifts should fit together to provide comprehensive coverage. Popular shift choices are 7.5, 8, 8.5, 9, 9.5, 10, 12, and 12.5 hours. Shifts of odd lengths, such as 8 hours and 53 minutes, may add up to an even number of hours every two weeks, but they often result in wasted time. Case studies show that employees resent having to worry about small bits of time, so they ignore them. From an employer's standpoint it is much better to change the hours in the workweek to make the numbers come out even.

■ HOW WILL SHIFTS FIT TOGETHER?

If several crews are needed to operate a factory or hospital around the clock, shifts must be synchronized to provide the right pattern of coverage. Two twelve-hour shifts give full 24-hour coverage, but many organizations can get by with two shifts of nine hours each, or two shifts of ten hours each, plus a skeleton overnight shift. Another popular pattern is four days on and four days off. Continuous operation is also possible with a rotation of three days on, four days off, followed by four days on, and then three days off. Sometimes a mix of compressed and non-compressed schedules can be matched to provide better coverage of peak workloads. (See the sidebar on Designing a Staggered Hours Program, page 191.)

■ HOW MANY HOURS WILL THE WORKWEEK CONTAIN?

The length of the workweek is determined by the length of the shifts and the required pattern of coverage. Compressed workweeks of 35 or 36 hours seem to cause fewer problems than 38- to 42-hour workweeks.

■ WHAT DAYS OF THE WEEK WILL EMPLOYEES WORK?

Tuesday to Friday schedules make sense because they are seldom affected by statutory holidays. Employers are under no legal obligation to pay for a statutory holiday that falls on a nonscheduled workday, but some do so out of goodwill for the ease of Tuesday to Friday schedules.

■ HOW WILL FULL SERVICE BE ENSURED FIVE DAYS A WEEK?

This question applies to companies that provide direct service using only one shift of workers. The usual practice is to divide the workforce in half. One group works Monday to Thursday, the other group, Tuesday to Friday. All staff must be cross trained to help customers and to take a front-line position if necessary. Some organizations bolster their Monday and Friday coverage by asking for volunteers from among the staff to take a midweek day off.

In case studies of the compressed workweek, participants report that they found their jobs much more challenging and interesting when they were given the chance to learn new skills and to perform different tasks.

■ HOW WILL CONTINUITY WITH CLIENTS AND SUPPLIERS BE MAINTAINED?

This is not a problem for facilities that operate continuously, but it can be a problem for companies that operate with only one shift. One solution is to keep all or part of the sales and office staff on a standard five-day schedule. Another solution is to have part of the office staff and part of the security/maintenance staff on compressed schedules at opposite ends of the week.

■ HOW WILL THE PROGRAM BENEFIT YOUR EMPLOYER?

A compressed workweek can be designed to provide extended business hours or better coverage at peak hours. It may also reduce

Designing a Staggered Hours Program

Staggering hours is often the best solution for a facility that operates continuously. The following steps are useful in designing a program.

❶ Establish an hours-of-work committee with representatives from management and labour;

❷ Conduct an informal poll of employees to establish the range of preferred starting times for the various shifts;

❸ Conduct a formal survey asking employees to choose a starting time from a range of options;

❹ Collate the results of the surveys. Match up sets of staff whose preferred shift patterns will fit together to provide continuous coverage. Let employees whose choices cannot be accommodated remain on the old starting time;

❺ Develop a policy for new employees. They should be assigned a starting time, but can request a change to a preferred shift when an opening occurs;

❻ Develop a system for staggering shifts before and after a temporary shutdown;

❼ Develop a policy for overtime rates and relief staffing, taking into account new shift schedules.

Businesses that do not operate continuously may also benefit from staggered hours if they need fewer people at the beginning and end of the day. In such a situation, an individual or small group of employees could propose a system of staggered hours. The design of such a system needs:

- A plan to ensure your duties are covered in the hours before or after your shift begins or ends. You may be able to arrange for someone on regular hours to cover for you, if necessary;
- A plan for arranging your duties in such a way that your employer benefits. You may be able to help with start-up or shut-down procedures, offer extended hours of service to the public, or handle special orders. Be aware that your duties might have to change if you want to start earlier or work later than everyone else.

overtime costs and cut time devoted to start-up and shut-down operations. The design of the program should incorporate some of these practical benefits that will help sell your employer on the idea.

■ HOW WILL THE PROGRAM BE IMPLEMENTED?

Four mechanisms will help in implementing a compressed work-week program.

Hours-of-work committee. This committee, made up of staff and management representatives, will oversee the design of the program and monitor, refine, and evaluate it.

Needs survey of potential participants. Case studies show employees have more positive attitudes toward a program if they can contribute suggestions on how it is going to work.

Written overtime policy. When shifts will exceed the standard eight-hour workday, the provincial ministry of labour must be consulted. If the workweek is less than standard it is important to decide when overtime rates apply.

Trial period. The trial period should be long enough to give workers time to adjust to the longer hours before evaluation begins.

Telecommuting

The success of home work arrangements depends as much on the personality of the job holder as on the nature of the work. For this reason, designs for telecommuting are highly individualized.

Use the following questions to help you design your plan.

■ FOR WHAT TASKS ARE YOU RESPONSIBLE?

Make a list of your duties. Include informal, incidental, or occasional duties as well as regular tasks. Maybe you are the unofficial fix-it person for the office, or the one who knows more than anyone else about the company's data processing system. Perhaps you have a flair for graphic art and are occasionally consulted on the design for a poster or brochure.

After you have identified all your contributions to your work and workplace, put an "H" beside those you can do at home without special equipment; put an "E" next to those you could do at home with special equipment, such as a computer; put an "O" beside those that need to be done at the office.

■ HOW MUCH OF THE TIME CAN YOU WORK AT HOME?

If your list contains only a few "E" and "H" items, it means you cannot spend much worktime at home. On the other hand, if it contains mostly "E" and "H" items you may be able to arrange for someone else to take over your "O" tasks, enabling you to work full time at home.

For some people, working exclusively from home is too isolating. You must think hard about how much contact with other people you need, and whether you will feel out of touch with what is happening at work. What balance between home and office work would best suit your needs? Would a satellite office be a useful compromise?

■ WHEN WOULD YOU WORK AT HOME?

Are there certain days of the week when it would be less disruptive for you to work away from the office? Should you work at home only part of the day? Perhaps you would prefer to have the freedom to go home periodically, as the need arises. Would you plan to be "on duty" during your regular office hours? Or do you want the option to work during the evenings or on weekends, and take time off midweek?

■ WHO WILL COVER FOR YOU AT THE OFFICE WHEN YOU ARE AWAY?

Ideally, it is best to delegate someone to handle jobs which come up at work when you are away and which cannot be postponed or attended to over the phone. It's also useful to think out in advance what ways you could structure your activities so that no one else is inconvenienced by your working at home. Forwarding your calls to home automatically from your extension at work could save co-workers and the switchboard operator from having to remember where you are. (Your telephone clients don't even need to know you're at home.) Keeping your files up to date and in good order is a must. Letting walk-in clients know when you'll be away from the office would also be a good habit to develop.

■ WHAT EQUIPMENT WILL YOU NEED?

Technology can make it easier for you to work at home, but there may be some extra expenses to cover. Upgrading telephone service to include an extra line, call alert, call forwarding, or conference calls can be costly if your residential service lacks these features.

Home and office computer equipment must be compatible. Perhaps you will have to buy a printer, modem, or fax machine to transfer material to and from the office, or sign onto a courier service. (Depending on what software you use, a fax card for your computer may fulfil your fax needs at less cost than a stand-alone fax.) If you're planning to tap into the office computer via a modem, check out in advance that the software required is easy to use and that it actually does what your computer expert says it's supposed to do.

Your employer may agree to pay for part or all of the costs involved, depending on the circumstances. If, for example, your move to home was welcomed by the company because it relieved overcrowding, your employer may agree to subsidize the costs.

■ HOW CAN YOU MAKE YOUR HOME WORK STATION COMFORTABLE?

A room that was adequate as a den or an extra bedroom may not be suitable for an office. For one thing, the lighting may be poor or your work chair too uncomfortable. If you have your computer keyboard and monitor on an old kitchen table, you will likely be straining your neck. If you can hear the kids arguing upstairs, concentration will be difficult. To work at home you need proper equipment, a comfortable work space, and freedom from distractions.

Comfort, quietness, and freedom from domestic concerns take on even greater importance if you are fully telecommuting from home. If your employer does not have to provide space for you at work, it might be possible to charge some rent for your home office to finance improvements.

■ HOW CAN YOU KEEP THE LEVEL OF DISTRACTIONS MANAGEABLE?

You do not want to move out of the office to get away from distractions only to find they are worse at home. If you have young children demanding attention, hiring someone to care for them while you are working may be necessary. Older children could be enrolled in after-school programs or in summer camp. Chatty neighbours, spouses who want your attention, and friends dropping by or calling during work hours can create havoc with your plans for a full workday. Firmness is a useful skill for telecommuters to cultivate. Sometimes it is necessary to cue others that you are working: "I'm in the middle of a project for work, so I can only talk for a minute now — I'll be free at five o'clock."

■ HOW CAN YOU KEEP IN TOUCH WITH YOUR WORKMATES?

For most people it is important to have relationships at work. For telecommuters, everyday functions that feel like a burden to regular staff take on a different significance. Attending staff meetings and work-related social events, serving on project committees, talking with co-workers by phone, even volunteering for union duties, all help to maintain the human connection with work. Connecting in these ways will afford you greater influence on decisions that are made. Your presence will be more visible at promotion time, and you will develop allies against unfair treatment should that ever occur.

■ HOW CAN THE ARRANGEMENT BENEFIT YOUR EMPLOYER?

Higher productivity and lower absenteeism are two obvious selling points for telecommuting; if you've already been doing some work from home, cite concrete examples of the benefits that resulted from doing so. Remember in your proposal to stress the fact that telecommuting is normal, not something out of *Star Wars*. Even your boss may have taken work home from time to time for the benefits that home work offers.

Telecommuting can relieve office overcrowding. Working at home on your own schedule can sometimes improve your access to scarce computer time, or extend hours of service. Salespeople can some-times reduce travel costs by operating out of a home office. Satellite offices are often much cheaper to rent than downtown real estate, and can make local access easier for your company's customers.

■ HOW WILL YOU IMPLEMENT YOUR HOME WORK PROGRAM?

As with other options, work from a written agreement. This is especially true if you are telecommuting on a full-time basis. The agreement should specify the conditions of your home work arrangement, and state explicitly that working at home will not alter your seniority or job status. It should include a contingency plan in case the telecommuting arrangement is cancelled.

You might have to devise a method for recording your hours. Make sure your home insurance policy covers office equipment. Consult an income tax specialist if you are getting rent from your company for your office space. Finally, before you burn any bridges behind you, consider whether a trial period might not be worthwhile.

■ WHAT POLICIES ARE NEEDED?

If you are telecommuting from a satellite office, you and your co-workers might need to establish some additional policies on special procedures for your particular working conditions. An hours-of-work committee can help put these guidelines together, and the committee can mediate any problems that may arise. In particular, it could look at eligibility criteria, the application process, a needs survey, and policies on who pays for home equipment, etc. It can also act as an informal watchdog to look out for the rights and job protections of telecommuters.

STEP SIX

GETTING WHAT YOU WANT

Planning Your Next Move

During this next stage you must convert your work option plan into an actual proposal. In many ways, this is the most crucial part of the process. You will have to marshal facts and resources, and perhaps develop a certain amount of fortitude if you wish to set your own working conditions.

Most people have to do some negotiating to get the flexible work schedule they want. Negotiation works, and thousands of Canadians have done it successfully, but it requires careful planning, good strategy, self-confidence, and a modicum of caution. In the words of the *I Ching*: "It is wise to pull the tail of the tiger with great humour."

Who Is On Your Side

The first step in negotiating is to analyze your situation. Find allies and identify obstacles. Identify the needs and values in your workplace that will help or hinder you. Start by taking an inventory of factors that can work in your favour. Check off each of the following statements that apply to you.

☐ *Are your skills and experience valuable to your employer?*

☐ *Are you considered a good worker?*

☐ *Do you have a positive relationship with your supervisor?*

Does your employer try to project an image of being ☐ *fair?* ☐ *innovative?* ☐ *progressive?* ☐ *efficient?* ☐ *caring?*

☐ *Is the personnel department concerned about employee morale?*

☐ *Do you have a good relationship with your union representative?*

☐ *Is your union or employee association likely to be supportive?*

☐ *Do you have an alternative plan if your proposal isn't approved?*

Checkmarks indicate strengths you can use in negotiating for what you want. (If you don't have any checks, are you sure you want to work there? Maybe you should be looking for another job.) Remember these strengths when it comes time to make a proposal to your employer. If your employer likes to be seen as fair-minded, make your request on the grounds of fairness. If your employer values efficiency, argue that your new work schedule is more efficient. Remember as well that it is in your employer's interests that you be satisfied with your working conditions; you'll be more productive and more fun to work with.

Now look at the obstacles you face.

☐ *Would you be easy to replace?*

☐ *Is your supervisor too busy to be receptive to changes?*

☐ *Is your supervisor unsupportive or unsympathetic to your needs?*

☐ *Does you employer project an if-you-don't-like-it-you-can-leave attitude?*

☐ *Is your employer slow to introduce new ideas?*

☐ *Does the personnel department do things "by the book"?*

☐ *Is your union unsympathetic to new work arrangements?*

This kind of inventory will give you a feeling for where you should tread cautiously, and who to approach for support and assistance. If you see that you have little leverage and a lot of inertia working against you, be prepared to be a little more flexible during the negotiating process, but don't lose heart. The Quakers have an expression: "Speak truth to power." If you ask for something that is fair and reasonable, and you persist in asking, the system will often give you what you want in the end. Never underestimate the effectiveness of a quiet truth.

How You Can Improve Your Chances

A well-organized written proposal is a powerful tool for getting what you want. There are several reasons why written (or more accurately, *typed*) proposals have a much better chance of approval than oral requests.

The process of writing a proposal helps you get your plan clear in your own mind. Writing ideas down, then organizing them for effect and logical sequence, is the best way of making sure all the details of your new schedule have been covered.

Supervisors often turn down requests for new work schedules because they imagine things that could go wrong. If a written proposal takes potential problems into account and suggests solutions, the new arrangement cannot be dismissed out of hand.

Supervisors usually have a heavy workload. When you present a carefully designed plan, your employer does not have to work out the details before agreeing to it. Saying yes should come more easily.

A written proposal is more difficult to ignore. Employers often sidestep verbal requests. A solidly written proposal shows that you are serious, sincere, and expect a response.

Proposals often require approval from two or three levels of administration. A written proposal is an effective way to carry your case to upper levels. It ensures that your ideas are presented accurately. It also gives your supervisor justification for pushing your application forward: "I have a written request from a staff member that requires some sort of response."

If you design the playing field, you have a better chance of con-

DAUNTING, ISN'T IT...?

trolling the game. If you create a reasonable framework for your new work schedule, including a suggested benefit package, your employer begins thinking about it within terms and conditions suggested by you, rather than in some other framework less to your liking.

Who Should Make the Proposal?

A proposal can be submitted by an individual, a group, or a union.

■ INDIVIDUAL PROPOSALS

This type of proposal is the easiest to get approved, possibly because employers feel that implementing an individual plan is less risky than making major adjustments to policy and procedure. Also, an individual proposal does not necessarily set a precedent for other employees. (This is even more true if you're the only person at your workplace with a particular set of duties.)

When only one person is involved, the stakes are relatively small. If you have a well-designed plan that doesn't require a precedent-setting change in financial benefits, you can often get approval from your immediate supervisor without involving the upper levels of the administration. This is the easiest route because the time and effort needed to get approval for a proposal tend to go up exponentially the more levels of management are involved.

Sometimes an individual can get special arrangements because of special circumstances. For example, let us say that your employer would generally be unwilling to grant phased retirement at full pay. However, suppose you had a chronically ill spouse who required expensive medical treatments and a lot of care and attention from you. Your employer may feel justified in making a special arrangement for you, without feeling the same conditions must be offered to all senior employees.

Organizations rarely make job sharing, permanent part-time, leaves of absence, or telecommuting available as a matter of policy unless they have had some previous experience with individual arrangements. If no one in your workplace has ever tried one of these

options, your best bet is to ask your employer to make an exception
for you. Usually an employer watches to see how well several such
experiences work before changing personnel policy.

Phased retirement, compressed workweeks, flextime, V-Time,
and banked overtime all tend to require changes to payroll structures. For that reason, individuals are apt to be less successful in
getting approval for these options unless they can formulate a plan
that minimizes structural changes, or can claim special circumstances such as a debilitating health condition.

As a general rule, individual proposals tend to have less force than
ones put forward by unions. The other point to remember is that
individuals have limited means of protecting their rights if someone
within the organization tries to change or undermine an agreed-
upon schedule. A union can invoke grievance procedures to protect
individual rights if an option was negotiated during the collective
bargaining process.

■ GROUP PROPOSALS

Organizing a group proposal takes time and energy, and you may
have to compromise on what you want. An organized group, particularly if it is a large one, may put some employers on their guard.

On the other hand, employers will sometimes accept a request
from a group that they wouldn't accept from an individual. For example, an employer is more likely to make alterations to the pension
plan if a dozen employees ask to phase into retirement, rather than
if one employee requests it. A job-sharing proposal from six employees may induce an employer to incorporate work options into company policy, where a request by only one or two staff might be turned
down.

Group proposals are better at getting an employer's attention.
Groups have more bargaining power than individuals, and they are
more effective in pressing for changes to company policy and/or the
structuring of personnel. If the work schedule you want requires
these changes, and if you do not belong to a union — or your union
is unhelpful — getting more people interested in your idea is the best
bet. This is almost always true for V-Time, banked overtime, and

compensatory benefit leaves, and it is usually the case with flextime, compressed workweeks, and phased retirement.

■ UNION PROPOSALS

Many unions are in favour of work options, but some are not. If you have a strong union that has a good working relationship with management and is supportive of flexible work schedules, you will probably want and need its support. If your union is philosophically opposed to work options, involving the union may not help your cause.

A union officer's knowledge of the in and outs of personnel policies, and his or her skill and experience in the negotiating process, can be helpful in arranging any of the options described in this book. In plans proposing paid time off, such involvement is essential. Sometimes your local shop steward can be a helpful source of advice and support, even when your union is not willing to involve itself officially.

An important point to remember is that your union does not have to be in agreement with your ideas to be of assistance. For example, for years the Canadian Union of Public Employees (CUPE) had a policy of opposing job sharing in principle, but nonetheless negotiated job sharing on behalf of its members on several occasions.

It is not always clear which of the three types of proposals — individual, group or union — would have the best chance of success. In many cases all you can do is make your best guess and cross your fingers.

If you decide to write a proposal that pertains to yourself alone, use the format in the next chapter. If you want to set up a work option program that would be available to a group of individuals or to all members of a bargaining unit, skip to the chapter on Writing a Collective Proposal.

Writing an Individual Proposal

Writing a proposal may seem overwhelming, but it is not so difficult if you take it one step at a time. You don't have to create a masterpiece of logic and persuasion; just think out a design carefully and write it up in an organized fashion.

Be concise. Your final proposal should not be more than three to five typewritten pages. If the format suggested here doesn't fit your style (or your organization), modify it accordingly. If head office must approve your proposal, you will need to make it more formal and detailed than if you're working for a smaller organization where only your supervisor's approval is required.

One last piece of advice: A proposal should propose, not threaten. Don't threaten to quit if you don't get what you want. That's more likely to offend your employer than increase your bargaining power. It is far better to state in your proposal why you need change. Maybe you are suffering ill health from burnout, or your child needs more attention. Maybe you feel an intense desire to finish your university degree. Whatever the reason, if it is compelling enough to cause you to consider leaving your job, get that point across in your proposal. Your intention to leave should only be raised after all other avenues are exhausted.

All individual proposals should have the following elements.

◼ INTRODUCTION

Begin with a short statement of purpose that outlines, in a sentence or two, the bare bones of what you want. It might read something like this: "I, John Thomas, marketing manager of the Agribiz Division, propose to share my position with Henrietta Shuster, currently my assistant, on a six-month trial basis, as outlined below."

◼ JOB DESCRIPTION

Draw up a detailed list of the tasks that comprise your job; use your official job description as a guide. Include the following:

- Job title;
- Status;
- Department;
- Location;
- Supervisor;
- A brief summary of your duties (25 words or less);
- Responsibilities and accountabilities — what (and who) are you in charge of?
- Job specifications — what are your specific duties?

When summarizing your tasks and responsibilities, be specific. State the tasks you do on your own, whether and how often you supervise others, and whether you work with confidential information or handle cash. Describe the complexity of tasks and the experience, training, and educational requirements needed to perform your job. Where relevant, indicate the degree of interaction with the public or co-workers.

This level of detail may seem unnecessary if your supervisor already has this information, but include it anyway because he or she may have forgotten some of the requirements of your job. Also, your proposal may eventually need the approval of someone in personnel or upper management who knows nothing about you or your position.

■ FILL-IN COVERAGE/REDEFINITION OF DUTIES

If you are writing a proposal for flextime, telecommuting, or compressed workweek, it is not necessary to include this section in your
proposal because you will not be changing the number of hours you
work. However, if you want to work fewer hours it is necessary to
describe a way to deal with the work that you will not be able to
handle yourself. At the very least you will need to suggest a framework for covering your duties. For example, a nurse who proposes
to go on a four-day week might say, "A part-time relief person could
be hired on a contract basis to work every Friday."

In many cases it helps to suggest a specific person who could fill
in for you. Management is more likely to accept your proposal if the
task of finding a qualified and trained replacement has already been
handled. By finding a qualified fill-in person you are comfortable
with, you also reduce the odds of being forced to work with someone
who may cause you grief.

In your proposal, briefly outline the qualifications of the suggested fill-in person, including:

- Experience and education;
- Skills and abilities;
- A brief description showing how closely these skills
  match/complement your own;
- An outline of the training or orientation the fill-in person
  will need;
- A copy of the individual's resumé, submitted as an appendix
  to your proposal.

If you are unable to suggest an appropriate person to fill in for
you, and expect to be working very closely with that person (as in
the case of job sharing or phased retirement), your proposal might
include a provision assuring you a role in the selection process. Perhaps something like: "The position will be advertised in the local
newspaper and applicants will be screened by a hiring committee
made up of the personnel manager, my immediate supervisor, and
myself, John Thomas."

Your proposal must also suggest how the work will be divided if someone else will be doing part of your job. Before tackling this matter, think about whether the work divides tidily into separate tasks or whether a process should be developed for sharing some tasks.

If the job needs to be split in a certain way, explain your rationale. For example, "Because of her greater accounting experience, my partner, Janice Jones, would handle bookkeeping. I would maintain continuity with customers by continuing to make all sales calls."

State clearly whether your fill-in person will be taking full responsibility for a particular area, or whether you will retain overall responsibility with the other person occupying the role of assistant. Indicate whether you want to have your work performances evaluated separately or as a team.

◾ TIME SCHEDULES

Describe your proposed work schedule in precise detail. If the fill-in person or job-sharing partner is covering part of your work, be equally specific about that person's schedule.

Think about whether you and your fill-in partner will require overlapping schedules in order to trade information about the job. What special arrangements should be made to accommodate staff meetings, statutory holidays, and vacation time? Do you want the right to trade time on occasion? The time-trade feature primarily applies to job sharing, but can also be a feature of phased retirement, permanent part-time, and leaves of absence.

◾ CONTINUITY AND/OR COMMUNICATION CONCERNS

If you will be rearranging your work hours (flextime or compressed workweek), changing your workplace (telecommuting), or reducing your hours (all other options), you must describe a plan for minimizing disruptions to work continuity and information flow. What information could get lost in the shuffle? How will you pass on important information from customers, clients, supervisors, and staff meetings?

In your proposal, acknowledge all the potential problems in continuity and communication that could arise because of your new schedule. For each potential problem either suggest a mechanism to correct the problem, or show why the current system would be adequate to prevent the problem. (Reviewing the notes you made in Step Five can be helpful in this regard.) The following areas may require some comment:

- Staff meetings and memos.
- Schedule postings. How will others know when you're in or out?
- Front-line coverage. Are you on call for any duties?
- Unfinished tasks and follow-up. Describe how uncompleted tasks will be finished or handed over smoothly.
- Client continuity. If you're not always available, how can you make sure your clients feel that they are getting consistent service?
- Information Exchange. How will you exchange important information with your job-sharing partner or fill-in staff?

This is a key section of your proposal. You must try to address your employer's objections before they occur by presenting solutions to all potential communication and continuity problems in your proposal. It will be harder for your employer to turn you down if potential problems have been identified and dealt with in advance.

■ SUGGESTED BENEFIT PACKAGE

Flextime, telecommuting, compressed workweeks, and banked overtime have no effect on benefit packages because the standard number of working hours does not change. However, statutory holidays do become an issue when proposing a compressed workweek.

People who want short-term leave of less than 90 days, paid leave, phased retirement, or cuts of 10 percent or less in worktime can ask for full benefits. Older workers should also protect their pension plans. For example, you might state, "Contributions to the pension plan will continue at the normal rate for full-time employment." Ask for full or *calendar* seniority. (You may need to be prepared to settle for prorated seniority later in the negotiating process.)

For options not mentioned above it is best to ask for a benefit package that is prorated according to the number of hours worked. Prorated benefits add to the persuasiveness of your proposal because they will result in little or no increase to your employer's payroll.

In this section of your proposal you need to list all your present benefits and indicate how the new work schedule might alter them. It may be expedient at this point to remind your employer, by way of a short policy statement, of the conditions under which you are currently receiving benefits. You might, for example, quote from the organization's policy manual, or include a short statement of principle such as: "Fringe benefits are part of an employee's total wage package and, therefore, any employee on reduced hours should be entitled to a proportionate share of benefits or receive a cash payment in lieu of partial benefits."

To understand how your benefits might be affected, check the list below. If you do not know whether you receive a particular benefit, ask your union steward or your personnel manager. (You should also review the chapter What Will Happen to Your Benefits? in Step Four.)

Unemployment Insurance(UI), Canada Pension Plan (CPP) and Workers' Compensation. Contributions to these plans are based on a percentage of your income. In your proposal you can simply say "UIC, CPP, and Workers' Compensation prorate automatically when income is reduced." [**AMERICAN READERS: Substitute Social Security for CPP.**]

Vacation and sick leave. Normally these will be prorated as a proportion of the standard full-time allotment.

Statutory holidays. The number of statutory holidays differs from province to province, and from state to state. In British Columbia, for instance, there is a provincial statutory holiday the first Monday in August which is not a holiday in some other provinces. For this reason it is difficult to give detailed guidelines for writing this benefit into a proposal.

It is also complicated to prorate statutory holidays for a shorter workweek. The simplest method is to say: "If a statutory holiday falls on a scheduled workday, the employee will receive payment for the number of hours the employee would be expected to work." If you work Mondays you will come out ahead with this arrangement; if not, you will be somewhat penalized. (Job-sharing partners often trade days so that statutory holidays will be apportioned fairly.)

An alternative approach is to say: "All statutory holidays will be prorated." In this case, if you work three-quarters time you will get three-quarters of a day's pay for each stat holiday whether you were scheduled to work that day or not. This approach is fairer, but it tends to cause paycheque fluctuations. The fluctuations are smaller when the holiday falls on a workday and larger if it falls on a day when you are not scheduled to work. Sometimes employees arrange to adjust their work hours in the weeks that contain a stat holiday in order to equalize paycheques.

The following items refer to supplementary benefits. Most supplementary benefits are extremely difficult, if not impossible, to prorate. The usual solution is to alter the entire package of supplementary benefits so as to reduce its cost by the same percentage as the reduction in your work hours. For example, if your work hours are to be reduced by 25 percent, you will have to find ways to cut the overall cost of your supplementary benefits by one-quarter. Try to retain the most important benefits and those that would be more expensive if you were to purchase them privately. Where fill-in staff are known in advance, participants with coverage through a spouse may forego specific benefits as a way to keep overall benefit costs in line.

Before you can propose a supplementary benefit package that would be divided fairly and accurately, you should ask your union or personnel department for the exact cost of each of these benefits. Failing this, you will have to estimate the costs and negotiate the final details later.

Registered Retirement Savings Plans (RRSPs). RRSP's can be purchased privately for about the same price. **[AMERICAN READERS: IRAs are the U.S. equivalent of RRSPs.]**

Company pension plans. Before you write your proposal it is extremely important that you ask your shop steward or the personnel manager for information about the company's plan and how calculation of benefits might be altered if you reduce your work hours. It is advisable to get a written assessment from your personnel department. In some instances your benefits may not be affected at all; in others, working less than full time might exclude you from the plan or greatly reduce the size of your pension.

The kind of statement you make about company pension benefits will depend on the particular circumstances. It might be possible to use the official wording in the pension plan contract to describe the arrangement you prefer. Or it might be wise to say: "This proposal is contingent upon arrangements being made which will ensure that there is no adverse effect on my future pension."

Most plans have what's called a *vesting period;* you must contribute to the plan for a specified number of years before you are eligible to receive any pension. If you're planning to leave your current employer before your pension would be vested, you might be as well advised to let go of the pension in order to hang on to other benefits. (You can contribute to a private RRSP instead.)

Provincial medical insurance premiums. If you are covered by your partner's medical plan, you can trade medical coverage for a benefit elsewhere. Or you might be able to pay all or part of the cost of your medical insurance premiums as a payroll deduction. Another option is to drop coverage through your employer and pay privately. Perhaps you can waive other benefits in exchange for retaining full medical coverage. Think through these factors before you start to write. [AMERICAN READERS: This is the benefit you most want to hang on to, particularly if your partner or a child has a medical condition that would make them difficult to insure privately.]

Extended medical coverage/dental insurance plans. These are expensive to buy privately. If you think you might need them, don't trade them away unless you are covered by your spouse's plan. You may have to offer to pay some or all of the cost as a payroll deduction.

Group life and disability/short-term illness insurance plans. Normally these are based on a percentage of income, so they prorate automatically when income is reduced. However, some plans exclude part-time employees. Other plans allow part-time employees to continue contributing as though they were working full time.

Profit-sharing plans. Profit-sharing dividends are usually calculated as a percentage of income, so they also prorate automatically.

Other benefits. These may include stock options, health club memberships, and other perks. Although these may be valuable to you, they are often hard to evaluate in dollars and cents. It is better not to set a price on them and not to mention them in your proposal.

If working on the benefits section of your proposal makes you feel confused, overwhelmed, or hopeless, don't be alarmed: this is normal. Do the best you can and plan to work out final details with the help of the personnel department after your proposal has been approved.

■ COSTS AND SAVINGS

Employers often fear that non-standard work schedules will cost them money. Itemizing costs and potential savings usually makes it clear that the expense is manageable. Consider the following costs.

- If your proposal involves adding another part-time position, the cost in added paperwork will be approximately $100 per year;
- If you are asking to retain full benefits, itemize the benefits and, if possible, indicate the cost. (The personnel manager and your union financial agent should both have this information);
- When positions with a salary significantly over $25,000 per year are reduced in hours and backfilled, the result is a slight increase in employer UIC, CPP, and Workers' Compensation payments due to the effect of contribution ceilings. (No extra cost is incurred if the salary is $25,000 or under);
- If your proposal requires extra office space, equipment rental, higher costs for in-service training, extra staff meetings, or overlap time, list these costs and an estimated dollar value.

Your proposal should make a separate accounting of any start-up costs, including the cost of hiring and training fill-in staff and the cost of any extra equipment that must be purchased.

The following areas are sources of possible savings:

- If your proposal involves hiring a less-experienced employee, his or her wage package may be less than yours.

(This situation occurs most frequently with the phased retirement option);

- Using part-time employees may mean that your employer has to pay less overtime. If you know how much overtime an average full-time employee works, you can often attach a dollar value to these savings;
- If your organization already has part-time staff and keeps records on absenteeism, you can make a dollar estimate of the expected savings resulting from reduced absenteeism.

Try to collect enough hard numbers to make a clear statement, such as: "This job-sharing arrangement will have an estimated net cost of $600 per year, primarily in increased benefit costs." It is also a good idea to mention factors that will mitigate costs: "Because my proposed job-sharing partner has recently retired from a similar position, training costs will be minimal."

■ ADVANTAGES AND DISADVANTAGES

List all the advantages and disadvantages that might be associated with implementing your work option. Mention any concerns you have dealt with in the design of your program: "A clear division of duties along with weekly cross-over meetings will minimize the possibility that one of the partners may overlook some task."

Possible advantages include:

- Reduced absenteeism and staff turnover;
- Improved morale;
- Increased productivity;
- Better coverage during peak workloads;
- Extended hours of coverage;
- Better lunch hour, holiday, or vacation coverage;
- Emergency and overtime coverage;
- Improved employee health and safety;
- Extra skills/specialized skills;
- Cost savings.

(Remember to include appropriate statistics from the Conference Board Survey data reported on page 15.)

Disadvantages might include problems and costs associated with:

- Continuity and communication;
- Training and supervision;
- Co-worker attitudes;
- Uneven skill levels;
- Arranging meetings and all-staff communication sessions;
- Scheduling confusion;
- Extra costs.

Try to be even-handed in assessing advantages and disadvantages. Work options should not be presented as a panacea but rather as workable trade-offs in which the advantages outweigh the problems. (Note: In some proposals this section may be called "Rationale" and would fit best immediately after the introduction.)

■ LOCAL EXAMPLES

Your case will be stronger if you can name other employers who have had success with the system you are proposing. It helps if you can find examples which are a) fairly local, b) in the same occupational area, and c) in the same industry.

To find these examples, question professional acquaintances and your union representatives. Call personnel departments of other organizations. You might uncover a sterling example that will strengthen your case and, perhaps, give you good ideas to incorporate into your own plan.

Sometimes the best you can do is offer successive approximations. For instance, if you are a public health nurse who wants to work permanent part-time, you might be able to cite a local example of medical orderlies working permanent part-time, and a program for part-time public health nurses in another city.

■ IMPLEMENTATION

An implementation plan proposes a starting date and suggests procedures for finalizing the new arrangement. It might also propose a trial period before full-scale implementation.

When you suggest a starting date, it indicates to management that a decision needs to be made within a specified period of time. A trial period protects you and your employer by allowing both parties to test the arrangement before making a decision that might be irrevocable.

Finalizing your work option can be simple. A good wording for this is: "In consultation with the personnel department, my supervisor and I will draw up a written agreement outlining the details of this arrangement. This agreement will not come into force until it has been approved by the personnel manager and my department head."

Suggesting that you and your supervisor will draw up the agreement allows you to stay involved in the design process and keeps decision-making within your grasp. This approach assigns responsibility for tasks and assures you the protection of a written agreement.

For a more concrete idea of what a work option proposal involves, take a look at the sample proposal starting on the next page.

TO: Jim Gordell, Manager, Driver Registration
               Ministry of Transport, Sidney, B.C.
FROM: Sharon Belz and Jocelyn Wain
DATE: September 30, 1994
SUBJECT: Job-Sharing Proposal

We, Sharon Belz and Jocelyn Wain, would like you to consider our proposal to share one of our keypunch operator positions.

Job Description: Our jobs are classified as KP02. We work at the Royal Avenue office, Driver Registration Department, Ministry of Transport, Sidney. Our immediate supervisor is Helene Smyth.

Duties: Our duties include using a Wang computer system to enter motor vehicle data such as accident reports, speeding tickets, name and address additions, changes, and renewals, plus other vehicle-related documents. We do our work independently and in systematic order; each item is logged and checked. Other duties may include some clerical work.

Task Analysis: We have both worked in the same offices doing the same work for approximately seven years. We know our jobs well and feel that sharing our duties would be easy. The keypunch operator job lends itself easily to sharing because the tasks are not complex and require little communication. The current procedure is to log all incomplete tasks at the end of a shift. This makes changeover with a partner very easy. We both know all the aspects of our job and feel confident with each other as work partners. We have no hesitation in starting or completing one another's work and taking responsibility for any task.

Fill-in Coverage: Any one of a number of former employees of the department could be rehired to fill the position that would open up when the two of us share one of our jobs. This person should be hired on a contract basis until the end of the trial period.

Time Schedules: We would like to share the workweek by working one-week-on/one-week-off, changing over on Wednesdays. A calendar of our proposed 1995 schedule is enclosed. If for any reason one of us needs more than one week off, we would like to be able to trade time. We would have to reach agreement with our supervisor before any time could be traded. We feel that this would be a good schedule; it would be simple to follow and everyone would know which partner was working on a particular day.

Communications: Any important information to be passed on, such as changes or updates, would be kept in a specific file. Our job does not require a lot of communication about the work in progress, but if necessary a phone call can be made for clarification. A calendar of the days when we would be working will be given to our supervisors and payroll so both would know when we were working. We would also give advance notice of any change in our schedule.

Benefits: Statutory benefits (Unemployment Insurance, Canada Pension, and Workers' Compensation) would automatically be prorated. Compensatory benefits (sick leave, statutory holidays, and vacation time) would be divided in half. Jocelyn, who now gets twenty days vacation per year, would get ten; Sharon now has fifteen days and would get seven and a half. Maternity leave remains the same. We would like to have the option for one partner to return to full time for the duration of the other's maternity leave. (This would mean the department would not have to find a replacement.)

If one of us is sick, the other partner could cover for that sick day so no time is lost to the employer. The sick person would in turn take a day to work for the partner. Under our union contract, the supplementary benefits (Medical Services Plan premiums, dental plan, extended medical, short-term illness protection, group life insurance, and pension plan) are paid by the employer. Our pensions would be prorated. We wish to keep our seniority as calendar seniority.

Cost: Costs to the employer would be minor. Our salaries are the same; no extra costs there. Statutory and compensatory benefits prorate; no extra costs. There would be extra costs in carrying a second set of supplementary benefits (about $800/year), but these could be offset by sick-time coverage. Other special leaves for dentist, doctor, and specialist appointments would be almost nil because they could be arranged on time off. There is a small paperwork cost in keeping an extra employee on the payroll. There would be no cost to the employer for training, equipment, or supervision. If either of us worked extra hours it would be at straight-time pay, which would be a cost benefit to the employer.

Advantages: Sharing our job would be good for us and the department. We feel at this time that part-time work would be more appropriate for our family lives and would also leave room for a more enthusiastic approach to our work. We could do our work with fewer fatigue-related mistakes. There would be lower absenteeism because the fill-in system could be implemented. If there is an overload of work we could come in on our days off. This would alleviate stress with deadlines and help the employer as well as fellow employees. The department would keep two valuable employees who know their job well and enjoy their work; two people would be available to give helpful input and ideas. A former employee of the department could be recalled from lay-off to fill the one vacant full-time position. Our supervisor seems agreeable and believes this job arrangement would work well. A letter of recommendation is attached.

Other Examples of Job Sharing: There are job-shared positions in several government departments: Ministry of Finance, Office of the Comptroller General, the Purchasing Commission, and the Provincial Treasury. There are clerks, accountants, and systems analysts who job share. There seem to be positive feelings and results wherever it has been tried.

Implementation: To begin our job sharing, we would suggest a starting date of April 1, 1995. We would like to have a trial period of six months to see how the situation works out. At the end of six months either side could terminate the arrangement if it is not to their satisfaction. If the arrangement were terminated at the end of the trial period, each of us would return to full time and the contract staff person would be laid off. We hope to continue job sharing for quite a few years but should one of us leave, the remaining partner would like to have the option of returning to full time.

Once details of the arrangement are finalized, a written agreement would be drawn up so that both sides would be clear about the terms of the arrangement.

Thank you for your time and your consideration of this proposal. Sharon and I both feel positive that job sharing will work in our situation, and we are looking forward to receiving your answer.

Two attachments enclosed.

Writing a Collective Proposal

If several employees want the same work option, they will need to draft a written proposal whether they are negotiating directly with management or though their union. Collective proposals are extensive in scope, usually encompassing the following ten elements.

■ INTRODUCTION

Begin with a short statement of purpose that outlines the objective in a sentence or two: "This proposal recommends the establishment of a trial job-sharing program for Clerks 1 and 2 in the Health Services Branch."

■ ELIGIBILITY CRITERIA

This section usually includes:

Eligible classes of employee. Eligibility may be defined on the basis of occupation, age, length of service, or type of responsibilities. Sometimes the criteria for eligibility changes according to the complexity of the job: "All Health Care Workers 1 and 2 with one year or more of service would be eligible for the program. Health Care Workers 3 and 4 would require the permission of immediate supervisors and the Personnel Committee in order to be eligible."

Sometimes there are two levels of eligibility: "This phased retirement option would be available to any employee age 60 or over with fifteen or more years of service, and to any employee age 55 and over with twenty or more years of service."

Quotas. Many programs limit the number of participants: "In order to maintain continuity, no more than 25 percent of the service representatives in any department would be allowed to job share."

An approval process. This clause describes the way in which employees would apply to participate in a program: "Employees would make written application to the Personnel Manager who would be in charge of confirming eligibility and securing all levels of approval."

A veto provision. Many programs give the department head or the participant's immediate supervisor the right to veto an individual's participation, either temporarily or permanently: "The department head may refuse entry into the program for any employee, temporarily or indefinitely, if operational considerations make that employee's participation impractical. If an employee is refused entry, the department head must provide that employee with a written explanation outlining reasons for the refusal."

Veto clauses are a mixed blessing and should be used with caution. While management is more likely to approve a program if it includes the right to say no in certain circumstances, escape clauses are open to abuse by inflexible managers.

A redress procedure. Sometimes protection against abuse of the veto clause can be built into the program: "Employees who feel they have been unfairly denied access to the program can file a grievance with the flextime umpire."

Provision for outsiders. Such a clause might read: "Employees not normally eligible for the program may apply for inclusion. Such instances will be decided on a case-by-case basis, at the discretion of the department head."

■ FILL-IN COVERAGE AND/OR REDEFINITION OF DUTIES

(This section is not necessary for flextime, compressed workweek, and telecommuting proposals.) Several decisions must be made if employees will be reducing their work hours under the proposed work option. How will participating employees' duties be reassigned, shared, or divided so that workloads are commensurate with their new hours? Will additional staff be required to fill in for participating employees? How will fill-in staff be selected?

These issues must be resolved on a case-by-case basis. The proposal should suggest a mechanism (usually a job redefinition committee) that will ensure these issues are decided fairly. The section might read something like this:

> *The employee, the employee's immediate supervisor, and a designated representative of the personnel department would constitute a committee to redesign the participant's job description in a way that is commensurate with the employee's new hours. If new staff is to be hired to fill in for the participating employee, this committee would also be responsible for approving the appointment.*
>
> *The committee would produce a written plan which must be approved by both the head of the department concerned and that department's union steward. The department head would be in charge of ensuring that the plan will allow the company to meet its normal operating goals. The union steward would be responsible for ensuring that the plan does not place unfair demands on either the participating employee or the employee's co-workers.*
>
> *Where possible, fill-in employees would be hired from the recall list on a seniority basis. If the fill-in arrangement involves a significant sharing of duties, the compatibility of the regular and fill-in employees would supersede seniority as a hiring criteria.*

■ TIME SCHEDULES

Describe the kinds of work schedules that are possible under the program, noting any legal restrictions. Describe appropriate mechanisms for determining individual schedules. (This task usually falls to the job redefinition committee.) Mention any provisions for overlapping schedules or trading hours, and any special arrangements for staff meetings, in-service training, vacation time, and statutory holidays.

■ JOB CONTINUITY AND COMMUNICATION

How will the new work arrangement affect office procedures and patterns of staff communication? Describe any general rules, for example: "Staff meetings will be attended by the job sharer who is on duty at the time. That person will be responsible for communicating the results of the meeting to the off-duty partner."

Describe measures for maintaining job continuity in explanatory paragraphs: "All job sharers will be expected to complete tasks and return files before the end of their shift. If necessary, partners will use a changeover file to transfer information."

In programs where poor communication and lack of continuity can create major problems (job sharing, phased retirement), it may be useful to designate the job redefinition committee to troubleshoot problem areas: "The job redefinition committee will try to foresee potential communication/continuity problems and suggest mechanisms to avoid or overcome them."

To ensure good communication and job continuity, improved mechanisms may be needed in the following areas:

- Staff meetings and staff memos;
- Posted schedules;
- Dealing with urgent calls and crisis;
- Finishing tasks and following up on uncompleted business;
- Client continuity;
- Information exchange between regular and fill-in staff.

■ BENEFITS

Flextime, telecommuting, compressed workweeks, and banked overtime have no effect on benefit packages because the standard number of working hours does not change. However, statutory holidays do become an issue when proposing a compressed workweek.

For workers wanting short-term leave of less than 90 days, paid leave, phased retirement, or cuts of 10 percent or less in worktime, ask for full benefits. Older workers' pension plans must be protected.

For example, the proposal might state: "Contributions to the pension plan will continue at a normal rate for full-time employment, and the letters patent for the pension plan will be changed to base payouts on contributions rather than salary."

For options not mentioned above it is best to ask for a benefit package that is prorated according to the number of hours worked. Asking for prorated benefits contributes to the persuasiveness of the proposal because prorated benefits add no cost to the employer's payroll. Ask for full or *calendar* seniority for participants where possible — and settle for prorated seniority where necessary.

In this section list all present benefits and indicate how the new work schedule might alter them. At this point it may be expedient to remind your employer, by way of a short policy statement, of the conditions under which the workers are currently receiving benefits. For example, quote from the organization's personnel policy manual, or include a short statement of principle such as "Fringe benefits are part of an employee's total wage package and, therefore, any employee on reduced hours should be entitled to a proportionate share of benefits or receive a cash payment in lieu of partial benefits."

The method of prorating benefits depends on whether your employer uses a cafeteria-style benefit plan or a fixed-menu plan. In a fixed-menu plan, everyone gets a standard benefit package. In cafeteria style, new employees are allowed to build their own benefit package from a range of options.

If your organization has a cafeteria-style system, the proposal should state that participants will be able to tailor their benefit packages to suit individual needs: "In consultation with the job redefinition committee, participants will select their own benefit package, the cost of which cannot exceed an hour-based proration of the normal full-time allowance."

If your organization has a standard benefit plan, benefits for all participants in the work option program will need to be prorated in the same way. In that case, the proposal should suggest a standard formula for prorating them. It is sometimes useful to survey potential participants to find out which benefits they want to keep in full, which benefits they are willing to have prorated, and which they will let go or pay for out of their own pockets.

The easiest way to organize this section is to list all current benefits and describe how they would change under the program.

Unemployment Insurance (UI), Canada Pension Plan (CPP) and Workers' Compensation. Contributions to these plans are based on a percentage of income. Simply state that "UIC, CPP and Workers' Compensation prorate automatically when income is reduced." [AMERICAN READERS: Substitute Social Security for CPP.]

Vacation and sick leave. Normally these are also prorated as a proportion of the full-time allotment.

Statutory holidays. Statutory holidays differ from province to province, and from state to state. The number of stats can vary even within the same province depending on what a union has negotiated for its membership. In some workplaces, for example, employees get Easter Monday off. For these and other reasons it is difficult to give detailed guidelines for this benefit in a proposal.

It is also extremely complicated to prorate statutory holidays for a shorter workweek. The simplest method is to say: "If a statutory holiday falls on a scheduled workday, the employee will receive payment for the number of hours the employee would be expected to work." Employees working most Mondays will come out ahead with this arrangement; those who do not will be somewhat penalized. Job-sharing partners often trade schedules so that statutory holidays will be apportioned fairly.

An alternative is to say that all statutory holidays will be prorated. In this case, an employee who works three-quarters time would get three-quarters of a day's pay for each stat holiday, whether the employee was scheduled to work that day or not. This approach is fairer, but it tends to cause paycheque fluctuations. The fluctuations are smaller when the holiday falls on a workday, and larger if it falls on a day when an employee was not scheduled to work. Sometimes employees arrange to adjust their work hours in the weeks that contain a stat holiday in order to equalize paycheques.

Supplementary benefits, such as company pension plans, medical, dental, and life insurance plans, are extremely difficult, if not impossible, to prorate. The usual solution is to alter the entire package of supplementary benefits in such a way that their cost is then equivalent to the reduction in work hours. For example, if work hours are reduced by 25 percent, the overall cost of supplementary benefits should be reduced by one-quarter. Try to retain the most important benefits or the ones that would be more expensive if they had to be purchased privately.

Ask the union or the personnel department for the exact cost of each supplementary benefit so that the package can be divided fairly accurately. Otherwise, make a rough estimate and negotiate the final details later.

Registered Retirement Savings Plans (RRSPs). RRSPs can be purchased privately for about the same price. [AMERICAN READERS: IRAs are the U.S. equivalent of RRSPs.]

Company pension plans. Company pension plans vary greatly in structure and the way in which pension income is calculated. Some pension plans are administered by the employer; others by an outside pension fund. In the latter case, changing the rules is much harder.

Before writing the proposal it is important to obtain information about the plan and how calculation of benefits might be altered if work hours are reduced. In some instances, benefits may not be affected at all; in others, working less than full time might exclude employees from the plan or severely affect the size of their pensions.

It is advisable to get a written assessment from the personnel department. If information about the plan is not available, or if there is any doubt about what options are available, it is often wise to say: "This proposal is contingent on arrangements being made so that participants' future pensions will not be adversely affected."

Provincial medical insurance premiums. Provincial medical insurance premiums can be dealt with in a number of ways. Because participants can buy their own coverage directly from the province, this is a reasonable benefit to trade for a full benefit elsewhere. All or part of the cost of medical insurance premiums can be covered by a payroll deduction. Coverage can be prorated from family to self. Full coverage can be retained by waiving other benefits. [AMERICAN READERS: Top priority must be given to retaining this benefit due to the costs and difficulty of obtaining insurance privately.]

Dental insurance plans and extended medical coverage. These are expensive to buy privately so they should be retained in full if possible, either by waiving other benefits or by increasing the employee's share of premiums through payroll deductions.

Group life, disability, and short-term illness insurance plans. These are normally based on a percentage of income, so they prorate automatically when income is reduced. However, some plans exclude part-time employees. Other plans allow part-time employees to continue contributing as if they were working full time.

Profit-sharing plans. Profit-sharing dividends are usually calculated as a percentage of income, so they prorate automatically.

Other benefits. These may include stock options, health club memberships, and other perks. Although they may be valuable to employees, they are often hard to evaluate in dollars and cents. It is better not to set a price on them and not to mention them in the proposal.

■ COSTS AND SAVINGS

Employers often fear that non-standard work schedules will be costly. Itemizing costs and potential savings usually makes it clear that the expense involved is manageable. Your proposal should take into account the following start-up costs:

- The hiring and training of fill-in staff;
- The purchasing of extra equipment;
- The company time spent designing and implementing the program.

These ongoing costs that should also be itemized:

- The cost in paperwork of adding additional part-time employees will be approximately $100 per year per added employee;
- If you are asking to retain full benefits for participants, itemize those benefits and, if possible, indicate cost;
- When positions with salaries over $25,000 per year are reduced in hours and filled by relief staff, the result is a slight increase in employer UIC, CPP, Workers' Compensation payments due to the effect of contribution ceilings;

- If implementing the proposal calls for renting additional office space, more in-service staff training, extra meetings, overlapping schedules, or leased equipment, list these as expenses, giving an estimated dollar value if possible.

The following are sources of potential savings.

- If the proposal involves hiring less experienced employees as fill-in staff, total wage costs may be less. (This situation occurs most frequently in phased retirement programs);
- Using part-time employees may mean that the employer has to pay less overtime. If it is known how much overtime an average full-time staff person works, a dollar value can often be assigned to these savings;
- If your organization already uses part-time staff and keeps records on absenteeism, it may be possible to make a dollar estimate of the savings expected to result from reduced absenteeism.

Try to collect hard numbers to make a clear statement. Example: "This job-sharing arrangement will have an estimated net cost of $300 per year for every job affected, primarily because of increased benefit costs." It's also a good idea to mention aspects of the proposal that will avoid additional costs: "Because the organization has a large pool of former employees who can be recruited as fill-in staff, training costs will be minimal."

■ ADVANTAGES AND DISADVANTAGES

List all the possible advantages and disadvantages that the work option program will create for your employer. Mention concerns that have already been dealt with in the design of the program. Example: "Some modified workweek programs have experienced difficulties with Monday and Friday coverage, but allocating days off by means of a rotation system will ensure equal coverage throughout the week."

Refer to any valid test situations that may be considered relevant to an advantage or a possible concern, for example: "One potential concern relates to the possibility that part-time operating room nurses might get out of practice in dealing with emergency procedures. However, this problem has not developed in situations where nurses employed on a casual basis work a similar number of shifts."

Possible advantages are:

- Reduced absenteeism and staff turnover;
- Improved morale and easier recruitment;
- Increased productivity;
- Better coverage during peak workloads;
- Extended hours coverage;
- Better lunch hour, holiday, and vacation coverage;
- Emergency and overtime coverage;
- New or specialized skills brought into the organization;
- Improvements in employee health and safety;
- Cost savings.

(Remember to include appropriate statistics from the Conference Board Survey data reported on page 15.)

Areas in which problems might arise are:

- Job continuity and staff communication;
- Training and supervision;
- Uneven skill levels;
- Co-worker attitudes;
- Scheduling confusion;
- Added costs.

Try to be even-handed in assessing advantages and disadvantages. Work options should not be presented as a panacea but rather as workable trade-offs where the benefits outweigh the drawbacks. (In some proposals the Advantages and Disadvantages section may be called "Rationale" and would follow the introduction.)

■ LOCAL EXAMPLES

Your case will be stronger if you can name other employers (or individual exceptions in your own organization) who have successfully implemented the system you are proposing. It helps if you can find examples which are a) fairly local, b) in the same occupational area, and c) in the same industry.

To find these examples, question professional acquaintances and your union representatives. Call personnel departments of other organizations. You might uncover a solid example that will strengthen your case and, perhaps, give you good ideas to incorporate into your own plan. Sometimes the best you can do is offer successive approximations. For instance, if your police force wants to set up a job-sharing program, you might be able to cite one informal job-sharing situation within your own department and a job-sharing program for firefighters in another city.

■ IMPLEMENTATION

An implementation plan proposes a starting date and suggests procedures for finalizing the new arrangement. It might also propose a trial period before full-scale implementation.

Suggesting a starting date indicates to management that a decision needs to be made within a specified period of time. A trial period protects you and your employer by allowing both parties to test the arrangement before making a decision that might be irrevocable.

Suggesting a method for reaching a final agreement is important. The structure should allow a reasonable amount of consultation. A committee made up of a union representative, a representative of the personnel department, a management representative, and someone who represents prospective participants can provide a forum for negotiation, compromise, and resolution of the sometimes irksome details that inevitably arise. This committee can also be recalled as needed to deal with problems or changes.

The final agreement often takes the form of a memorandum of agreement between the employer and the union. It states that the program is temporary, that it must be evaluated before the next contract talks, and includes the understanding that terms for continuing the program would be made part of the next collective agreement.

In the initial proposal it is not necessary to go into a great deal of detail about how the program will be implemented; much of that can be worked out in committee. However, any essential aspects of the implementation procedure should be spelled out. For example: "The phased retirement program will not begin until the necessary changes in the pension agreement have been made and approved by an outside legal authority."

Features of the program which would facilitate the implementation process should also be mentioned, for example: "To minimize misunderstandings, participants in the V-Time program should receive an orientation package that describes the effect of the program on their wages, benefits, seniority, and duty assignments."

For a more concrete idea of what a collective work option proposal involves, take a look at the sample proposal starting on the next page.

Proposal for a Three-Quarter Time Program

Introduction
This is a proposal for an expanded permanent part-time program for the nursing staff in the emergency operating room (EOR) unit of the King William Hospital. The proposed program would be built around a rotation whereby four staff would split three current full-time positions.

Eligibility Criteria/Participants
Initially the program would involve three members of the current full-time staff (Sylvia Bains, Joanne Hopkirk, and Carol Casey) plus a former staff member (Marie Chasse) rehired on a contract basis. If the three-quarter time option proves successful we hope the hospital will offer the same arrangement to other teams of nurses who request it.

Fill-in Staffing/Job Redefinition
When the three current staff cut back to three-quarter time, one additional three-quarter time nurse will be needed to cover the shortfall in hours. Marie is trained in EOR procedures and has a good work record. Duties and responsibilities would be the same as for full-time nurses.

Schedules
Four part-time nurses will split three full-time rotations. Instead of working 32 twelve-hour shifts in a ten-week period, each part-time nurse would work 24 twelve-hour shifts every ten weeks. To show how the schedule would work in practice, we have drawn up a sample duty roster for a three-week period in January.

Under the current arrangement the schedule for these three weeks is as follows:

Day of Month	01	02	03	04	05	06	07	08	09	10	11	12	13	14	15	16	17	18	19	20	21
Sylvia		D	D	N	N						D	D	N	N						D	D
Joanne	N	N					D	D	N	N						D	D	N	N		
Carol	D	D	N					D	D	N	N							D	D	N	N

D = Day Shift; N = Night Shift

Under the proposed arrangement the schedule for the same period would be:

Day of Month	01	02	03	04	05	06	07	08	09	10	11	12	13	14	15	16	17	18	19	20	21
Sylvia		D	N	N							D	N	N								D
Joanne	N	N					D	N	N							D	N	N			
Carol	D	D	N					D	N	N								D	N	N	
Marie		D				D		D		D					D		D		D		

This schedule was designed to fit Marie's preference for working days only. The schedule would be different under other circumstances.

Communication/Continuity Concerns
The new arrangement should not affect continuity of patient care because patients are rarely on the EOR unit for more than 24 hours.

Existing communication systems and procedures could easily accommodate the new arrangement. (All hospital communication systems are designed to be able to accommodate a complete changeover of staff every twelve hours.) The new schedules will be somewhat more irregular than the standard full-time shift rotation. However, any member of staff can consult the monthly register to find out which nurses will be working at a particular time.

Suggested Benefit Package
UIC, CPP, Workers' Compensation, pension benefits, and long-term disability insurance would all be prorated automatically because contributions and benefits are based on a percentage of wages.

Sick leave, vacation, maternity leave, and holidays would all be prorated according to the formula for part-time staff contained in the collective agreement.

According to provisions for part-time staff contained in the existing collective agreement, the hospital would continue to pay full medical, dental, extended medical, and group life insurance premiums.

For purposes of accumulating service increments, pension credits, and seniority, every 1875 hours worked would be considered equivalent to one year of service, as per the terms of the existing collective agreement.

Cost Analysis

Employer contributions to UIC, CPP, Workers' Compensation, the pension plan, and long-term disability insurance all prorate automatically. No extra costs would be involved.

Vacation, holiday pay, and maternity leave all prorate automatically. No extra costs would be involved.

For every three full-time positions filled by four people, the hospital would have to fund four sets of supplementary benefits packages. This would increase costs by about $82 per month or $1000 per year (medical plan = $20/month; dental plan = $40/month; group life = $7/month; extended medical = $15/month).

Labour Canada estimates the cost in paperwork of adding one more person to the payroll at approximately $100/year.

The cost of in-service training for one extra staff member is difficult to estimate, but would probably not be more than $100 per year.

The hospital will save money on sick leave benefits because part-time staff use less sick leave than full-time staff. Over the past year, full-time staff took an average of 100 hours of sick leave but part-time staff took an average of only 85 hours of sick leave per full-time equivalent (FTE). If the four part-time staff on this program use 45 hours less sick leave per year (100 - 85 x 3 = 45), the hospital will save $700/year (45 hours x $16/hour = $700).

The hospital will save money on overtime pay because three-quarter time staff would usually work extra hours at straight-time pay. Last year, full-time staff worked an average of 70 hours of overtime at time-and-a-half rates. If the four part-time staff work a total of 150 extra hours at straight-time rates, the hospital would save $1200 per year (150 hours x $8 premium for overtime = $1200).

Total additional costs under the new arrangement would be more than offset by estimated savings. Costs would equal $1200 for 3 FTEs or $400 per FTE. Estimated savings would equal $1900 for 3 FTEs or about $600 per FTE. Despite higher benefit costs, overall personnel costs would be less.

Advantages

REDUCED STRESS: Nursing is physically and emotionally demanding. Although the twelve-hour shifts allow longer periods of time off, they also cause more fatigue, particularly among older nurses and those with family responsibilities. EOR positions are particularly stressful. The workload is unpredictable and patients are often severely injured. In many cases the work requires quick thinking and a high level of concentration; there is little or no room for error.

REDUCED TURNOVER AND EASIER RECRUITMENT: More than half of the nurses on the EOR unit say they plan to leave within the next two or three years if they can't find a way to lighten their workload. Most of these nurses say that they would stay if they were offered positions at three-quarter time. Several nurses who have left the unit for health or family reasons say they would be willing to return to a three-quarter time schedule. As well as reducing turnover, the three-quarter time option would be a powerful recruiting tool. Lower rates of turnover and absenteeism would mean fewer trainee and casual staff on the unit. This is an important consideration on a unit where quick and accurate response to a crisis is essential.

EMERGENCY BACK-UP: The use of three-quarter time staff would also provide a trained reserve in the event of a major medical disaster.

The drawbacks of the program would be minor. Some additional support services might be required for a somewhat larger staff. The work schedules of nurses on three-quarter time would also be somewhat less regular and predictable.

Local Examples
Many B.C. hospitals use three-quarter time positions for peak coverage, with no apparent problems reported. Split rotations are also not unusual; for example, the Pearkes Clinic of the Queen Alexandra Hospital employs five health care workers who split 3.5 positions in a manner very similar to that described in this proposal, and the arrangement has proved satisfactory for all concerned.

Implementation
We would suggest that the new arrangement be given a trial period of three rotation cycles (a total of 30 weeks) starting January 1.

If the program were cancelled at the end of the trial period, the contract for the person rehired would not be renewed. The new arrangement requires no changes to the collective agreement. We recommend that all parties sign a trial agreement that outlines the terms of the arrangement, its effect on scheduling and benefits, and contingency plans.

We also recommend that the supervisor in charge of scheduling shifts coordinate the evaluation of the trial program. In addition to collecting feedback from the participating nurses and their supervisors, she would also be asked to tabulate absenteeism and overtime use for the purpose of making a proper cost analysis.

STEP SEVEN

PUTTING WORK IN ITS PLACE

Expediting the
Approval Process

Tactics are important in getting a work option proposal approved. In a large organization the approval process may take anywhere from six to eighteen months, but there are ways to speed the process.

With individual proposals, the first question is where to send your proposal. In most cases it should be given to your immediate supervisor. However, if you know that your immediate supervisor is opposed to the idea, send it to someone at a higher administrative level. This is a risky strategy, but it has worked on occasion.

If a union is involved, someone from the union should get a copy of your proposal. If you know of someone in the union leadership who has been responsive to your needs in the past, send a copy to that person. If the personnel department is likely to be supportive, send a copy there too. You want to make sure that all people who might back you and who might intercede on your behalf know about your plan.

Write a short covering letter to go with each copy of the proposal. That will make it seem less formal. It also gives you a chance to say why that person is being sent a copy and what action you are hoping will follow.

Group or union proposals usually go to the head of the personnel department and to someone in senior management. Again, send a copy to prospective supporters. If the proposed program is large or complex, suggest that the personnel department buy a copy of

Barney Olmsted and Suzanne Smith's *Creating a Flexible Workplace* to help with the nitty-gritty of designing forms, schedules, agreement language, etc.

It is not a good idea to introduce work option proposals in contract bargaining talks. In most cases, work options start as temporary experiments under a memorandum of agreement between the union and management. However, the collective agreement may contain a clause to the effect that: "Work scheduling experiments may be conducted from time to time during the life of this contract by mutual agreement between the union and the employer."

There are at least three reasons why contract talks are not a good place to initiate work option programs:

- The atmosphere in contract talks is often adversarial;
- It takes more time to set up a good option program than is available during contract talks;
- Most option programs need time to settle in. Until a program is running smoothly it should not be cast in stone by including it in the collective agreement;

After an option program has had a couple of years to mature, both sides are usually willing to make it a part of the collective agreement without argument.

Once you have submitted your proposal, you have to be diplomatic about pushing for approval. Without some urging from you — or someone who is backing you — your proposal could get stuck in the pipe. On the other hand, too much pushing will arouse antagonism. Make your interventions within a framework of curiosity or helpful concern. ("I had hoped to hear something about my proposal by now. Can you tell me what's holding it up?" or "I understand that my proposal has gone to you for consideration. If you have any questions, I would be happy to answer them.")

Sometimes management will try to discourage you by stalling on a decision. If that happens, your union may need to intercede.

Your employer may make a counter-proposal. Think about what compromise arrangements you would be willing to accept.

You should also consider what you would do if your employer refuses to negotiate. Will you quietly begin looking for another job?

Will you quit outright? Will you raise the issue with your union? Will you look at self-employment or going back to school?

If you are convinced that you have other options, you can often press your case more vigorously. Sometimes management will say yes simply because it becomes harder and harder to keep saying no. The process of shepherding a proposal through to approval almost always requires patience, tenacity, and nerve, particularly in large organizations.

A final note to those who are worried that a request for flexible hours might cost them their jobs: a proposal to change your hours is not a refusal to fulfil your contract. A proposal simply says, "If we can both agree, I would like to change my work schedule." If your employer were to fire you for submitting a proposal, you could sue for wrongful dismissal and you would probably win.

···IT'S A NOTE FROM FARMER JONES ··· HE AGREES
TO ALL OUR DEMANDS EXCEPT MATERNITY LEAVE
FOR THE HENS ···

Implementing Your Program

Your work option proposal should include a basic plan for implementation. Once your proposal has been approved, all you have to do is make sure you cover all the steps in your plan.

Implementing an individual program usually involves little more than drawing up a written agreement and getting it signed. Read the paragraph below on written agreements for a checklist of items to include.

Implementation of group programs will involve some or all of the following items. If the proposed program is large or complex, invest in a copy of *Creating a Flexible Workplace*; it'll save you considerably in staff time — and grief. (For multiple option programs, see the chapter The Flexible Workplace on page 271.)

■ NEEDS SURVEY

A needs survey will determine how many employees are interested in the program and how they would prefer to arrange their hours. Before arranging relief coverage for a banked overtime, flextime, or V-Time system, you will need some idea of the expected pattern of use. A needs survey is usually a short, anonymous questionnaire which provides rough estimates to use in the planning stage.

■ HOURS-OF-WORK COMMITTEE

An hours-of-work committee serves several purposes. It can draft a final agreement, produce policy and briefing documents, screen applicants, settle disputes, monitor results, and coordinate housekeeping tasks.

■ WRITTEN AGREEMENT

A written agreement ensures that both sides have the same understanding of the rules. The written agreement should contain the following clauses.

- Describe clearly any changes in your benefit package, especially your pension;
- Describe any effects on your seniority, job classification, and salary;
- List any changes in your duties or responsibilities;
- Describe specific features of your new schedule, including any agreements about statutory holidays, vacation time, or time-trading provisions;
- Define the conditions under which you would be entitled to overtime pay;
- Specify a trial period and a starting date;
- Describe what will happen if the program is cancelled, and outline the circumstances which would justify cancelling the program before the end of the trial period.

■ LEGAL REVIEW

Before signing any agreement, ask the labour standards branch of your provincial ministry of labour to confirm that it satisfies all legal requirements. [AMERICAN READERS: Most U.S. states have a comparable government department. The U.S. Department of Labor can help you locate it.]

■ APPLICATION PROCESS

An application process, and application form, for people wanting to take advantage of the work option must be prepared. This involves developing explicit eligibility criteria and procedures for approving applications, job redefinition, relief coverage, changes to the benefit package, and so on. Every successful applicant to the program should have an individualized written agreement similar to the document described above.

■ BRIEFING MATERIAL AND POLICY STATEMENTS

All those directly or indirectly affected by the new program should receive advance notice of the changes and a basic orientation in the operation of the new system. Any policy changes, such as changes in overtime, should be clearly defined. Participants should have the name of a contact person who can answer questions or deal with problems. Supervisors should also be briefed on the program so that their expectations are realistic.

■ COMMUNICATION MECHANISMS

What changes in the filing system and office procedures will be required to accommodate the new system? How will staff meetings be scheduled? Will there be a special communications log or a tape recorder to pass along information? Is an overlap in schedules needed? Is a scheduling calendar needed and if so, who should receive a copy?

■ RECORDING SYSTEMS/PAPERWORK

How will set hours of work be recorded under the new system? If changes in the mechanics of the payroll structure are required, these will have to be spelled out. What changes are needed in pension plans, insurance policies, or the after-hours answering service? Do signs listing office hours need to be updated?

■ EQUIPMENT

Are any special equipment purchases required? Who will be responsible for purchasing such equipment? Are extra keys, uniforms, desks, or computers needed? Does the phone or switchboard system need upgrading?

■ FILL-IN STAFFING

Who will hire fill-in staff? How will they be recruited? What method will be used to schedule fill-in staff? Who will be responsible for scheduling? How much training will the new staff need? Who will be responsible for training?

Evaluation and Follow Up

Work option programs are rarely free of problems. It is almost impossible to foresee all the circumstances that could interfere with the smooth running of a plan, but the bugs usually show up within the first year. Time and effort spent evaluating and adjusting your program during the trial period can often mean the difference between wholehearted support from your employer and reluctant acceptance or even rejection of the plan.

It is useful to solicit early feedback from your supervisor, co-workers and clients. By asking whether your new schedule has troubled or inconvenienced them in any way, you may uncover minor problems and resentments before they escalate into major issues. If you then ask, "Is there any way this problem could be avoided in the future?" you may be able to involve the other person in finding ways to make the program more effective. People who are consulted feel included, and are less likely to attack the program when it is being evaluated.

Minor changes in office procedures often enhance the advantages of the new schedule and minimize the difficulties. Your program does not have to be problem-free at evaluation time, as long as it appears to have more advantages than drawbacks.

During the trial period you can monitor "vital signs" and collect a file of positive comments. Look for information that can be used at evaluation time. Is absenteeism down measurably? Have fewer customer complaints been recorded? Have there been fewer delays in filling orders?

It's also important to be aware of your own reactions during the trial period. Sometimes the results of a change in hours are unexpected; the reality of the new schedule may not live up to expectations. The end of the trial period is a natural time to ask for changes which would make the program work better for you, or to ask for cancellation of the program if that is your decision.

Communication patterns usually require some adjustment in order to get the best results. Sometimes the problems involve feelings rather than the actual exchange of information. If someone (you, a co-worker, or your supervisor) feels out of touch or thinks they have lost control of the situation, the strain may have less to do with the efficiency of the system than with friendships in the workplace or the power relationships between people. Going out to lunch together, or calling in at the pub after work, may improve the personal relationships that are also a part of the workplace. The personal relationship aspect is particularly important for job-sharing partners.

Programs designed for a single individual do not require an elaborate process of evaluation. A one-page survey for co-workers and selected clients, if that is appropriate, can provide useful feedback. The kind of questions to ask include:

? *How has the new arrangement affected you?*

? *What problems have you found with the new arrangement?*

? *Are these problems manageable? How could they be minimized?*

? *What benefits do you see in the new arrangement?*

? *Do you see any reason why the new arrangement should not continue?*

? *Do you have any other comments or suggestions?*

You and your supervisor should also answer the survey in order to establish a basis for your discussion. Collect any available data on absenteeism, productivity changes, overtime use, etc.

You and your supervisor may be the only people who need to take part in the formal evaluation. However, if you suspect that your supervisor does not want the program to continue, you may want to ask that someone from your union or the personnel department be present at the evaluation meeting. It can be useful to have an objective third party lead the discussion in any case.

The evaluation meeting should result in a report which summarizes the findings and then makes one of three recommendations:

❶ The program should continue on an ongoing basis.

❷ The program should be revised and run again for another trial period.

❸ The program should be cancelled.

The report may be written by anyone who was present at the evaluation meeting. Before being submitted to upper management, it should be ratified by everyone who took part in the evaluation process.

A more elaborate evaluation procedure is necessary when work option programs involve several participants, or if the program is a pilot project. In this case, one person may be delegated to study the program and prepare a report. The report forms the basis for discussions in the hours-of-work committee, which makes recommendations about the future of the program.

The report writer is usually a member of the hours-of-work committee, or a representative of the personnel department. Outside consultants may also be used. In addition to administering written questionnaires to participants, their co-workers, and supervisors, the report writer should conduct telephone or face-to-face interviews. The review will be more positive in outlook if both the report writer and the hours-of-work committee approach the evaluation by asking how the program can be made more effective, rather than whether the program should be continued.

A more objective assessment of the program might be achieved if control data can be obtained. This data can be taken from records compiled before the program started, or by monitoring a comparable unit still on a traditional schedule. One of the difficulties of analyzing the effects of work option programs is that results are often coloured by subjective attitudes and feelings about the program. Hard numbers on absenteeism rates, turnover rates, orders shipped per shift, etc., make for a more credible analysis of results.

After the hours-of-work committee has accepted the report and made the necessary additions, changes, and/or recommendations, the report should be submitted to management and the union executive for further action or comment. It is also advisable to circulate copies of the final report to those who participate in the evaluation.

When a work option is to be expanded from the pilot stage to a full-scale program, it is wise to phase in changes in stages so as to minimize confusion and continuity problems while the new system is settling in. An exception to this rule involves compressed workweeks, where a mixture of old and new schedules may be more problematic than revising everyone's schedule at the same time.

Once a program has final approval it should be included in both the collective agreement and the personnel policy manual. The program then becomes integral to an organization's operating policy.

SPECIAL CASES AND FURTHER RESOURCES

Work Options as an Alternative to Layoffs

Layoffs are usually preceded by rumours, hints, and official warnings. Instead of waiting passively for the axe to fall, employees at many workplaces have used this time to explore work options as a way of avoiding impending layoffs.

In most organizations, some people will welcome the opportunity to work less than full time. By allowing these employees to reduce their hours, work options can make more work available to others. Job sharing, leave programs, V-Time, banked overtime, and retirement options have all been used to reduce or eliminate layoffs.

Employers know that layoffs are bad for morale and that concern about job security has a negative effect on productivity. Although this atmosphere is bad in every other way, it can be good for introducing the idea of a work option program. Employers and unions who wouldn't normally agree to innovations in work scheduling will often listen when it's clear that changes could save jobs. If you have been turned down for a work option before, this would be a good time to try again.

When work options are being considered as an alternative to layoffs, as many people as possible should be involved in the discussions. In these situations, signs of strong support on the shop floor will often influence the decision of management.

Start by forming an organizing committee made up of people who have some interest in the concept. Circulate a memo about the formation of a committee. This will strengthen awareness of the threat of layoffs, and enable supporters of alternative approaches to find you. Do not assume that management or the union will take the initiative in suggesting work options as a solution for layoffs. In most cases the initiative has to come from an informal group of employees.

The various work options are not all equally effective at preventing layoffs. Job sharing usually appeals to 5 or 10 percent of employees, and can preserve half that percentage of jobs. More people are likely to participate if the workforce is largely female or if it includes a large number of older workers. V-Time and permanent part-time, which allow smaller cuts in worktime, appeal to more people and may increase job opportunities by as much as 10 percent.

Leave programs — either deferred salary arrangements or unpaid educational leave — appeal to about 5 percent of the workforce. From 25 to 50 percent of workers over age 55 will be interested in phased retirement programs or opportunities for early retirement with a bridging pension. (This constitutes a legitimate use of the surplus money that many pension funds now contain.)

If compulsory banked overtime is used to convert overtime hours and premium rates into time off, the number of jobs created will depend on the average amount of overtime in your workplace. Because men are usually less interested than women in reducing their hours of work, compulsory banked overtime may be the least painful and most effective way to reduce staff levels when the workforce is predominantly male. This alternative is less attractive than voluntary work options, but it is obviously preferable to layoffs.

Programs that combine more than one work option can increase the number of jobs saved. Job sharing, short-term leaves, phased retirement, and permanent part-time can all be offered under the general umbrella of V-Time. For this reason, V-Time is usually the preferred multiple-option approach. V-Time and banked overtime can fit together neatly if one set of relief staff can be used for both.

When you are first thinking about work options as an alternative to layoffs, a needs survey can help determine which options should be offered. In addition to explaining the way different options work, the survey should mention any safeguards and protections to be included in the program.

Safeguards can help to encourage maximum participation. Voluntary programs should be free of any real or perceived compulsory features, and seniority should be based on a calendar system so that employees who reduce their hours will not lose their place on the seniority list. An automatic right to return to full time after six months or a year is another reassuring feature. Older workers are unlikely to participate unless the pension plan is altered to protect their retirement incomes. Maintaining full benefits for those who make small cuts in worktime is an added incentive to participate.

If the number of planned layoffs is large (20 percent or more), voluntary work options may not have enough impact to avoid layoffs. In these circumstances, work sharing may be a better alternative, particularly if the layoffs are temporary. Work sharing involves an across-the-board reduction in work hours. The typical solution is a four-day week, although cuts are sometimes greater than this.

Compulsory reductions in work hours always cause emotional and economic upheaval, but a sense of solidarity can develop when everyone faces the same reductions. Besides, working less does not damage a person's self-respect as much as unemployment does. Sometimes extra free time is welcome despite the income loss. Work sharing is never entirely voluntary because it occurs only in the shadow of impending layoffs, but it usually occurs because everyone has accepted the need to work less in order to avoid layoffs for some.

When all employees agree to reduce their hours equally to avoid temporary layoffs, they become eligible for the federal government's Work Sharing Program, which allows them to collect unemployment insurance for the days they do not work. Under this program, employees on a four-day week would take home about 92 percent of their full-time income. Employees on a three-day week would take home approximately 83 percent of the usual income. An employee who is eventually laid off becomes eligible for full unemployment insurance benefits with only a small penalty. The Work Sharing Program has a number of eligibility rules. All employees in a given unit must participate voluntarily; in an organized workplace the union must approve the program, and the reduction in work hours must be temporary. Contact your local Canada Employment Centre for more information. [AMERICAN READERS: California and a number of other states have work-sharing programs, sometimes under the title of "Short-Time Compensation."]

Options for Job Seekers

Everything we have said so far has been directed towards working people who want to reduce or rearrange their hours. What if you are unemployed and want part-time work or flexible hours? It's not easy to go looking for an alternative work arrangement but it's not impossible, either. Job seekers have had success using the following strategies.

■ JOINT JOB SEARCH

If you are sure that you do not want full-time work, why not try to find a compatible partner and look for work as a team. Sometimes this will put you at a disadvantage compared to other candidates, but not always. Occasionally an employer will favour a pair of applicants over an individual. In one case, for example, a shipper-receiver position went to two sisters because the arrangement gave the employer the capacity for double coverage on heavy days. In another case, a teaching position went to two teachers who jointly offered a range of specialties rarely available in a single teacher.

To be successful at a joint job search, you must do much of the "partnering" work in advance. First find a partner with whom you feel comfortable, preferably someone you have worked with in the past and know well. Figure out your preferred schedules and the mechanisms you intend to use to exchange information. Discuss the way you each like to organize things and your philosophy of work. Get to know each other's work history and likes and dislikes on the job, so that by the time you get to a job interview you will already be functioning as a team.

If you plan to split your hours unequally, look closely at how you would divide the work and how you would share authority. Discuss in advance the extent to which you are willing to cover for each other for vacations or illness, and whether you are willing to work over-time to cover peak periods. These can be important selling points for an employer, but do not promise anything you cannot deliver.

Your job search will help develop the teamwork necessary for a good partnership. Two people's ideas, energy, and enthusiasm can make the process of finding a job easier. Looking for a job together is also an excellent opportunity to learn how to support one another.

Joint job search involves developing a team presentation. List your qualifications and your work histories side-by-side in a joint resumé. Mention briefly how you would work as a team, and the advantages of a team approach. Have a friend pretend to be an employer and practise operating as a team in a mock job interview. Make sure you are well informed about job sharing so that you can answer employ-ers' questions.

■ FIND A PARTNER WHO HAS A JOB

Talk to your friends, professional associates, and employees at for-mer places of employment. Who feels overloaded and wants to cut back? Lend this book to friends who are employed. Don't feel embarrassed about asking to share someone's job. You're not trying to take their job away from them, nor are you looking for charity. You are looking for someone who has a good reason for wanting to work less. (If you want to work closer to full-time hours — say, four days a week — you may need to find more than one partner.)

A proposal for a change in work scheduling should come from the person who is working, but there is no reason why you couldn't do most of the work involved in writing and designing the proposal, since you are unemployed and presumably have more free time. Just be sure that the plan you develop accurately reflects the job and your partner's needs and wants.

Your resumé should be submitted as an appendix to the proposal. Be aware that even if your potential partner's employer accepts the idea of job sharing, it does not necessarily follow that you will be the one hired. You still need to win that employer over to you with a good resumé and a good interview.

■ NEGOTIATE AT JOB INTERVIEWS

If you are applying for a full-time job on the basis that you would be willing to work regular hours if necessary, you may be able to negotiate different hours during the job interview. You may discover that your preferences and the needs of your prospective employer are well matched.

■ NEGOTIATE AT THE POINT OF HIRING

If you are willing to work regular hours if you have to, you can wait and try negotiating when you have been offered a position. Under the right circumstances, flextime, compressed workweeks, V-Time, partial telecommuting, and banked overtime can all be negotiated at the point of hiring. Sometimes an employer will suggest that the work option proposal be postponed until the end of your probationary period.

■ PAY YOUR DUES AND THEN ASK

Sometimes the only way to get the work schedule you want is to take a full-time job and then, after a year or so of proving yourself to be a dependable employee, ask for a change in hours. If you adopt this approach, it might be wise to enquire about future prospects for a more flexible work arrangement during the job interview — before making a big investment of time.

■ FREELANCE OR WORK ON A CONTRACT BASIS

Freelance and contract staff enjoy a degree of flexibility in their work schedules that is seldom accorded to regular staff. The disadvantage is that freelancers and contract workers have little or no job security.

■ LOOK FOR PERMANENT PART-TIME EMPLOYMENT

A growing number of employers offer good wages, benefits, and job security to part-time employees. Many employers do not bother to advertise part-time jobs. Instead they hire from applications on file. By targeting the companies you would like to work for and making sure they have you listed as available for part-time work, you can tap the hidden market for permanent part-time jobs.

■ LOOK FOR A RELIEF STAFF POSITION

If you prefer to work part time, if you thrive on variety and have a wide range of skills, you may be able to convince an employer to hire you as relief staff. Large employers often recognize the fact that semi-permanent relief staff can reduce the chaos that descends whenever regular people are on holiday. Because most employees take their vacations in the summer, a relief position is best suited to those who want to take time off during the winter months. Relief staffing can also be a stepping stone to a permanent part-time job.

Compensatory Benefit Leaves

Compensatory benefits are rights of employment. They are almost always negotiated through the collective bargaining process. There is seldom any point in approaching your employer directly about a compensatory benefit program. However, if you feel strongly that one of the benefits listed is worth fighting for, you can propose that your union include it in the next round of contract talks. Use Steps Five and Six to develop your proposal, remembering, of course, that you are trying to persuade your union instead of your employer.

Compensatory benefits include vacation time, statutory holidays, sick leave, compassionate leave, and maternity, paternity, parental, and adoptive parent leaves. For more information on your legal rights to leave see the *Canadian Master Labour Guide* from CCH Canadian Ltd. **[AMERICAN READERS: Most states have their own labor codes, differing from state to state, in addition to federal regulations, so you'll need to get specific information from your state government.]**

■ VACATIONS

Although Canadian employers are not legally required to give employees time off for vacation, they must provide a minimum of two weeks' vacation pay each year, which is equivalent to 4 percent of yearly wages. Many employers offer longer paid vacations based on the number of years of service with the organization. North America has low vacation allotments compared to Europe. In France, for instance, the legal minimum is six weeks of paid vacation each year. This suggests that increased vacation time is an appropriate target for collective bargaining.

■ STATUTORY HOLIDAYS

Canada has nine statutory holidays each year: New Year's Day, Good Friday, Victoria Day, Canada Day, Labour Day, Thanksgiving, Remembrance Day, Christmas Day, and Boxing Day.

A number of provinces designate an extra statutory holiday, commonly the first Monday in August. Some collective agreements require additional paid holidays (including, in some cases, the employee's birthday). Employers are legally required to give you the day off (unpaid) to attend your own or a son or daughter's wedding.

Employers are not required by law to pay for a statutory holiday unless it falls on one of your normal workdays, but many collective agreements have more inclusive eligibility rules. As with vacations, employers are not legally required to grant time off for statutory holidays. If you work on a holiday, however, you are entitled to receive holiday pay at time-and-a-half, in addition to your regular daily wage.

■ SICK LEAVE

Sick leave usually consists of a fixed number of days off each month or year; for example, one day per month, or ten days each year. Some sick leave allowances are based on a percentage of hours worked. This system accommodates both part-time employees and those who work a lot of overtime.

In most sick leave programs, employees cannot draw against future sick leave allowances. They can claim only the amount of sick leave they have accumulated before becoming ill. Some programs allow employees to bank all their sick leave; others set a maximum that can be carried over from year to year. Some programs pay for unused sick leave, and some allow unused sick leave to be rolled over into vacation time. In other programs the rule is "What you don't use, you lose."

Sick leave is not popular with employers. It can be costly and inconvenient, and some employers are concerned about abuse of the system. Absenteeism is a serious problem that results in many more lost workdays each year than strikes or work stoppages.

Unions often have to pay a high price at the bargaining table to negotiate a sick leave plan. Employers are often more willing to agree to a plan if it is designed to reward the healthy (see the information about Earned Time Off on page 274).

■ COMPASSIONATE LEAVE

Unpaid compassionate leave is a legal right in federal government jurisdictions and in some provinces. Many workplaces have some sort of compassionate or bereavement leave that allows employees to visit dying relatives or to attend funerals. Sometimes these conditions are written into company guidelines for personnel or into collective agreements. At other workplaces there is tacit agreement that compassionate leave is granted at the discretion of the supervisor.

Usually, but not always, compassionate leave is paid leave. Often it falls under the guidelines for sick leave or personal leave. These guidelines usually define eligible relatives, just cause, and the length of leave allowed. Guidelines for compassionate leave should also ensure that a request can be approved quickly and easily. People in the midst of grief should not have to cope with unnecessary paperwork or delay.

Your union steward or personnel manager can tell you what compassionate leave arrangements exist at your workplace. In the absence of such provisions, make a written request to your supervisor to the effect that you need time off to visit a dying relative or attend a funeral. (Depending on your supervisor and your workplace, such leave may be unpaid. Be prepared for that possibility.) If your supervisor refuses on the grounds that granting such a request is outside his or her authority, take your request directly to the personnel manager.

If there is an adequate sick leave program at your place of employment, perhaps the least cumbersome arrangement is to make bereavement leave a legitimate use of sick leave. This usually requires the addition of only a few clauses to the sick leave guidelines. From a bargaining perspective, it is often easier to modify an existing benefit than to create a new one. The disadvantage is that taking time off for a bereavement will cut into your illness allowance.

■ PARENTAL LEAVE

Although parental leave is more widespread in the United States and Europe than in Canada, a number of Canadian companies now allow parents to take time off to care for their sick children. Such arrangements are sometimes paid and sometimes unpaid.

As with bereavement leave, the immediacy of the situation may mean that you will have to apply for personal leave in order to get time off if there are no parental leave provisions where you work. If you propose to establish a parental leave program there are a number of possible designs to suggest.

The most straightforward method is to incorporate a codicil into the sick leave plan allowing employees to use their own sick leave to care for sick children. In many cases this only legitimizes what is already happening when parents call in "sick" when it is really their children who are ill. Again, the obvious disadvantage is that it decreases the amount of sick leave available should illness strike that employee. It is also important to consider the effect of this approach on short-term illness insurance plans.

A second method of granting parental leave is to set a separate paid leave allowance, similar to sick leave, of a half-day each month. This is a more cumbersome approach and requires additional record keeping. Also, it frequently increases employer costs and may create resentment from non-parents. However, if either the employer or the union has strong pro-family values, such an arrangement will sometimes be approved.

A clause in the personnel guidelines will be enough to establish unpaid parental leave. This method is inexpensive for the employer. If an employee is willing to forego income in order to attend to the needs of a sick child, parental leave is not likely to be used frivolously. The obvious disadvantage from the employee's perspective is that most parents cannot afford many days without pay. However, if neither of the first two options is possible, unpaid parental leave at least acknowledges that parenting responsibilities are a legitimate reason to miss work.

■ MATERNITY LEAVE

Maternity leave is a legal right in all Canadian provinces, although the time allotted is not consistent. All provinces allow at least seventeen weeks; Quebec, Saskatchewan, Alberta and British Columbia allow eighteen weeks. The Northwest Territories has no provision for maternity leave. Woman who are eligible for maternity leave can collect up to fifteen weeks unemployment insurance.

Some unions have a collective agreement which requires the employer to supplement Unemployment Insurance payments by 25 percent, which is the maximum allowed under UI regulations. This increases a woman's income while on leave to 72 percent of her regular salary. Some collective agreements also allow women to remain off work for up to an additional six months, unpaid, with a guaranteed right to return to work and the continuation of at least partial benefit coverage.

Today the trend is for women to start their families later in life, have fewer children, and to return to work more quickly after the birth of a child. This trend has helped control the potential costs of maternity leave provisions. It has also underlined the growing importance of the female workforce in our economy, and the need for employers to assist women in finding ways to combine work and motherhood. Adequate maternity leave provisions are a significant part of making women's place in the workforce more equitable.

■ PATERNITY LEAVE

In Canada, since 1990, ten weeks of Unemployment Insurance parental leave benefits are available to fathers as well as mothers who qualify for this benefit. Within federal jurisdictions and in some provinces, paternity leave is a legal right. Some collective agreements also allow fathers a period of leave to spend time with a newborn child. The period varies from a few days to several weeks, and the leave may be paid, partially paid, or unpaid, depending on the terms of the agreement. A limited number of non-unionized workplaces have personnel guidelines for paternity leave. Your union steward or personnel manager should be able to tell you whether your employer provides this benefit.

If there is no paternity leave where you work, you can make a proposal to institute such a program. If your need is immediate, apply for personal leave as a substitute.

The most straightforward way to design a paternity leave program is to model it after your firm's maternity leave program. However, paternity leave differs from maternity leave in two important respects. There is no physical condition on which to base the conditions of leave as there are for women qualifying for maternity leave, and there are grey areas concerning eligibility. For instance, should the benefit extend to a father who is not married to the mother having the child, or to a father who is not living with the mother?

Despite problems in determining eligibility, paternity leave programs have three important influences. First, they allow fathers time to bond with their newborn children. Second, they give fathers the opportunity to take over more of the housekeeping load while mothers are recovering from childbirth. Third, by equalizing the cost of benefits for men and women, they help counteract unconscious prejudices against hiring women.

■ ADOPTION LEAVE

Unpaid adoption leave is a legal right in federal government jurisdictions and in most provinces. However, only the largest workplaces grant paid leave for adopting parents to bond with the newly adopted child. The most obvious reason is that adoption happens so seldom. In a small workplace the need for adoption leave rarely, if ever, arises.

Where adoption leave provisions exist, the benefits are usually similar to those for maternity and paternity leave. Adopting parents have the same rights to unemployment insurance as a birth mother, but the claim can only be made on behalf of the adopting mother because, under the current legislation, maternity unemployment insurance does not extend to fathers.

The most common way of establishing adoption leave is to write a codicil into the maternity and paternity leave guidelines, giving adopting parents the same rights as birth parents. Most employers, however, do not establish a policy on adoption leave until they receive a request for one.

The Flexible
Workplace

As more people demand reduced or flexible work schedules, organizations will have to adapt in order to attract and retain some of the most productive and highly qualified employees. A number of innovations can facilitate a flexible workplace.

■ CAFETERIA-STYLE BENEFITS

Many companies are finding that standardized benefit packages do not meet the diverse needs and wants of their employees. An alternative approach is to allow new employees to select their own benefit packages from a range of possible choices. An employee's salary at any given time would comprise the gross hourly wage multiplied by the number of hours in a pay period, minus the cost of benefits. Computers make such a system easier to administer.

With cafeteria-stye benefits, employees can be fairly remunerated and have the benefit plan of their choice, regardless of the number of hours they work. Even temporary staff are treated fairly, though most will opt to keep their full hourly wage rather than taking benefits. A cafeteria-style plan also more fairly remunerates employees who work overtime.

■ FLEXIBLE PENSION ARRANGEMENTS

Employees on reduced work schedules should be able to contribute to the pension plan as though they were working full time. This feature is essential for employees who are approaching retirement age. Pension plans which allow employees some flexibility in the amount they contribute and the size of their pension are an important part of any cafeteria-style benefit plan.

■ HOURS-OF-WORK COMMITTEE

When all work scheduling issues go through a single, ongoing committee, it is easier to develop coherent policies. One standing committee can develop more expertise and understanding of the issues than multiple ad hoc committees. A standing committee is also able to monitor programs over time and to catch problems before they escalate. The committee should include representatives from labour, management, and the personnel department. Often one member is empowered to act as an arbitrator to settle smaller disputes.

■ EFFICIENT USE OF MEETING TIME

A two-hour staff meeting takes up only 5 percent of a full-time worker's week, but 10 percent of a half-time worker's week. The more people work reduced hours, the more important it is that meetings make the most efficient use of time. Using a timed and prioritized agenda, and delegating unworkable items to smaller committees, can speed up meetings. Ricardo Semler's book *Maverick* has good suggestions for shortening or eliminating meetings.

■ CROSS TRAINING OF STAFF

The more flexibility an organization offers its staff, the more often employees will be required to do one another's work. Cross training promotes teamwork and better understanding between employees. It provides insurance against having no one to fill a position if an employee suddenly becomes ill or has an accident. In management positions, cross training prepares people to move up the ladder.

■ PERMANENT RELIEF STAFF

Leaves, V-Time, and banked overtime all work best with a permanent relief staff. A permanent relief staff means that fill-in staff are competent, committed, and well versed in the company culture.

■ SELF-DIRECTED STAFF

The more people work independently and organize their own hours, the more important it becomes to train employees to supervise themselves. John Naisbitt and Patricia Aburdene discuss this issue in their book *Re-Inventing the Corporation*.

■ FLAT PAY GRADIENTS

Pay differential should be altered in a couple of ways. First, differences across occupations should be minimized if employees are going to stand in for one another more frequently. Second, casual and part-time employees should get the same total hourly remuneration as full-time workers. Otherwise employers will try to expand the lower-priced end of the gradient, and employees will gravitate to the higher-paid end. I recommend prorated rather than full benefits for part-time staff.

■ ACCESSIBLE INFORMATION

More information must be stored in written form if employees are going to fill in for one another. Good message-taking habits need to be practised. Files must be returned to their original locations. Organizations with telecommuting staff find it helpful to store information electronically rather than as hard copy.

■ EARNED TIME OFF

Once employees have the ability to bank time or make up for lost time, a paid sick leave program becomes unnecessary. Instead, the average amount of sick time per year is added to the employee's vacation allowance. This becomes *earned time off*. Earned time off (ETO) can be used as sick leave or as vacation time. An ETO system rewards employees who stay healthy by allowing them extra vacation time; the usual system rewards employees who get sick by giving them paid time off. ETO gives all employees more equal use of sick time. Unscheduled absenteeism usually decreases with ETO, and planned vacations increase, making for easier relief staffing.

■ PROFESSIONAL DEVELOPMENT

If an employer wants a staff that stays and grows, ongoing training and career development should be offered to all employees. Vocational counselling, in-service courses, and paid educational leave can all be used to encourage professional development within an organization.

For a more complete discussion of the flexible workplace, see Naisbitt and Aburdene's *Re-inventing the Corporation* or Olmsted and Smith's *Creating a Flexible Workplace*.

Dead Heroes:
Men and Work

There is an abundant literature for women on how to combine work and family life, how to balance work and play, and how to achieve personal wholeness. As yet, there is very little literature on these subjects for men.

Most of what is written for men pushes them in the opposite direction. To be "a winner," a man is expected to give all he has to his work — to become a workaholic.

On average, North American men die about eight years younger than North American women. Most people assume that this gap is based on biological differences. In fact, prior to about 1800 the gap in life expectancy between men and women was quite small. In many of the world's cultures today, men live as long as women.

Men in North America die young not because of their biology but because of their behaviour. The trends that have accompanied the women's movement offer further evidence of this. As more women join the ranks of workaholics, they are starting to succumb to the so-called male illnesses of heart attacks, ulcers, and strokes.

We men wear out before our time because of our compulsion to overwork. However we try to rationalize it, the compulsion to work all the time is a slow form of suicide. In a way we are like lemmings rushing headlong toward our own destruction.

What do you suppose lemmings might say if we could interview them on their way to the sea? If the CBC were there with a microphone, the interview might go something like this:

"Excuse me! Could you tell our listeners why you're running into the sea?"

"Because you just can't buck the system."

"I'm the manager. I've got to set the example."

"I'm doing it for the wife and kids."

"Sorry, I don't have time to think about that. I've got a deadline to meet."

"Don't pick on me. I'm no different from anyone else."

"I have to keep up with my competition."

We can produce a whole raft of apparently rational, hard-nosed reasons why we must work ourselves into early graves. But these reasons are only rationalizations. The real reason for our behaviour lies in our romantic vision of what it means to be a man.

The Hero Myth

Underneath our apparent rationality, most men are incurable romantics, and the romantic fantasy that most entrances us is the myth of the hero. These are the basic elements of the hero myth.

- Heroes cannot die because they are protected by forces of good;
- To succeed, heroes have to be tough and fearless;
- The hero who ignores his limits will have no limits;
- Heroes must struggle and suffer for a long time without recognition and reward;
- When he finally finds the Holy Grail, the hero will be loved and revered by all.

The hero myth is a wonderfully inspiring and uplifting fantasy. The problem is that we forget it is a myth based on wishful thinking. This is not surprising given that we are surrounded by wishful thinking, whether we are in the board room, the locker room, the lunch room, or the TV room. John Wayne, Audie Murphy, James Bond, Rambo — they are all the same story dressed up in different clothes.

The hero myth is a powerfully seductive fantasy. It tells us that no harm can come to us if we're on the side of goodness and right; that the man who acts as though he has no limits, has no limits; that life may be hell now, but once you rescue the fairy princess you'll receive half the kingdom. No wonder Sylvester Stallone can make the same movie over and over again and earn $100 million a pop. Hollywood knows how addicted we are to our fantasies.

There is a joke that says it all about this issue. Two journalists are drinking in a bar on the top floor of a 40-story hotel. One says to the other, "You know, Mac, this is a very special building. It's designed so that if you fall over the railing the wind currents will pick you up and bring you back to the top."

The second guy say, "Aw, you're putting me on."

The first guy replies, "I'll bet you $100 it's true."

"You're on," replies the other.

The first guy goes out on the balcony and jumps over the railing. He plummets toward the ground, then gradually slows to a halt, floats back up, and lands gently on the balcony.

The second guy is awestruck. He hands over the $100 without a word. Then a glint appears in his eye and he thinks, "I could make a fortune with that trick."

He says to the first guy, "That's fantastic. Let's both try it." They both climb up on the railing and jump off. The second guy plummets all the way down and goes *SPLAT!* all over the pavement. The first falls halfway and then wafts back up to the balcony. He walks into the bar, slaps down the $100, and orders another drink.

The bartender shakes his head and says, "You know, you can be a real jerk sometimes, Superman."

That joke is the story of our lives. We keep fooling ourselves into thinking we can do what Superman does, and then we go Splat all over the pavement. Take a look at the obituary column in your daily paper. There are a lot of us pretending to be Superman and going Splat at age 60 or 50, and sometimes even at 40.

Here is an analogy that illustrates the extent of male wishful thinking. Imagine that you own an English sports car — a red MG with a tachometer that redlines at 6000 RPM. How would you treat it?

You would probably drive with an engine speed in the 2000 to 4000 RPM range because that would give the smoothest ride and the best gas mileage, and it would create the least wear and tear on the engine. You might take the engine up to 5500 RPM to pass or accelerate, but you wouldn't run it in that range for an extended time.

On rare occasions you might take the engine right up to or even over the red line for a few minutes, just to see what the car could do. But you would be watching the tachometer closely and listening carefully to the engine. You would change the oil regularly and consider it false economy to scrimp on preventative maintenance.

Now consider how most of us treat our bodies — our biological sports cars. We continually drive our biological engines at 5500 RPM because we foolishly believe that doing so will make us stronger. We regularly take ourselves well over the red line with our eyes closed because we think that if we don't see the red line, no red line exists. We skip preventative maintenance activities like sleep and vacations under the illusion that no harm will come to us because we are hard working and noble.

And we wonder why our MGs age more gracefully than we do.

The Virtue of Toughness

One part of the hero myth that deserves particular attention is the idea that heroes are supposed to be tough. Heroes are supposed to ignore fatigue and grit their teeth against pain, to steel themselves against cowardice and rise above doubt and despair.

"Real men" are supposed to suppress negative emotions through sheer will. Actually, we rarely use willpower alone. That approach is probably workable for Superman, but mere mortals must rely on other techniques.

The most basic way we suppress feelings is known as the *startle response*. "President John F. Kennedy has just been shot." Can you remember how your breath caught in your throat when you first heard that announcement? Central to the startle response is a sharp constriction of the chest muscles which numbs feeling and thereby dampens panic.

We have been conditioned to believe that we are not supposed to have certain feelings. Over the years we develop a chronic tightness in the chest — a kind of permanent startle response. Exercise is problematic because as soon as we start to breathe deeply, the chest opens up and we start to feel things we've been taught not to feel. As a result, we often find ourselves avoiding exercise without really knowing why.

Overeating is another way of suppressing "unmasculine" feelings. Whenever we eat something, our bodies release small amounts of endorphins — natural morphine-like substances which aid digestion by tranquillizing the emotions. Alcohol also works very effectively to depress the central nervous system. The nicotine in cigarettes and the caffeine in coffee both create a buzz in the nervous system which tends to obscure other feelings. We think of food, alcohol, and cigarettes as addictive substances, but it is important to recognize that what we're really addicted to is the suppression of feeling. What is frightening about this wholesale suppression of feeling is how unconscious and automatic it is, and how deeply rooted. For a great many of us, feeling normal could more properly be described as feeling numb.

This learned pattern of suppressing feelings has some useful advantages in particular situations. Bursting into tears at a board meeting, for instance, is not likely to win a promotion. Having control of our emotions also enables us to deal with some awful but necessary tasks — like working in a slaughterhouse, for example. In emergencies it prevents us from succumbing to panic. And it enables us to temporarily push ourselves beyond our normal limits.

The ability to suppress feelings has some real advantages if used consciously in specific circumstances. But it has immense disadvantages if we do it automatically all the time. As a way of life it has some fatal drawbacks.

Loss of inner wisdom. Feeling and intuition add greatly to our power to make good decisions. Our emotions will often alert us to potential problems long before our reason sees anything wrong. When we habitually cut ourselves off from our feelings, we lose this emotional wisdom.

Unsatisfactory relationships. People bond on a feeling level. Whether we're talking about a parent-child, husband-wife, or friend-friend relationship, it will be lifeless if the channel to our feelings isn't open.

Alienation from our bodies. Our bodies have intricate feedback mechanisms to tell us what their needs and limits are. Men make it a virtue to ignore all this crucial information. Then we wonder why we age so quickly.

Damage to our bodies. The dangers of alcohol, nicotine, and obesity are well known. Tense chest muscles constrict the heart and put it under extra strain. They also constrict breathing and leave the body chronically short of air. Cells that do not get enough oxygen are at risk of becoming cancerous. Next time you see a John Wayne movie, watch how shallowly the Duke breathes. John Wayne died of cancer; the two things may not be unrelated.

Loss of positive feelings. Unfortunately, the mechanisms that suppress feeling are non-selective. We lose good feelings as well as bad ones. When we try to be tough by suppressing "unmasculine" feelings, we end up dead from the neck down. That's the real tragedy of men's lives. Too often our "heart" dies many years before we do.

As children we experience life in full vibrant colour but, little by little, our culture trains us to tune the colour out. Often we end up living in black and white. We may even grow to believe that what we see is all there is to life.

It's not easy to stay alive in our culture. Survival requires a conscious and continuous effort to break free of the male straitjacket. The following is a list of ways to take better care of yourself.

Ten Ways to Save Your Own Life

❶ *If you live with lemmings, don't follow the crowd.*
Our culture socializes men to kill themselves emotionally so they will not know that they are killing themselves physically. Many of our cultural role models, and much of the advice we get from the media, friends, and co-workers, lead us to violate our real selves in pursuit of an unreal, idealized fantasy. An excellent guide on how to stop hurting yourself is *Compassion and Self-Hate* by Theodore Rubin.

❷ *Stop trying to be a hero.*
The hero delusion is fool's gold — all glitter and no substance. It is

a siren song that leads us to become dead heroes. In order to enjoy the pleasure of being ourselves, we must let go of our romantic fantasies. A thought-provoking book on the male myth is *He* by Robert Johnson.

❸ *Get physical.*
Body-centred activities are one way to revive feelings. Regular exercise, stretching, yoga, tai chi, and outdoor recreation can all help focus attention on the body. If all else fails, breathe deeply.

❹ *Live more with less.*
Our possessions possess us. How many of us own fancy cars or luxurious houses, only to find that we spend so much time working to pay for them that we're too tired to enjoy them? Joe Dominguez and Vicki Robin's book *Your Money or Your Life* is an excellent guide to simplifying your life.

❺ *Seek balance.*
Men tend to put all their eggs in one basket. A man who puts his whole life into his job is an excellent candidate for a heart attack when he retires, or for suicide if he loses his job. If you have several areas of meaning and satisfaction in your life — work, family, friends, hobbies, and volunteering — your sense of self-esteem will stand on a much broader base.

❻ *Create safe spaces.*
Many people will not support your efforts to become a feeling human being, so you need to seek out friends with whom you can be yourself. A men's support group can be a source of strength and comfort. Herb Goldberg's *The Inner Male* is a safe space you can keep on your bookshelf. Keeping a daily journal of thoughts and feelings provides a private safety zone.

❼ *Track your defences.*
We block some of our feelings so quickly that the only way we can get in touch with them is by looking for the tracks they leave. Whenever you find yourself smoking, drinking, or eating too much, begin to monitor your thoughts. What were you thinking just before you decided you needed a drink? This is one way to discover and face the feelings that you automatically avoid.

❽ *Nurture others and yourself.*

Women are generally better at taking care of themselves, partly because they get more practice in nurturing. When you practise giving attention to others and showing compassion for them, it's not so hard to extend the same attention and compassion to yourself. Gender roles are changing. It used to be the case that men produced and women nurtured. Now women are both producers and nurturers. This change takes part of the load off men as breadwinners, but it also means that we must improve our nurturing skills in order to keep the gender seesaw in balance.

❾ *Value resilience over toughness.*

When something is tough, it's strong but brittle. Push it past its limits and it shatters. On the other hand, something that is resilient immediately bounces back when pushed too far. In this sense, resilience means survival. To put it concretely, consider the difference between an egg and a tennis ball. If you try to depress the surface of an egg, it resists but it eventually breaks. It's tough. Push on a tennis ball and it gives way, but springs back when the pressure is released. It's resilient. Life tends to knock human beings around a certain amount. Which fares better under pressure, toughness or resilience? If you admire Humpty Dumpty, model yourself after the egg. But if you would like to keep your bounce as the years go by, you'd better know how to give a little.

❿ *Work less.*

The human body is not designed to work 50 to 80 hours per week on a regular basis. Most men can arrange to work less if they approach their employer in the right way. (This book shows you how!) Self-employed people who are overloaded should consider taking in a partner. Your business may be better off if you give it your best instead of your all.

Further Resources

■ **Step One: Thinking Clearly About Work**

WORK IN THE PAST

Sahlins, Marshall. *Stone-Age Economics* (Hawthorne, NY: Aldine de Gruyter, 1972).

Schor, Juliet B. *The Overworked American: The Unexpected Decline of Leisure* (New York: Basic Books, 1991).

Terkel, Studs. *Working* (New York: Avon, 1983).

WORK IN THE FUTURE

Benimadhu, Prem. *Hours of Work: Trends and Attitudes in Canada: Report 18-87* (Ottawa, Conference Board of Canada, 1987).

Bosch, Gerhard, Peter Dawkins, and Francois Michon. *Times are Changing: Working Time in 14 Industrialized Countries* (Geneva: International Institute for Labour Studies, 1993).

Canadian Mental Health Association. *Work and Well-being: The Changing Realities of Employment* (1984. Available from the Canadian Mental Health Association, 2160 Yonge Street, Toronto, ON M4S 2Z3).

Conference Board of Canada. *Attitudes Towards New Work Patterns* (Ottawa: Conference Board of Canada, 1986).

DuRivage, Virginia (Editor). *New Policies for Part-time and Contingent Workers* (Washington, DC: Economic Policy Institute, 1992).

Naisbitt, John, and Patricia Aburdene. *Re-inventing the Corporation: Transforming Your Job and Your Company for the New Information Society* (New York: Warner Books, 1985).

O'Hara, Bruce. *Working Harder Isn't Working: How We Can Save the Environment, the Economy and our Sanity by Working Less and Enjoying Life More* (Vancouver: New Star Books, 1993).

Yankelovich, Daniel. *New Rules: Searching for Self-Fulfillment in a World Turned Upside Down* (New York: Random, 1981).

WOMEN AND WORK

Canape, Charlene. *The Part-time Solution: The New Strategy for Managing*

Your Career While Managing Motherhood (New York: Harper and Row, 1990).

Cassedy, Ellen, and Karen Nussbaum. *Nine to Five: The Working Woman's Guide to Office Survival* (1983. Available from the National Association for Working Women, 614 Cleveland Ave. NW, Cleveland, OH 44113).

Lowman, Kaye. *Of Cradles and Careers: A Guide to Re-Shaping Your Job to Include a Baby in Your Life* (New York: Penguin, 1985).

Shaevitz, Marjorie. *The Superwoman Syndrome* (New York: Warner Books, 1985).

Shom-Moffat, Patti, and Cynthia Teffler. *The Women's Workbook* (Toronto: Between the Lines, 1983).

WORK AND FAMILY

Canadian Employment and Immigration Advisory Council. *Workers With Family Responsibilities in a Changing Society: Who Cares* (Ottawa: Supply and Services Canada, 1987).

Catalyst. *Resources For Today's Parents* (New York: Catalyst, 1990).

Conference Board of Canada. *Work and Family: Employment Challenge of the 1990s* (Ottawa: Conference Board of Canada, 1990).

Galinsky, Ellen, et al. *The National Study of the Changing Workforce* (New York: Families and Work Institute, 1993).

Johnson, Laura C., Elka Klein, and Cathy Paperny. *The Working Families Project: Sourcebook on Work-Related Day Care in Canada* (1985. Available from the Social Planning Council of Metro Toronto, 950 Yonge St., Toronto, ON M5E 1V8).

Lewis, Suzan, Dafna N. Izraeli, and Helen Hootsmans. *Dual-Earner Families: International Perspectives* (London: Sage, 1992).

Magid, Renee Y. *When Mothers and Fathers Work: Creative Strategies for Balancing Career and Family* (New York: AMACOM, 1987).

Morgan, Hal, and Kerry Tucker. *Companies That Care* (New York: Simon and Schuster, 1991).

National Academy. *Work and Family: Policies for a Changing Workforce* (Washington, DC: National Academy Press, 1991).

O'Hara, Bruce. *Work and Family Employment Policy: Bibliography Arranged by Subject* (Courtenay, BC: Work Well Publications, 1990).

Rose, Karol L. *Work & Family: Program Models and Policies* (Colorado Springs, CO: Wiley Law Publications, 1993).

Work and Family Institute. *The Corporate Reference Guide to Work-Family Programs* (New York: Work and Family Institute, 1991).

■ **Step Two: Surveying Your Options** (see Step Five)

■ Step Three: Choosing Your Time

CAREER CHANGES/LIFE DIRECTIONS

Bolles, Richard. *What Colour is Your Parachute?* (Berkeley: Ten Speed Press, 1986).

Sher, Barbara, and Annie Gottlieb. *Wishcraft: How to Get What You Really Want* (New York: Ballantine, 1983).

Sinetar, Marsha. *Do What You Love and the Money Will Follow: Discovering Your Right Livelihood* (New York: Dell, 1989).

ASSERTIVENESS

Paul, Jordan and Margaret. *Do I Have to Give Up Me to be Loved by You?* (Minneapolis: CompCare Publications, 1983).

Smith, Manuel J. *When I Say No I Feel Guilty* (New York: Bantam, 1985).

STRESS MANAGEMENT

Hanson, Peter. *The Joy of Stress* (Islington, ON: Hanson Stress Management Organization, 1986).

TIME MANAGEMENT

Covey, Stephen R., and A. Roger Merril. *First Things First* (New York: Simon and Schuster, 1993).

PERFECTIONISM

Rubin, Theodore. *Compassion and Self-Hate* (New York: Macmillan, 1986).

■ Step Four: Deciding About Money

MONEY

Dominguez, Joe, and Vicki Robin. *Your Money or Your Life: Transforming Your Relationship With Money and Achieving Financial Independence* (New York: Viking Penguin, 1992).

Long, Charles. *How to Survive Without a Salary* (Toronto: Summerhill Press, 1988).

Longacre, Doris. *Living More With Less* (Scottsdale, PA: Herald Press, 1980).

BENEFITS

Campling, Robert F. *Employee Benefits and the Part-Time Worker* (Kingston, ON: Queen's University Industrial Relations Centre, 1987).

Catalyst. *Flexible Benefits: How to Set Up a Plan When Your Employees are Complaining, Your Costs are Rising and You're Too Busy to Think About It* (New York: Catalyst, 1986).

■ Step Five: Designing a Program

JOB SHARING

Lee, Patricia. *The Complete Guide to Job Sharing* (New York: Walker & Co., 1983).

McGuire, Nan, and Barney Olmsted. *Job Sharing in Health Care* (San Francisco: New Ways to Work, 1984).

Meier, Gretl S. *Job-Sharing: A New Pattern for Quality of Work and Life* (Kalamazoo, MI: W.E. Upjohn Institute for Employment Research, 1979).

Moorman, Barbara. *Job Sharing Through Collective Bargaining* (San Francisco: New Ways To Work, 1982).

Moorman, Barbara, Suzanne Smith, and Suzie Ruggels. *Job Sharing in the Schools* (San Francisco: New Ways to Work, 1980).

Office of Staffing Policy and Operations. *Job Sharing for Federal Employees* (Washington, DC: United States Office of Personnel Management, 1990).

Olmsted, Barney, and Suzanne Smith. *The Job Sharing Handbook* (San Francisco: New Ways to Work, 1994).

Russell, Thyra K. *Job Sharing: An Annotated Bibliography* (Metuchen, NJ: Scarecrow Press, 1994).

State of Wisconsin. *Project JOIN Final Report: A Demonstration Project to Develop and Test a Job Sharing and Flexible Time Arrangement in the Wisconsin Civil Service* (Madison, WI: Wisconsin Department of Employment Relations, 1979).

Walton, Pam. *Job Sharing — A Practical Guide* (London: Kogan Page, 1990).

PERMANENT PART-TIME

Catalyst. *Flexible Work Arrangements II: Succeeding With Part-time Options* (New York, Catalyst, 1993).

Nollen, Stanley D., and Virginia H. Martin. *Alternative Work Schedules, Part 2: Permanent Part-time Employment* (New York: AMACOM, 1978).

Part-time Work in Canada. Report of the Commission of Inquiry into Part-time Work. (Ottawa: Labour Canada, 1983).

Rothberg, Diane S., and Barbara Ensor Cook. *Part-time Professional* (Washington: Acropolis Books Ltd., 1985).

LEAVES OF ABSENCE

Abrams, Don. *The Time Buyer: How to Get Time Off Your Job Without Loss of Income* (Toronto: Deneau, 1986).

Axel, Helen. *Redefining Corporate Sabbaticals for the 1990s* (New York: Conference Board, 1992).

Catalyst. *The Corporate Guide to Parental Leaves* (New York: Catalyst, 1987).

Von Moltke, Konrad, and Norbert Schneevoight. *Educational Leaves: European Experience for American Consideration* (San Francisco: Jossey-Bass, 1977).

V-TIME

Moorman, Barbara, and Barbara Olmsted. *V-Time: A New Way to Work* (San Francisco: New Ways to Work, 1985).

BANKED OVERTIME

Working Times. The Report of the Task Force on Hours of Work and Overtime. (Toronto: Ontario Ministry of Labour, 1987).

PHASED RETIREMENT

Axel, Helene. *Job Banks for Retirees: Research Report No. 929* (New York: Conference Board, 1989).

Dennis, Helen. *Retirement Preparation: What Retirement Specialists Need to Know* (Lexington, MA: Lexington Books, 1984).

Doeringer, Peter B. (Editor). *Bridges to Retirement: Trends in the Labour Market for Older Workers* (Ithaca, NY: ILR Press, 1990).

Jacobson, Beverly. *Young Programs for Older Workers: Case Studies in Progressive Personnel Policies* (New York: Van Nostrand Reinhold, 1980).

Page, Cynthia L. *Your Retirement: How to Plan for a Secure Future* (New York: Acro Publishing Inc., 1984).

Paul, Carolyn E. *Expanding Part-time Work Options for Older Americans: A Feasibility Study* (Los Angeles: Employment and Retirement Division, Ethel Percy Andrus Gerontology Center, University of Southern California, 1983).

Rostow, Jerome, and Robert Zager. *The Future of Older Workers in America: New Options for an Extended Working Life* (Scarsdale, NY: Work in America Institute, 1980).

Swank, Constance. *Phased Retirement: The European Experience* (Washington, DC: National Council for Alternative Work Patterns, 1982).

FLEXTIME

Nollen, Stanley D., and Virginia Martin. *Alternative Work Schedules, Part 1: Flexitime* (New York: AMACOM, 1978).

Silverstein, Pam, and Jozetta H. Srb. *Flexitime: Where, When, and How* (Ithaca, NY: ILR Press, 1987).

Simcha, Ronen. *Flexible Working Hours: An Innovation in the Quality of Working Life* (New York: McGraw-Hill, 1980).

COMPRESSED WORKWEEK

Nollen, Stanley D., and Virginia Martin. *Alternative Work Schedules, Part 3: Compressed Work Week* (New York: AMACOM, 1978).

Poor, Riva. *4 Days, 40 Hours: Reporting a Revolution in Work and Leisure* (Cambridge, MA: Bursk and Poor, 1970).

TELECOMMUTING

Atkinson, William. *Working at Home: Is It For You?* (Homewood, IL: Dow Jones-Irwin, 1985).

Gordon, Gil (Editor). *Teleworking Explained* (New York: John Wiley and Sons, 1993).

Gordon, Gil, and Marcia Kelly. *Telecommuting: How to Make It Work for You and Your Company* (Englewood Cliffs, NY: Prentice-Hall, 1986).

Nilles, Jack. *Making Telecommuting Happen* (New York: Van Nostrand Reinhold, 1994).

Schepp, Brad. *Telecommuting Handbook* (New York: Pharos Books, 1990).

Telecommuting Review: The Gordon Report (Newsletter available from Telespan Publishing, 50A West Palm St., Altadena, CA 91001).

Telework Canada (Newsletter available from KLR Consulting Services, Suite 200, 4170 Still Creek Drive, Burnaby, BC V5G 6C6).

The Worksteader News (Newsletter available from 2396 Coolidge Way, Rancho Cordova, CA 95670).

HOME WORK

Arden, Lynie. *The Work-at-Home Sourcebook* (1994. Available from Live Oak Publishing, P.O. Box 339, Boulder, CO 80306).

Edwards, Paul and Sarah. *Getting Business to Come to You: Everything You Need to Know to Do Your Own Advertising, Public Relations, Direct Mail, and Sales Promotion, and Attract All the Business You Can Handle* (Los Angeles: Jeremy Tarcher, 1991).

The Whole Work Catalogue: Options for More Rewarding Work (Newsletter available from The New Careers Center, P.O. Box 339, Boulder CO 80306).

◼ Step Six: Getting What You Want

CASE STUDIES
(SEE ALSO WORK AND FAMILY AND PROGRAM DESIGN)

Christensen, Kathleen. *Flexible Staffing and Scheduling in U.S. Corporations: Research Bulletin No. 240* (New York: Conference Board, 1989).

English, Kathy. *The Options at Work Case Study Series* (Courtenay, BC: Work Well Publications, 1989).

Johnson, Laura C. *Working Families: Workplace Supports for Families* (Toronto: Social Planning Council of Metropolitan Toronto, 1986).

McCarthy, Maureen, and Gail S. Rosenberg. *Work Sharing: Case Studies* (Kalamazoo, MI: W.E. Upjohn Institute for Employment Research, 1981).

Nollen, Stanley D. *New Work Schedules in Practice: Managing Time in a Changing Society* (New York: Van Nostrand Reinhold, 1982).

Paris, Helene. *The Corporate Response to Workers with Family Responsibilities: Report 43-89* (Ottawa: Conference Board of Canada, 1989).

LEGAL CONSIDERATIONS

Canadian Master Labour Guide: A Guide to Canadian Labour Law (Don Mills, ON: CCH Canadian Ltd., 1987).

EMPLOYER ATTITUDES

Belous, Richard S. *The Contingent Economy: The Growth of the Temporary, Part-time and Subcontracted Workforce* (Washington, DC: National Planning Association, 1989).

Harwood, Paul. *Adaptive Organizations and People* (Ottawa: Supply and Services Canada, 1991).

Peters, Thomas J. *In Search of Excellence: Lessons from America's Best Run Companies* (New York: Harper & Row, 1982).

Rogers, Judy. *Attitudes Towards Alternative Work Arrangements: A Qualitative Assessment Among Employers in Metropolitan Toronto* (Toronto: Social Planning Council of Metropolitan Toronto, 1986).

PROGRAM DESIGN AND IMPLEMENTATION

Bureau of National Affairs. *Alternative Work Schedules: Changing Times for a Changing Workforce* (Washington, DC: Bureau of National Affairs, 1988).

Catalyst. *Flexible Work Arrangements: Establishing Options for Managers and Professionals* (New York: Catalyst, 1990).

New Ways to Work. *Change at the Top: You Can Be a Manager and Work Less than Full Time!* (London: New Ways to Work, 1994).

————. *Changing Times: A Guide to Flexible Work Patterns* (London: New Ways to Work, 1993).

Olmsted, Barney, and Suzanne Smith. *Creating a Flexible Workplace: How to Create and Manage Alternative Work Options* (New York: AMACOM, 1994).

Work Well. *A Manager's Guide to Work Options Series* (Courtenay, BC: Work Well Publications, 1990).

■ Step Seven: Putting Work In Its Place

NEGOTIATING

Fisher, Roger, and William Ury. *Getting to Yes: Negotiating Agreement Without Giving In* (Boston: Houghton Mifflin, 1981).

■ Special Cases and Further Resources

THE FLEXIBLE WORKPLACE

Canape, Charlene. *Flexible Work Options: A Selected Bibliography* (Falls Church, VA: Association of Part-time Professionals, 1990).

Ivantcho, Barbara *A Selected Bibliography on Work Time Options* (San Fransisco: New Ways to Work, 1989).

Naisbitt, John, and Patricia Aburdene. *Re-inventing the Corporation: Transforming Your Job and Your Company for the New Information Society* (New York: Warner Books, 1985).

Olmsted, Barney, and Suzanne Smith. *Creating a Flexible Workplace: How to Create and Manage Alternative Work Options* (New York: AMACOM, 1994).

Semler, Ricardo. *Maverick* (New York: Warner Books, 1993).

MEN AND WORK

Dominguez, Joe, and Vicki Robin. *Your Money or Your Life: Transforming Your Relationship With Money and Achieving Financial Independence* (New York: Viking Penguin, 1992).

Goldberg, Herb. *The Inner Male: Overcoming Roadblocks to Intimacy* (New York: Penguin, 1988).

Johnson, Robert A. *He: Understanding Masculine Psychology* (New York: Harper Collins, 1989).

Keen, Sam. *Fire in the Belly: On Being A Man* (New York: Bantam, 1991).

Rubin, Theodore. *Compassion and Self-Hate* (New York: MacMillan, 1986).

PROMOTING WORK OPTIONS

O'Hara, Bruce. *WORC Well: A Guide to Creating Worktime Options Resource Centres* (Toronto: Canadian Mental Health Association, 1987).

■ Organizations

American Association of Retired Persons, 215 Long Beach Blvd., Long Beach, CA 90801. Telephone (310) 496-2277.

Association for Part-time Professionals, Crescent Plaza, Suite 216, 7700 Leesburg Pike, Falls Church, VA 22043. Telephone (703) 734-7975.

Canadian Association of Pre-Retirement Planners, 10429 143rd St., Edmonton, AB T5N 2S5. Telephone (403) 455-0501.

Canadian Association of Retired Persons, 27 Queen St. E., Suite 1304, Toronto, ON M5C 2M6 Telephone (416) 363-8748.

Catalyst: National Network of Career Resource Centers, 250 Park Ave. South, New York, NY 10003. Telephone (212) 777-8900.

Ethel Percy Andrus Gerontology Center, University of Southern California, University Park, MC0191, Los Angeles CA 90089-0191.

Families and Work Institute, 330 Seventh Ave., New York, NY 10001. Telephone (212) 465-2044.

International Society for Work Options, c/o New Ways to Work, 785 Market St., Suite 950, San Francisco CA 94103. Telephone (415) 995-9860.

Leisure and Life Quality Institute, Lumbers Bldg., Faculty of Environmental Studies, York University, 4700 Keele St., North York, ON M3J 1P3.

New Careers Center, P.O. Box 339, Boulder, CO 80306. Telephone (303) 447-1087.

New Ways to Work, 785 Market St., Suite 950, San Francisco, CA 94103. Telephone (415) 995-9860.

New Ways to Work (London), 309 Upper St., London N1 2TY, U.K.

Work Well and **Work Well Network**, Box 3483, Courtenay, BC V9N 6Z8. Telephone (604) 334-0998.

■ **Journals**

Conditions of Work Digest (2 issues per year, available from International Labour Organization Publications, Geneva, Switzerland).

Flexibility (10 issues per year, available from The Home Office Partnership, The Jeffrey's Bldg., St. John's Innovation Park, Cambridge CB4 4WS, U.K.).

International Flexwork Forum (4 issues per year, available from the Institute for Economic and Financial Research, Toranomon NN Bldg., 1-21-17 Toranomon Minato-ku, Tokyo 105, Japan).

New Ways to Work Newsletter (4 issues per year, available from New Ways to Work, 309 Upper St., London N1 2TY, U.K.)

The Whole Work Catalogue: Options for More Rewarding Work (2 issues per year, Available from the New Careers Center, P.O. Box 339, Boulder CO 80306).

Work Times (4 issues per year, available from New Ways to Work, 785 Market St., Suite 950, San Francisco CA 94103).

Index

absenteeism 45, 55, 63, 70, 128, 144, 174, 217, 251, 266
Aburdene, Patricia 273, 274
additional income 120
adoption leave 35, 154, 269-270
agricultural economy 4-5
alcohol 279, 280
analysis of job 136-139
anticipatory time off 49, 172
application process 249
approval process 225, 243
Arden, Lynie 78
assembly line workers 68
automatically eligible 179
auxiliary staff 170

balanced life 59
bandwidth 65, 180-181, 185
banked hours 74
banked overtime 15, 49-55, 68, 123, 133, 169-174; at Canadian Hydrographic Service 52; definition 13; employer benefits 173-174
benefits 57, 123-128, 144, 156, 164, 213-115, 221, 227-131; and banked overtime 54; and leaves of absence 36, 38, 41; and permanent part-time 28; in lieu of 228
bereavement leave 35, 154
breadwinner 7, 282
budgeting 118

bugs 251
burnout 47, 48, 53, 55, 68, 72, 73, 128, 150; avoiding 40; reducing 45

cafeteria-style benefit plan 228, 271, 272
caffeine 279
calendar seniority 212, 228, 259
Canada Employment Centre 259
Canada Pension Plan (CPP) 124, 144, 213, 216, 229, 231
Canadian Auto Workers union 155
Canadian Master Labour Guide 264
Canadian Union of Public Employees (CUPE) 207
care and nurturing leave 37, 156
career part-time 28
cash-in-lieu payments 128
casual employment 29, 127
casual worker 30
CCH Canadian Ltd. 264
changeover 142, 143, 159
changes in workplace 8
client continuity 212
codicil 267
collaboration 24
collective agreements 36, 38, 41, 254
collective bargaining 206, 264
communication 25, 221
communication mechanisms 249
communication patterns 252
commuting 66, 68, 77

Company pension plans 125, 214, 229, 230
company-paid programs 57, 175-176
Compassion and Self-Hate 280
compassionate leave 35-36, 154, 266
compensatory benefits 144, 221, 264
compensatory leaves 35-36, 154
compensatory time off 49, 51
compressed workweek 16, 69-74, 123, 188-192; at Royal Jubilee Hospital 71; definition 13-14; employer benefits 190, 192
compulsory banked overtime 258
computers 8
Conference Board of Canada 10, 14, 17
contingency plan 197
continuous entry 163, 164
continuous staffing 73
contract work 78
contract workers 262
contract bargaining talks 244
contribution ceilings 216, 231
control data 253
Cook, Barbara 149
core hours 64, 181, 183
Corporate Response to Workers With Family Responsibilities, The 14
cost of living 119
cost analysis 238
cottage industry 77
counter-proposal 244
Creating a Flexible Workplace 168, 244, 247, 274
cross training 150, 152, 159, 171, 272, 273
customer complaints 252

deferred earnings 38, 40, 154, 258
dental plans 126, 144, 215, 229, 230
disability insurance 126, 215, 231
discretionary leave 35, 36, 154, 155
division of labour 141, 210-211
division of time 142
Dominguez, Joe 122, 281

earned time off (ETO) 274
educational leave 36, 38, 154; unpaid 258

electronic cottages 75
eligibility criteria 224
eligible-with-permission 179
emergency back-up 239
employee training and development 156
employee-paid programs 57, 175-177
enforced savings 39
Equal Opportunities Commission 17
equipment 82, 250
ethic of success 9
European lifestyle 5, 7
evaluation 251, 253
ex-employees 172
excessive overtime 55
exercise 281
extended leave 36, 37-38, 154-156
extended vacation 45, 56, 57, 154, 171

family 4
fears 110
feedback 251, 252
fieldwork 52
fill-in coverage 210, 220, 226, 250
financial picture 117-122
five-for-four 38
fixed-menu benefit plan 228
flex-day 182, 183
flex-month 182
flex-week 182
flex-year 182
flexibility 24
flexible hours 63
flexible quitting time 65
flexible starting time 65
flexitime 63
flextime 16, 63-68, 123, 133, 179-187; at National Life of Canada 64; definition 13
flextime machine 185
fool's gold 280
40-hour workweek 69; alternatives 13
Four Days, Forty Hours 69
four-day week 259
4/40 compressed workweek (4/40 CWW) 69-70, 74
freelance workers 262
freelancing 78

full telecommuting 75
full-time employees 127
full-week rotation 142
furlough 156

gender roles 7, 10
Goldberg, Herb 281
grievance process 37, 206
group programs 133
group proposal 206, 243

H 281
hero myth 276-280
high-stress jobs 18
holiday pay 265
home work 75, 78
home work station 195
hours banking 66, 68
hours-of-work committee 180, 185,
    187, 192, 197, 248, 253, 254, 272
housewives 7, 32
hunter-gatherer economy 3-4

I Ching 201
implementation plan 218, 222, 234, 247-
    250
inactive status 37, 156
indefinite leave 37
Independent Retirement Accounts
    (IRA) 125, 214, 230
individual proposal 205, 243
industrial economy 5, 7
ineligible 179
information exchange 212
Inner Male, The 281
integrated option 175, 178

job continuity 227
job description 209, 220
job protection 127
job redefinition committee 226
job security 257, 262
job seekers 260
job sharing 15, 17-26, 123, 127, 150; ap-
    peal 258; at a dental practice 26; at
    Western Community Outreach 21;
    definition 13, 17; employer atti-
    tudes 19-20; employer benefits 144-

145; minimizing costs 145; popular-
    ity 17; reasons for 18; suitability
    considerations 22-25
union attitudes 20; vs. work sharing
    19; work schedules 18-19
Job Sharing for Youth programs 19
job-sharing proposal, sample 220-222
job splitting 149
Joe-jobs 29
Johnson, Robert 281
joint job search 260

Kammerer, Christel 63
Kennedy, John F. 278

Labour Canada 238
Landsman Community Services 121
layoffs 44, 48, 165, 257, 259
leave of absence 156
leave without pay 36, 37, 156
leaves of absence 15, 35-43, 154-160; at
    Greater Nanaimo School District
    39; definition 13, 15, employer bene-
    fits 160; reasons for 35; replacement
    staff 157-158 suitability considera-
    tions 40-43
legal requirements 248
life insurance 126, 215, 229, 231
Local Exchange Trading System
    (LETS) 120
Lowman, Kaye 79

male support group 281
maternity leave 35, 154, 268
Maverick 272
maximum participation 258
medical plans 126, 144, 215, 229, 230
memorandum of agreement 234, 244
midday flexibility 65, 181-182
minimum workweek 120
modified workweek 69, 72, 188-192
Monday to Thursday schedules 190
morale 63, 173; improving 45
mortality rates 275
multiple-option approach 258

Naisbitt, John 9, 273, 274
natural breaks 138

needs survey 136, 161, 163, 192, 247, 258
negotiation 201, 262
New Ways to Work 17, 168
New Rules 9
nicotine 279, 280
nomadic life 4
North American work ethic 5, 7
notice of intent to return 37

Of Cradles and Careers 79
older workers 18, 56, 59, 74, 212, 227, 259
Olmsted, Barney 168, 244, 274
organizational skills 24
overeating 279
overlapping schedules 73, 143, 211
overtime 49, 51, 53-55, 63, 72, 238, 271
overtime legislation 185
overwork 275

paperwork 249
paperwork cost 216
parent/student job sharing 18-19
parental leave 35, 154, 267
Paris, Helen 14
part-time employees 231
part-tme employment 29, 126, 127, 263
part-time professional 149
partial pension schemes 57, 60, 175, 177-178
partial telecommuting 75
partner selection 145-148, 151, 260
paternity leave 35, 154, 268
pay differential 273
peak periods 29
pensions 59, 60, 144, 272; and leaves of absence 37; and permanentpart-time 34; and phased retirement 56
perfectionist 107
permanent part-time 15, 27-34, 123, 127, 149-53, 258; at Bentall Group 31; benefits 28-29; definition 13, 27; employer attitudes 29-30; employer benefits 152; popularity 27; suitability considerations 32-34; union attitudes 32; work schedules 27
permanent part-time relief work 170

permanent relief staff 273
personal leave 36-38, 154-56, 266
personnel policy manual 38, 254
phased retirement 15, 56-62, 123, 175-78; at Victoria General Hospital 61; definition 13
policy statement 213
Poor, Riva 69
post-retirement work pools 59, 175, 178
pre-retirement planning 56, 59
predictable schedules 127
preventative maintenance 278
productivity 144, 257
professional development 274
professional workers 68
profit sharing 126, 215, 231
progressive corporations 9
promotion opportunities 22, 33, 54
Proposition 13 44
prorated benefits 128, 213, 228

Quakers 203
quotas 225

Re-Inventing the Corporation 9, 273, 274
"real men" 278
recall list 226
recording systems 249
recruitment 239
redress procedure 225
reduced hours 225; effect on benefits 123-126
refusal to negotiate 244
Registered Retirement Savings Plan (RRSP) 125, 214, 230
relief staff 49, 51, 55, 150, 158, 163, 167, 170-171, 174, 263
religion 4
report writer 253
retired workers 59, 178
retirees 172
retirement 58
Revenue Canada 38, 40
right to return 42
rights of employment 35, 264
Robin, Vicki 122, 281
rota system 66
Rothburg, Diane 149

Rubin, Theodore 280

sabbaticals 36, 38, 40, 154, 155
safeguards 258
safety margin 122
Sahlins, Marshall 4
salaried employees 53, 54, 174
Santa Clara County Employees Union
    44
satellite telecommuting 76, 196, 197
seconded 155
self-discipline 79
self-employment 78
self-fulfilling prophecy 32
Semler, Ricardo 272
seniority 37, 41, 156, 165, 259
service economy 7-8
settlement periods 65, 66, 182
shop steward 207
short-term illness insurance 126, 215,
    231
Short-Time Compensation 259
shorter workday 45, 47, 112, 189
shorter workweek 9, 45, 56, 57, 113, 229
sick leave 35, 125, 144, 154, 213, 229,
    238, 265-266
sick-time coverage 221
situation analysis 201-203
skeleton staff 184, 189
Smith, Suzanne 168, 244, 274
Social Security Contributions 124, 144,
    213, 229
social service leave 155
soft loading 171
split rotation 240
split-week rotation 142
splitting duties 149
staff meetings 272
staggered hours 69, 73, 191
Stallone, Sylvester 277
standing committee 272
start-up costs 231
starting date 218, 234, 278
statement of purpose 209, 224
Statistics Canada 53
statutory benefits 221
statutory holidays 35, 125, 144, 154,
    212, 227, 229, 265

streamlining 150-151
stress 239
students 29
supermarket employees 28, 32
supplementary benefits 229
support staff 188

tardiness 63, 144
task analysis 220
technology: and telecommuting 75,
    194-195; effect on human labour 7;
    effect on workweek 5, 8
teenagers 29, 32
telecommuting 16, 75-82, 123, 193-197;
    at *Monday* magazine 81; definition
    14; employer attitudes 76-77; em-
    ployer benefits 196; union attitudes
    77
temporary leave 36
temporary staff 170
3M Canada 51, 72
three-quarter time program proposal
    236-240
3/38 compressed workweek (3/38
    CWW) 69, 72
time/income trade-off 44
time management 87 114
time schedules 220
time-and-a-half 265
time-buyer plans 36, 38, 156
Time-Buyer, The 40, 157
time-dependent tasks 137
time-independent tasks 137
time-off patterns 161
time-trade 18, 211, 221
Toffler, Alvin 75
trial period 136, 185, 192, 219, 234, 251,
    252
troubleshooting 133
Tuesday to Friday schedules 190
turnover 55, 63, 72, 128, 144, 174, 239

umpire 166, 168, 185, 187
underemployment 54, 128
unemployment 9, 216
Unemployment Insurance (UI) 124,
    144, 213, 229, 231, 259, 268
union proposal 207, 243

unions 55, 126, 146, 154, 155, 175, 206, 243, 266, 268; and job sharing 20; and permanent part-time 32; and telecommuting 77; and V-time 48; United Food and Commercial Worker's Union (UFCW) 32
United Way 40
University of Alberta 57

V-time 15, 35, 44-48, 123, 133, 161-168, 258; at B.C. Ministry of the Environment 46; definition 13; key elements 45; sample chart 164, 165
V-Time: A Matter of Time 168
vacation 35, 124, 144, 154, 213, 229, 264
vacation pay 264
vesting period 215
veto provision 225
vital signs 251
voluntary reduced worktime 44, 161

wage slaves 5
wage structure: three-tiered 127
Wayne, John 280
wedding 265
weekend relief shift 51
women: in workforce 7-9; re-entering workforce 18
work 1-10; and career 89; and men 275-282; attitudes 10; in agricultural economy 4; in future economy 8-9; in hunter-gatherer economy, 3-4; in industrial economy 5; in service economy 7-8; work schedules 9

work ethic 5, 7, 9
work experience 29
work habits 24
work option resource centres 146
work options 13-83, 257; effectiveness in alleviating human resource problems 15; percentage usage in organizations 14
work schedules 143, 152
work sharing 19, 259
Work Sharing Program 259
workaholic 275
Work-at-Home Sourcebook, The 78
workday length 189
Workers' Compensation 124, 144, 213, 216, 229, 231
workforce 8, 29
Working at Home 78
Working Harder Isn't Working 9
workplace tolerance 33
workweek: length of 5, 8, 189; reduced hours 56, 113
writing a collective proposal 224
writing an individual proposal 208-235
written agreement 248
written proposal 203, 205
wrongful dismissal 245

Yankelovich, Daniel 9
Your Money or Your Life 122, 281

zero balance systems 66
Zetterberg, Carol 78